THE
POWER
OF
BEING
SEEN

THE
POWER
OF
BEING
SEEN

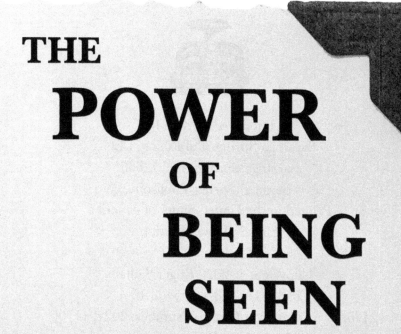

ROGER SAILLANT

Published in 2022 by
Saratoga Springs Publishing, LLC
Saratoga Springs, NY 12866
www.SaratogaSpringsPublishing.com
Printed in the United States of America
First Softcover Edition

Copyright © 2022 Roger Saillant
ISBN-13: 978-1-955568-10-4
Library of Congress Control Number: 2022911706
Written by Roger Saillant
Graphic Design by Patrick Jankowski
Cover design by Anthony Richichi
Publisher & Book design by Vicki Addesso Dodd

Saratoga Springs Publishing's books are
available at a discount when purchased in quantity for
promotions, fundraising and educational use. For additional
information, book sales or events contact us at
www.rogersaillant.com or
rsaillantpublications@gmail.com

Dedications

To all adults–never pass up the opportunity to see a marginalized child and encourage them.

To all marginalized children–do your best to be open to the wisdom and guidance offered by adults who see you, and you sense are trying to help you.

Contents

CONTENTS

It's darkest before the dawn ...
-English theologian, Thomas Fuller

Chapter 1
Possible Escape

The sounds of cicadas crooning in the hedgerows and our pitchforks clinking against stones were all that cut through the pall of hot stillness. Leafy dust from the clover hay rose up and stuck to our sweaty faces and arms, transforming us into scaly mummies. When I scanned the sky for storm clouds, I saw two buzzards searching for a meal, but no clouds. The sky offered no relief. Gathering and stacking hay in mid-July was hot work.

The three of us worked silently, since speaking in the oppressive heat would have required too much effort. Besides, we didn't like each other. Richard, my older foster brother, frequently bullied me, and Mr. McClelland thought we didn't work hard enough.

I daydreamed about other kids swimming in the nearby creek or being on vacations instead of working. The unmistakable sound of wheels crunching across gravel interrupted my jealous fantasies. Cars and trucks on our lane usually meant deliveries or pickups since we had no vehicles of our own. Mr. McClelland's curiosity about visitors always lured him from the fields. He told us to keep working while he checked things out. We slowed our pace as he walked away and stopped completely when he disappeared behind the farm buildings. We couldn't hear voices, but the barking dogs indicated that it was a stranger. "I can't hear anyone talking. Do you?" I asked.

Richard shrugged and started stacking again. "They must've gone inside. We'd better get to work again before the old man comes back and yells at us for standing around."

I started pitching hay again and asked, "Was it a car or a truck?"

"Probably a car. Sounded too light to be a truck," came the reply. Richard had been placed on the farm when he was three; he was over four years older than I was and had more experience at sizing situations up.

Time passed. We stacked hay. We measured time by the number of haystacks we built. We had stacked three and were about to start on a fourth when Mr. McClelland appeared in the distance and yelled, "Boys, come in here. Now!"

We looked at each other, smiled with relief, and walked quickly toward the house, knowing that a reprieve had been given and our sentence had been reduced, but without knowing why.

When we got to the back of the house, Mr. McClelland grabbed me by the arm and said, "Go to the well, clean your face and arms, son, and then come inside."

He added, "Don't dawdle!"

I hated it when he called me "son" because I was not his son. He used the word "son" as a way to imply a closeness between us that didn't exist. He was trying to manipulate me. If I'd been his son, I would probably have been about forty years old, not eleven, since he was in his late sixties.

He turned to Richard and said firmly, "Grab the egg baskets and finish collecting the eggs that Mum couldn't finish because of the visitor."

"Who's here?" Richard asked.

"None of your damn business. This has nothing to do with you. Just go!"

Then he commanded Richard in an even firmer tone, "When you finish collecting the eggs, stay outside away from the house." He repeated, "This has nothing to do with you."

Richard obeyed even though he was fifteen, very tall, and had big muscles. I often wondered why he was so obedient. He shrugged, mouthing an obscenity on his way to the hen houses. He knew better than to say anything when Mr. McClelland was incensed.

Something had really set Mr. McClelland off. He was acting as though he was going to "cuff" or "strap" one or both of us. At first, he would curse us, and then he would use his favorite quick punishment—to swat us across the back of the neck.

An example of big trouble was the time we slipped away to the creek during his nap time and went swimming instead of hoeing. He brought out the razor strap and used it on our bare backs. Usually by the time we got the strap, there was enough ruckus that Mrs. McClelland would hear it and come to our aid.

She could stop him just by saying, "John, why are you hitting them? Does what they did warrant the strap?"

He would back away. It was a mystery how such a frail woman could have so much power over him.

Going to the well got me away from him. I used the hand pump to pull up a bucket full of water and stuck my head in it. The cool water felt great. I put my hands and arms in the bucket and let them soak. While I cooled down, I wondered what had provoked him.

I didn't recognize the car parked in the driveway. *Why am I being singled out?* My mind raced over the past few days, trying to recall if I'd recently done something wrong. There were some things I'd done alone or with Richard that could have unpleasant repercussions if discovered. Maybe someone had come to report how we'd broken into a house.

Over the past week or so, I believed that I hadn't done anything that warranted punishment. Maybe they wanted me to rat out Richard? He'd recently stolen some model airplanes from the Doylestown Hobby Shop. I knew that it would be a bad idea to tell on Richard because he would retaliate by beating me up. I was determined not to confess to anything. I knew that not speaking at all was the best strategy. I grabbed an old towel off the stone wall and dried my head and arms.

I was glad to be out of the ferocious sun, but my pumping heart was warming me up again. When I stepped onto the porch, I glanced in the kitchen window and saw Mr. and Mrs. McClelland sitting with their backs toward me, facing a woman whom I'd never seen before.

Feeling lightheaded and apprehensive, I went inside. Everyone looked at me. I looked nervously around the kitchen to see if anything was out of place in the crowded room.

The house had been built in two stages. A Pennsylvania Dutch family had constructed the original thick stone-walled section in the early 1800s. The wooden frame addition had been built before the Civil War, and that was where the kitchen was located with its typical low-ceilinged farmhouse appearance. With one quick glance I saw the table with six chairs resting on the linoleum-covered floor whose true colors had long ago been soiled into a blotchy grayness. The black coal stove was opposite the table near the sink. An overstuffed chair rested in the corner where Mrs. McClelland cleaned eggs and read the Bible every day. Buckets of eggs had been placed near the chair ready to be cleaned. There were two electric appliances against one wall, a stove and a refrigerator. Across from the door where I stood and on top of an old bureau was the prized new RCA black-and-white TV purchased to catch hog and egg prices, the news, and the Friday night fights. The mood in the room was as uncomfortable as the furnishings looked.

"Come, sit here, son," Mr. McClelland said in an uncharacteristically soft tone. His seeming warmth alarmed me.

As I sat down, Mr. McClelland said, "This here is Miss Fleming. She's from the Children's Aid Society and has come to see you with some news."

She reached out as I rose slightly and shook her hand politely. She looked at me, or rather looked me up and down, and withdrew her hand as if to avoid contamination. She looked at the McClellands with a hint of disapproval. Social workers rarely, if ever, came to the farm unannounced. We were usually cleaned up and ready to meet them wearing good clothes, not dirty work clothes, and the meetings took place in the parlor, not in the kitchen.

Miss Fleming began, "This is my first trip this far from the city. The area is so beautiful." She stretched out the word "beautiful" to emphasize how impressed she was.

What crossed my mind was that city people were such phonies. I smiled at her. *Maybe I should mention how beautiful our pig pens and barnyards are?*

Richard told me that the Aid Society only placed kids who lacked promise on farms. They believed that the loser kids could be trained to be farmhands and would be able to support themselves when they aged out. Richard and I knew we'd been placed in the losers' category.

She looked young, inexperienced, and like she was trying hard to make a good impression. The Aid Society had a lot of turnover, which meant that Richard and I had a new social worker almost every time we met one, which was about every other month. Richard had said, "We always get the rookies because we're in the *farm system*."

"Miss Fleming has something to discuss with you," Mr. McClelland said, trying to move things along. For my part, I was happy to spend the rest of the afternoon sitting silently at the table, considering that the alternative was haying.

Miss Fleming spoke up. "I've come here today to meet with you. I've already had a conversation with your foster parents about some important news for all of you and especially you, Roger." As she said that, she pushed a light-yellow envelope across the waxy tablecloth to me. It was addressed to me in care of the Children's Aid Society of Pennsylvania with a return address from Florida.

Miss Fleming spoke to me in that flat institutional tone so common with the Aid Society people. "I've discussed the contents of this letter with your foster parents. The letter is from your mother."

"What?" The question jumped out of me. I was stunned. *How could this be?*

My mind raced. The McClellands told me multiple times that she was dead. That she'd been killed in prison. Then, it came to me in a flash—maybe she'd written the letter before she'd been killed.

"I thought she was dead."

"No," the aid worker said, "She's not dead. This letter arrived last week. We took our time to decide what was best for you. We concluded that at your age it would be only right that it be given to you. After all, she is your mother and she has the right to communicate with you."

My body froze. My thoughts swirled. *I have a real living mother who wrote to me? Why? Why now? How could this be?* It didn't make sense, none of it. If this were true, then I'd been lied to. Why? This was crazy.

I took the opened envelope and teased the letter out too slowly, I guess, because Mr. McClelland growled at me with irritation, "Just take it out and read the damn thing."

I looked up and caught Miss Fleming shooting a disapproving look toward Mr. McClelland. Mrs. McClelland winced, too.

The letter had a faint scent of flowers. I was told that she'd been a prostitute before she'd died. I wondered if prostitutes used perfumed letters. The flowery handwriting covered a single page.

Dear Roger,   *July 14, 1953*

    I am your mother. I live in Miami Beach, Florida. I work for the Hotel Employees Union which is a great position for me. I also deal in antiques which allows me to travel.

    I placed you with the Aid Society when you were nearly nine months old. My personal situation was very difficult at that time, and I knew I could not have given you a good home. I have been in contact with the Aid Society through the years to see how you are doing. I know that you have been in several homes, which were hard for you, but now I know you are doing much better on a farm.

    You have an older brother named Rory who lives with me. He is a very good swimmer and a wonderfully talented artist. You also have a sister named Karen who lives in Philadelphia in a foster home like you. She is a very gifted singer and the Aid Society staff believe that she has a wonderful future as a vocalist.

    I look forward to learning more about you. I would like to meet you.

    Please write.

    Love,

    Mom

I was in disbelief. I read it again. The letter had transformed me from being an abandoned kid without any connection to blood relatives living with foster parents—to one with a living mother, a brother, and a sister. *Now what? Does this mean I'll leave the farm? Who will I live with next, my mother?* Various implications flooded through my mind. I wanted some space.

Mr. McClelland interrupted my thoughts. "Son, we're your parents now. She left you long ago. We are the ones who really care for you." His tone was soft again.

What were the implications for him? What was he up to? He was almost pleading with me. I looked at him, Mrs. McClelland, and the social worker, trying to read their faces so that I would know what to say or do. My life was suddenly a mess. I wanted someone to rescue me from this situation.

"What do you want me to do?" I asked. "Now what happens?"

Miss Fleming jumped in and said, "Roger, we think it is important that you meet your younger sister in Philadelphia first. Let's see how that goes, and then we can decide what the next steps should be."

"Does my sister know about me?"

"No, not yet," she replied.

"When will you tell her?"

Mr. McClelland spoke up, "Son, we should go very slowly. This is really big news, and we should take our time to think this through."

I looked at Mrs. McClelland and Miss Fleming again, hoping that they would say that it was all up to me.

No one spoke.

The idea of meeting my sister and my brother was appealing to me. *What do they look like? Since they each have talent, maybe I can learn something from them if I don't have to work on the farm.* I felt indifferent about meeting my mother, especially one who signed her name using the word "love" when she didn't even know me. She'd given me up. *What were her real motives for reaching out to me? Could she want me to work for her?*

Although everyone in the room controlled me in one way or another, I was beginning to sense that I had some real power for the first time in my life. Maybe Mr. McClelland knew it. If I found a way to leave the farm, he would have one less worker. He would lose the Aid Society money, too. On different occasions he'd told both Richard and me that no one else in the world cared for us except for him and Mum (Mrs. McClelland), and that we should be grateful to be on the farm. This was our home. The implication was that working was a way to show our gratitude to be part of his family. This letter showed me, at least, that someone else might care for me.

"Roger, would you like to meet your sister?" Miss Fleming asked.

For the first time, Mrs. McClelland spoke, "Miss Fleming, would it be all right to wait a few days, or do you need an answer from Roger now?"

"I think that this has been a lot for Roger to absorb. He should take his time," said Miss Fleming.

"A lot for him to absorb," snorted Mr. McClelland. "What about us? Besides, why don't you tell him about why she abandoned him and that she's a 'fallen woman'?" He slurred the last phrase like a curse.

Miss Fleming ignored Mr. McClelland and said, "Certainly, he should take some time. We on the staff think that he should eventually meet his sister, especially since she lives nearby in Philadelphia. We believe in keeping families together where possible."

She'd repeated herself about meeting my sister as a first step. I wondered if it really mattered what I thought. Was it really my choice whether I was willing to meet my sister first and, perhaps, my brother and mother at a later date? Or was that what they were going to have me do anyway? Had they decided to move me away from the farm gradually? I needed to find out what "fallen woman" meant.

"Meeting his sister is one thing and keeping families together is important, but his mother abandoned him a long time ago. How can she just take him back now?" Mr. McClelland interrupted again.

At that point, Miss Fleming interrupted him, "Roger, I know that you're surprised or maybe even shocked by this news."

"'Shocked'—it sure seems like it could be more than that, lady," I thought.

"Things are happening so fast for you. You have a lot to think about for now. Why don't you go outside and play while I go over some things with your foster parents?"

"Play? If she only knew," I thought.

I wanted to be out of the kitchen and away from all of the sweet talk. This was extraordinary news and contradicted all that I'd been told about my real family. I wanted to jump up and scream. Instead, I stood up calmly and politely said, "Thank you, Miss Fleming, for bringing this letter. I guess I'll see you again soon."

"It was nice to meet you, Roger, and to see how you're doing. I'll be back."

I left the room and sucked fresh outside air into my lungs.

Mr. McClelland followed me out onto the porch and closed the screen door behind him. Two filled egg baskets sat near the door where Richard had placed them. Richard was seated, resting on the edge of the porch away from the door but probably within earshot of the kitchen conversation.

Mr. McClelland looked at Richard and said, "I thought I told you to stay away from the house."

Before Richard could answer he whispered forcefully, "You, boys, need to finish the haying. As soon as I get this business straightened out with this woman, I'll join you." He turned, grabbed the baskets of eggs, and went back into the kitchen.

The unspoken truth for me was the thought that I might be

able to get away from the farm. I knew escaping the work was only a possibility, but it was beginning to sink in that this might be a real way out. There would be no more stables to clean, manure to haul, cows to milk, water to carry, chickens to feed, corn to pick, fields to hoe, corn to husk. I might have a way to be like other boys—play baseball, go swimming, go fishing, go to the movies. I'd never before had another option. I knew about the world of other boys, but it had never been a possibility for me. Until now.

The more I thought about leaving the farm, the guiltier I felt. I was eleven years old, and the McClellands had given me a home since I was four. They were now in their sixties, and I knew that they depended on Richard and me to do a lot of work around the farm. I owed them.

Richard didn't interrupt my thoughts until we were back in the hayfield. "You got a letter from your mother. I thought she was dead. Do you think it's real? Do you have it on you?"

I realized that I didn't have the letter. "No."

"The old man seemed really upset," Richard said with a certain satisfaction. He had a knack for being able to call them "the old man and the old woman" behind their backs. The best I could muster was "Mr. and Mrs. McClelland" when I spoke when they weren't around. We both called her "Mom" to her face, which is what she wanted and which, over the years, came to feel fairly comfortable to me. Mr. McClelland wanted us to call him "Daddy," which we did but as little as possible. The idea of closeness to him made us both uncomfortable.

"Does this mean you're going to leave?" Richard rarely minced words.

"I'm not sure about anything yet."

"Look, you little shit, if you think you can just leave me with all this work, think again. You need to know that before you leave,

I'll kick the crap out of you. Understand?"

Chapter 2
Misdemeanors and Punishments

I lived in several foster homes before I was moved to the McClelland farm. I knew that my birth mother placed me in foster care before I was nine months old, and, as you would expect, I have no specific memory of that placement.

Some children who are abandoned by their mothers at such an early age die. Others are likely to suffer an anaclitic depression. The symptoms are characterized by intense fears of abandonment and feelings of helplessness and weakness. I've been told by social workers that I was generally listless and dull in my infant years in foster care. I eventually learned that my file contained the evaluation statement, "Roger shows little or no promise for a normal future." That assessment combined with some bad behaviors—for example, late potty training, biting, and crying more than normal—contributed to my farm placement.

My first clear memory is being spanked and put in a pantry because I had loaded my pants instead of the toilet. My potty-training failure took place in a home that housed several other foster children. Pantry-placement occurred when we were bad. Although some of the kids screamed a lot when they were closed in that dark space, I don't recall ever doing that. I do remember that it was quiet and smelled like spices, particularly cinnamon. When in the pantry, I would lie on the floor where I could see the light streaming through the crack beneath the door, watch children's feet, hear talking, and eventually fall asleep. It was a safe place.

In this same foster home there was a girl named Jill. She was older, skinny, and taller than I was with long dark hair. She picked on me a lot. We didn't get along. I'm sure that I was a pest to her, too.

I recall that tensions escalated between us to the point that out of frustration, I bit her hard. My teeth broke her skin. She screamed and ran away, crying and saying, "Roger hurt me. He bit me."

Our foster mother heard her and came for me. "Did you bite Jill?"

"Yes, 'cause she hit me."

My foster mother took me by the arm. "You apologize to Jill right now!"

She made me say I was sorry, but I wasn't. She spanked me because she was an honor graduate of the "spare the rod and spoil the child" school and I was not about to be spoiled. I was placed in solitary confinement in the pantry.

While I was curled up on the floor, the door suddenly sprang open; she grabbed me again and in one motion pulled me up and through the doorway. I thought that spanking and the pantry fit the high crime of biting, but I was wrong. She dragged me into the parlor and sat me down on the sofa.

A big man came into the room where I was seated and sat down beside me. He had a dark blue hat and wore a badge.

His stern look and his forceful words scared me.

"Did you bite Jill?" he queried.

"Yes," came my answer. When I started to follow with an explanation, he cut me off.

"If you bite Jill again or anyone else, I'll send you to jail. That's where bad boys are sent."

I knew that jail was worse than the pantry. He had my attention. I'd crossed the line, and my future was bleak.

The thought of jail was seared into my mind as though I had been branded with a hot iron. I did not need someone else to reinforce it. The incident became part of my internal oral history. Biting was bad. I knew that I did not want to go to jail for doing it or any other crime for that matter. Bad actions could lead to painful consequences.

Soon after, the Aid Society moved me to another foster family. Their name was Perry-Ferry. There were no other children living with them, which eliminated the biting risk. The Perry-Ferrys were old. I don't recall being spanked.

Mr. Perry-Ferry was a tall, slim man. His wife was heavyset with snow-white hair. They both were kind to me. I recall walking on icy sidewalks in Philadelphia beside Mr. Perry-Ferry. He used a cane and wore a dark hat. He held my hand whenever we walked to his favorite soda shop.

He was welcomed by everyone in the shop. He would order a glass of ginger ale for me. He would talk to his friends while I drank the ginger ale. Sometimes he bought me candy.

He would say, "You must keep this candy a secret just between us, okay?"

"Yes," I said, smiling and nodding.

The treats kept me quiet. When he had completed his socializing and I had finished my ginger ale, we walked back to the house where he placed his cane in a large open vaselike pot in the hallway near the front door. The container had other canes and umbrellas in it. Our coats and his hat were hung on hooks signaling that our little outing was over. I liked him and he liked me. I felt safe.

The Perry-Ferry household was quiet in contrast to where I'd lived before. Mrs. Perry-Ferry was always busy and let me play beside her. She talked to me and gave me cookies. When she brushed her long white hair, she would let me touch it.

"Your hair looks like snow."

"Yes, I know," she replied, "but it doesn't melt." Then she would look at me and say, "Sometimes you can melt my heart, though."

When she said that, I felt warm all over.

One morning the house was filled with strangers who moved about quietly. A woman whom I did not know took me into my foster parents' bedroom. Other men and women were there, too. Mr. Perry-Ferry was lying fully clothed on the bed on top of the covers. His feet were bare. The unknown woman took me up to a place beside the bed near his head.

She looked at me and said, "During the night your father went to Heaven."

I could hear Mrs. Perry-Ferry sobbing in the living room.

Everyone looked sad. Although I did not know what everything meant, I did sense that it meant that there would be no more trips to the soda shop.

I knew that I would never see him again. I was sad, too.

The bigger implications for me became quite clear very soon. The Children's Aid Society had a rule that one-parent households could not serve as foster homes. In addition, I did not know it at the time, but they must have evaluated me as well and determined that I was well below average in intelligence. Based on those facts, they decided that I should be placed on a farm where I would learn farming skills and be employable and self-sufficient when I aged out of the foster care system.

Within a few days after Mr. Perry-Ferry's death, a female social worker came to the house.

"Roger, I've come to take you to a farm." She spoke gently, but enthusiastically. "There will be many different animals there, and you'll have a big brother named Richard."

I stood silently, unsure about what was to happen next, until the social worker took me outside and opened a car door.

Mrs. Perry-Ferry handed a brown bag to the social worker and said, "Here are Roger's clothes." The social worker placed the bag on the back seat.

Mrs. Perry-Ferry bent down and hugged me. After the hug she gave me another brown bag. She opened it so that I could see what was in it and said, "Papa told me that you love ginger ale. Here are two bottles and a bottle opener. When you get thirsty on your long trip, you'll have something to drink."

She started to cry. I cried. The social worker gently pulled me away and guided me onto the car's front seat. I sat, holding onto the paper bag that held the bottles of ginger ale. I saw Mrs. Perry-Ferry near my side of the car waving as we drove away. I waved goodbye back.

The trip to the next family was underway. I sat on the front seat with my legs thrust out like a little Pinocchio, and like him, I was waiting for my new life to begin. I had no idea where I was going except that it was far away. My view of the world from the front seat was limited, but I could see the sky, which at first was filled with trolley wires, then only electric wires, and eventually branches of trees. The tree branches arched over us, forming a bright green tunnel. The windows were open, and occasionally I could smell the fragrances of spring.

The social worker broke into my daydreams when she said, "Roger, you must be getting thirsty by now. Wouldn't you like to have some ginger ale?"

I held the bag and said, "No, I'm not thirsty."

Further along on the trip she said, "You've been holding onto those bottles ever since we left the Perry-Ferrys. Don't you want to put them down or have a drink?"

I clutched them tighter and again said, "No."

"You know, Roger, that ginger ale is getting warmer. It won't taste as good when it gets warm. Don't you think we ought to drink it now?"

I heard the "we" in her request. I was not going to share anything with her. I gave her another no, but this time firmer still. We were in the car that she controlled, but I controlled the ginger ale.

While I sat stubbornly holding onto the bag, I heard a *putt-putt* sound growing louder outside the car. We were climbing up a hill, and the social worker had slowed in order to drive past the tractor coming our way on the narrow road, which gave me a good look. The big green and yellow tractor was driven by a man wearing a straw hat. What a sight —my first real tractor and farmer. I later found out that we were driving up Old Snake Hill Road, which today is called Pine Run Road. I think the old name was better since the road was so twisty.

After a few more twisty roads, we arrived at a long lane and turned down it. We passed a big red barn. The air was filled with strong unpleasant smells.

"Roger, we're here. This will be your new home with new parents and a brother."

When the car stopped, she leaned toward me and said, "Mrs. McClelland, your new mom, is a nice woman. Be good."

I did not know I'd been bad.

A woman opened the car door on my side and helped me get out. She was introduced as Mrs. McClelland. She was skinny, wore her brown hair in a bun, had glasses, and smelled fresh like soap. Dogs were jumping, barking, and trying to lick me. She quieted them and pushed them away because she could see that they were frightening me.

Although the social worker was talking to her, Mrs. McClelland was focused on me. "Roger, welcome to our farm." I studied her for a moment before I said, "Hello." Mrs. McClelland leaned down and said, "May I take your bag?" I shrugged and said, "No," and held onto it.

She coached me up the concrete walkway that lay between tall trees, toward a big white house with green trim and a porch. The building was huge with many doors and an attached shed that extended like an arm along one side of the sparse lawn. I learned later that part of the building was for storing wheat and tools and the other part held coal for the furnaces. Several cats that were curled up on the wicker furniture eyed the dogs and us as our procession moved toward the screened front door. I was more curious than they were about what would happen next. I was scared and excited.

"Richard is at school now. I know he's eager to meet you. Your birthday is in April, and his is in August. He is a little over four years older than you," Mrs. McClelland said as we entered the kitchen.

When we were inside, Mrs. McClelland took the bag from me and placed it on the tray of the kitchen cupboard. I never knew what happened to the bottles of ginger ale. Maybe the social worker got them after all. Maybe they were chilled in the refrigerator, and we drank them later when Richard came home. All I know is that I had held onto them as long as I could.

Chapter 3
An Apology of Sorts

I was sad and missed my old home. Mrs. McClelland consoled me by writing a letter to Mrs. Perry-Ferry saying that I missed her and how I was doing. She wrote back, and Mrs. McClelland read the letter to me. Hearing her words triggered memories, and I cried. Mr. McClelland, who was sitting outside on the porch, heard me.

Mr. McClelland was an average-sized man who wore light blue work shirts and dark blue dungarees held up by a thick black belt that was wrapped tightly around his thin waist. His unshaven face had many wrinkles. He had a corncob pipe stuck between his teeth as though he were ready to bite it in two. His appearance scared me, especially in contrast to the neatly dressed and always clean-shaven Mr. Perry-Ferry. When he burst into the kitchen, I felt a chill like it had suddenly gone from summer to winter.

He asked, "Boy, have you been hurt?"

I was sobbing and just shook my head and whimpered, "No."

"Then, what's the matter?"

Mrs. McClelland looked worried and said, "John, he's a little homesick. He misses Mrs. Perry-Ferry."

"This is his home now. Make him stop or I will."

My sobbing intensified.

Mr. McClelland grabbed me and marched me upstairs to my room. As he closed the door behind me, he looked at me and said, "If you know what's good for you, you'll stop crying now."

I began to wail. The door opened, and he stepped into the room with what I learned later was a slat from a bale of peat moss.

"I told you to stop it! This will teach you that I mean what I say." Mr. McClelland grabbed me again, bent me over his knee, and swatted me several times with the slat. The slat hurt. I was four years old.

I never saw another letter from Mrs. Perry-Ferry.

The next day after spanking me, when I was on my knees in the front yard making roadways in the dry dirt, using my hand as a plow, Mr. McClelland arrived in front of the house in a stranger's car. I hardly noticed them. Mr. McClelland then stood over me and said, "Look what I brought Mum for Mother's Day."

I looked and saw a tiny wiggling black furry ball with small black eyes. It was a puppy. He placed the puppy on the ground and pushed it toward me and said, "This here is a Toy Cocker Spaniel. You can take care of it for Mum."

I immediately liked the puppy whose tongue was licking my hands and chin. He was excited to meet me.

"What's his name?" I asked.

"He doesn't have a name. You can name him."

"How about we call him Rex?" Richard had arrived and spoken up. "He looks so tiny that he will never be king-sized, so he needs a name that would make him feel like a king."

Rex became my dog.

Over the years the farm became the home for many dogs. We lived about thirty miles outside of Philadelphia in rural Bucks County. When fall arrived, hunters from the city would come to hunt the abundant pheasants and rabbits. The hunters were usually friendly and cared for their dogs. Some did not. I was told that some hunters, usually city people, would only have their dogs for hunting and would just drive away and leave them when the season was over. Over the years a few of these abandoned dogs appeared in the yard as strays, looking for food and attention.

These multi-breed dogs accumulated on the farm and were given names like Trixie, Spot, and Lassie. They were all housebroken and friendly. Some preferred to stay outside. Richard gave them a lot of attention, but I only loved Rex.

I never saw papers for Rex, but he was true to his breed in size and color. The other dogs were just mutts, and all were huge compared to Rex. We had three to five dogs around the house, inside and out. There were females and males, dog fights, and sometimes puppies. The McClellands would find homes for some of the puppies with other farmers in the area. The remaining unplaced puppies disappeared.

Sometimes, Dr. Binswanger, the veterinarian, was called, and he would "fix" the females in exchange for produce. This stopped the arrival of puppies, but it did not stop the males from going off in the spring to fight other dogs in order to win mates. Rex ran away once and came back with a torn ear. I tried my best to keep him in the house during those times when he was most likely to run off. I was always afraid of losing him. Some of the other dogs never did return.

Rex was a great runner. He had a short tail like a rabbit except he was black as coal. His backside was so smooth that when he would run, he looked like a black cannonball with tiny legs. He would chase cows, other dogs, cats, cars, horses, and ducks. Anything that moved was considered fair game for a good chase. He would fetch tossed sticks and wait eagerly for another toss.

When there was time after the chores were done, there was time for long investigative walks in the fields and the woods around the farm. We would sit and enjoy the sight and smell of flowers, the sounds of insects and birds, and I would look at clouds while stroking his curly black hair. There was no purpose to our outings. There was no need for a purpose. We just existed together for those moments.

When I was in eighth grade, Rex developed a large, angry red tumor between his hind legs. Dr. Binswanger was long gone, having committed suicide several years earlier, and no one was available for treatment.

Mr. McClelland came to me and said, "Son, there is nothing that can be done to save Rex. You know what we have to do."

I looked at Rex and looked away. "Yes, I know."

"It might be better for you to go inside and let me handle this," replied Mr. McClelland. He already had the shotgun in his hand.

Chapter 4
Hypervigiliance

I arrived on the farm in early May, an innocent-to-the-ways-of-nature city kid. At four, I was about to learn about the world beyond cement sidewalks, cars, and loud streets.

The farm was a quiet place. The city's incessant traffic noises were replaced by the sounds of insects, birds, and the soft rustling of swaying tree branches. I soon learned that there were other differences between living in the city and living on the farm.

Upon arrival, I asked, "Where's the bathroom?"

"Outside," came the reply from Mrs. McClelland. "Come, I'll show you."

Mrs. McClelland took my hand and guided me down a path to a small wooden shed. There was a door with a latch and a hole. The latch was used to pull the door open.

"This is where we go to the bathroom," she said matter-of-factly.

"We close the door, lift the lid on the toilet, and do our business. We clean up using the papers," she explained.

She paused to be sure that I understood and said, "Afterwards, put the lid down and come outside."

I had never seen anything like it. The shadowy dark space inside was dirty and smelly; it was very uninviting. I did what I was told and climbed onto the wooden seat and went to the bathroom. I had no idea what else lay ahead for me on this "farm," but I felt apprehensive.

I learned that the shed was called an outhouse. The one the McClellands had was a two-seater. As I grew up, I wondered why two people would want to share the same small space while going to the bathroom with all the attendant noises and odors. I never saw two people in there at the same time.

The wooden outhouse on the farm was practical in every aspect. It had a door and a small window for light and ventilation. The seats each had a wooden lid on hinges, which were always left in the closed position when not being used. A small bag of lime rested on the floor with a cup inside to be used to add lime through the hole when you finished your business. The lime helped to suppress odors. Old newspapers rested beside the seat to be used for wiping.

The building was designed to be tilted back to allow for waste to be scooped out several times a year. At night it was really a scary place to be, especially in the summer when there were a lot of insect noises and strange animal sounds outside. In the winter it was too cold to stay long.

Soon after I arrived on the farm, I needed to use the outhouse urgently. I rushed in and sat down on the seat farthest from the door because I wanted as much privacy as possible; every inch away from the door seemed to matter to me. I did what I had to do and pulled up my pants. Pure pain shot through me. My bottom was on fire. I sprang out of the outhouse, screaming while dropping my pants. I was being stung by wasps that had been swept into my pants from the toilet seat cover.

I later learned that no one used that second seat. Disuse had allowed a family of wasps to set up housekeeping. They stung me aggressively. Those few stings had taught me several lessons. One, wasps really hurt and should be avoided. Two, I would never use the second seat again. And three, I would only use the outhouse when there were no other options.

Because of that experience, I was about to learn another lesson about living in the country. If you go outside, you use whatever is available to wipe. Leaves worked well although they tended to be smoother and less absorbent than newspapers.

Once, I found what I thought was a good spot in a hedgerow with lots of green leaves. I finished my business, cleaned up, and went home. That night my hands, arms, and bottom began to itch. I was covered with a red rash everywhere that the leaves had touched me. I was embarrassed to admit that I had gone to the bathroom outside, but I had to ask for help.

I went downstairs after dinner. "Mom, could you come here and help me?" I asked softly to avoid being heard by others.

She got up and came into the hallway. "What's the matter?" she asked.

I showed her my arms and my hands.

"Oh my, you have poison ivy!" she exclaimed. "Well, I know what to do about that."

"You do," I said with relief.

She looked closely as she held my hands and turned my arms. Then, she asked, "Do you have it anywhere else?"

I looked up at her sadly and nodded, knowing that I would have to tell her if I wanted to get relief. "Inside my pants, too," I said.

"How did you get it there?" she asked and then paused as understanding crossed her face.

The awkward moment passed as she went to work. She treated me by applying wet whitewash to the sores which helped dry up the oily residue from the poison ivy and soothe the irritated areas.

Mrs. McClelland must have called the Aid Society because the social worker who brought me to the farm came back a day or two after the whitewash treatment. She brought with her what she called a "remedy" in a dark bottle. She scolded me for what I had done and warned me to be careful in the future. She told Mrs. McClelland to give me one teaspoon of the liquid from the bottle mixed in water twice a day until it was empty. The treatment was designed to build up resistance to poison ivy. It worked.

The McClellands likely discussed with the social worker my misadventures with the wasps and the poison ivy as well as my overall adjustments because she stayed in the house for a long time on that visit.

Learning about the farm was a process. There were times when I learned by trial and error and other times when I learned a lot from Richard, who was good at telling stories and sharing his perspectives. While the social worker was inside talking to the McClellands, Richard told me a story.

"Have you seen the stuffed animals in the old cardboard barrel in their bedroom?" he asked.

"You mean the gray elephant and the donkey?" I replied because I'd seen them when I was snooping.

"Those toys belonged to another foster kid who lived here named Phillip," Richard said as he warmed up to tell the story. "He got killed right here on the farm."

"How?"

"The kid jumped on the side of a truck loaded with tomatoes. The dumb shit fell off when it went over a bump and got run over."

"Really!" He had my full attention. "Then what happened?"

"Well, Uncle Ted, who you know is the old lady's brother, was driving the truck to Campbell's Soup in Philadelphia. He didn't even know what happened until he came back two days later."

Richard went on, "The old lady took it hard, but the old man got very quiet. He didn't swear or anything. His real son got killed a few years back in another trucking accident. He's tough."

"Do you think they're talking about that now?" I asked.

"Could be. Maybe they are. Or maybe they're talking about how stupid you are and that you could get killed here, too."

At that moment and before I could react, the door opened and the social worker came out. She told us that she would be back in a few weeks and that we both should be careful around the farm.

I nodded, saying yes, while Richard just smiled. We never saw that social worker again. When the new one did come, she didn't refer to anything that had happened in the past. It was a fresh beginning.

Over the next year or so, changes began to happen. The farm had two active wells and one old one, which was covered with boards. The wells were designed to collect rainwater. One well was outside of the barn alongside the lane. When it rained, water would flow down the lane and be diverted by a channel in the driveway into the well. A heavy rain would almost always fill it up. The water from that well was used exclusively for the animals.

There was a second deeper well, which had been dynamited out, adjacent to the house. Water from the roof of the house and the porch was guided into the well by a series of gutters. That water could be pumped by hand at the well site for animals. We got our drinking water from it through the use of a hand pump in the kitchen.

One summer morning I was awakened by a pounding sound outside my bedroom windows. When I looked out, I saw a tall piece of machinery and two men guiding a heavy tube up and down. I got up and went outside to see what the unexpected banging was about.

"What are you doing?" I asked.

"This is a well driller. We're digging a well for your family, young man. This way you'll have water," one of the workmen said with a smile.

"We already have water," I said.

"Yeah, maybe, but this will be an artesian well, and there is nothing better than artesian well water."

The loud banging noise reminded me of the city. I stood and watched, fascinated by the well driller, which went *thump! thump!* and the gray-brown ooze that came out of the ground and pooled up on the grass.

The pounding went on for several days until the machine hit a vein of water. We all gathered around, drinking cold artesian well water for the first time. Mr. McClelland looked triumphant and said that we no longer had to worry about droughts.

The McClellands had many skilled relatives. They came and installed pumps and piping and faucets in the kitchen for the water. They even installed a bathtub at the end of a hallway between the kitchen and the parlor and connected water to it. We could take baths in a bathtub instead of bathing out of a bucket. However, there was no hot water. When we needed hot water, we heated a bucket of water on the coal stove and poured it into the tub. We would carry it quickly from the kitchen to the bathtub.

The following summer the skilled relatives, led by Uncle Hugh, built a septic system in the backyard. Uncle Hugh was Mr. McClelland's brother-in-law, who had come over from Northern Ireland about the same time as Mr. McClelland. He worked in a warehouse in Philadelphia during the week but enjoyed helping out on the farm on weekends. He'd been raised on a farm in the "old country" and loved being outside. Things always seemed easier when he was around.

Once the septic system was in place, they installed a toilet inside. That eliminated the need to use the outhouse. Not long after the work was completed, Uncle Hugh died of a heart attack.

I was adjusting to the farm, and the McClellands were adjusting to the twentieth century. I think that the Aid Society helped to catalyze movements toward modernization of the farm.

Chapter 5
Bugs, Worms, and Dust

My bedroom had two big windows—one facing north and the other to the west. The walls were stone and more than a foot thick. The glass windows, which were open on this hot day, had been installed long after the house had been built and did not fit tightly. They rattled in thunderstorms and heavy winds and, I was to learn later, were loose enough to allow snow to pass through and accumulate on my bedcovers in the winter.

One morning, I woke up in a fright due to the loud rattling of these windows. I climbed out of bed and saw an airplane roaring close to the ground in the tomato field. I thought it was on fire and was trying to land or was about to crash. Anxious, I dressed and raced downstairs to see what was happening.

Mom was standing at the kitchen window, not at all afraid. Richard and Mr. McClelland had been eating breakfast but had gotten up and gone outside. I was beginning to get used to calling Mr. McClelland, "Daddy," but it wasn't easy. They were standing behind the house watching the plane.

"What's happening?" I asked.

Mom replied without turning, "That plane is crop-dusting our tomatoes."

"What does that mean?"

I was disappointed to learn it wasn't smoke coming out of the plane and the plane wasn't going to land. Instead, it was just powdered pesticide. She turned and motioned to me to stand beside her and said, "Well, hornworms eat the leaves of the tomato plants. Spraying kills them. We get a lot more tomatoes when we spray."

"What are hornworms?" I knew about earthworms but had never heard of hornworms. The name made them sound dangerous.

"They're green and have a horn on one end. Eventually they turn into moths," she said patiently.

"Oh," I acknowledged her words without understanding. I decided to go outside and watch as the plane continued to spray the field. The spray settled like a white fog on the field.

"You boys need to stay away from the field for a few days. That spray is poisonous," instructed Mr. McClelland.

The bright orange plane had two sets of wings. The pilot made one last pass over the edge of the tomato field and then circled and flew toward us, dipping the plane's wings as he went low over the house. It was noisy but exciting.

The McClellands had a contract to grow tomatoes for Campbell's Soup. Under the contract, the company provided all the plants needed for the acreage assigned to the McClellands. The company sprayed the fields at their expense and even provided labor to help pick the ripe tomatoes. The Campbells people would send two dark-skinned men to come live with us. They slept for several weeks in one of the bedrooms on the third floor. That bedroom was hot in the summer. If the weather was good, the men would eat on the porch. They ate inside infrequently, but it was always after we'd finished eating ourselves. They kept to themselves.

The two men were hard workers. They spoke very little English. One of my first jobs on the farm was to carry quart bottles of water to them in the fields. They would drink the water quickly and motion for more. Mom felt sympathetic toward them.

When I was a few years older, she said, "Come upstairs with me to the third floor. I want to show you something."

We went to the third floor where she opened a door in the wall of one of the bedrooms and said, "Long ago the people who owned this house hid escaping slaves in this wall."

I was surprised because I hadn't seen the door before. "Why did people have slaves?"

"Slave owners were farmers just like us who needed help. But they were cruel to their helpers. The slaves had to escape in order to be free of their bad masters. It is not right for people to own other people as slaves." She paused. "Our house was part of what they called 'The Underground Railroad.' The man who owned this house hid the escaping slaves in this wall. He had a relationship with a man in New Britain who was a Quaker."

"Are the Puerto Ricans our slaves?" I asked.

"No, those men just work for us. But many of the Puerto Rican people used to be slaves," she said, pausing while she thought about what she would say next. "We must always be kind and respectful to other people, no matter what they look like, what they believe in, or where they come from. Jesus said, 'Do unto others as you would have others do unto you.'"

I liked it when she reminded me of Biblical teachings. I'd heard stories about slaves and slavery but did not realize that it was so close to home. Secretly, I'd worried that maybe the Puerto Ricans were slaves. I felt relieved that they were not. I felt pride that this home was used to help slaves escape. In the back of my mind, though, I wondered if Richard and I weren't a little like slaves since this was not our real family, we always had a lot of work to do, and Mr. McClelland would punish us if we did not do the work to his liking.

Within a couple of years of my arrival, we stopped growing tomatoes for Campbells. The fields were then used to grow corn, wheat, and timothy hay exclusively. We raised tomatoes for ourselves. Mrs. McClelland canned whole tomatoes, made tomato juice, and even fried tomatoes in the summer to serve on bread. We had tomatoes or potatoes in some form with lunches and dinners throughout the year.

Tomatoes had hornworms; potatoes had potato bugs. We didn't spray for potato bugs, which ate potato plants so voraciously that they could strip a plant of its leaves in a day or two. Picking potato bugs off the plants was one of my earliest jobs. I was five years old. Mr. McClelland believed that if you were alive and able, then you could work.

One day he took me to the potato field where Richard and he were hoeing. He held out a quart bottle with a little oil in the bottom of it.

"Here's what I want you to do," he said, pointing to the plants. "See these bugs with the black and white stripes on their backs and orange heads?"

"Uh-huh."

"I want you to take them off the leaves with your fingers like this and drop them in this bottle with the oil. You see," he said encouragingly as he repeated the process.

I touched one. It felt so slippery moving around between my fingers that I let it go.

"Oh, no! They won't hurt you. If you're going to be a farmer, you have to be tougher than that."

I picked another one off a leaf and held onto it and dropped it into the bottle.

"There, that's the idea. When I was about the same age as you, or younger, in the old country, I used to pick hundreds of these off plants in a day. They paid me one penny for every hundred bugs I picked. In fact, I've heard that President Herbert Hoover used to pick potato bugs to get money, too."

I didn't have any idea who Herbert Hoover was, and Mr. McClelland never offered to pay me any money. All I could see were long rows of potatoes and a lot of bugs. While they hoed, I picked bugs. I recall that I picked enough bugs that they were landing on top of each other. Some used the dead ones as rafts and floated around on the oil. Others began to crawl out of the jar.

Mr. McClelland, who'd been checking on my progress during the day, looked at what was happening and commented, "Son, those bugs are coming out faster than they're going in."

He was right. They were crawling out of the jar and onto the ground and heading back to the potato plants. I looked up sheepishly and said, "I guess I'm not as good as you and President Hoover."

"Well, that's about as bad a start at bug picking as I've ever seen," he surmised, snickering.

When the growing season for potatoes was over, harvesting began. The McClellands had a potato digger that was pulled by two horses. They pulled it up and down the rows of dying potato vines, exposing white potatoes on both sides of the furrow. I felt like I was on a treasure hunt, finding potatoes of all different shapes and sizes. Some of the shapes looked like human faces while others looked like animals. Some of the potatoes were tiny, but many were much larger than my hands.

I helped to fill the baskets, but the filled baskets were too heavy for me to carry. The McClellands stored the baskets in the cellar of the house, which was cool and damp. When the harvest was over, the cellar was stuffed with baskets filled with potatoes. We ate potatoes all winter long. Sometimes they were served mashed, sometimes boiled and served whole, and other times fried, especially for breakfast. When spring came, the potatoes in the cellar were beginning to sprout. Sprouting made the white insides turn black, and they tasted awful. We had to eat them anyway.

During the summer, my jobs included carrying water and coffee to the men in the fields. On one particular day, I was daydreaming, probably mesmerized by the quiet and the hot stillness of the afternoon. My daydreams were interrupted by a loud noise blasting in my ear. An insect had landed on my shoulder without me knowing it and had started singing its song.

I was so startled that I dropped the two bottles, swatted my shoulder, and ran for the house. The laughing men told me later that I'd just had my first direct encounter with what they called a locust, an insect that I learned years later was a cicada. I should add that the halcyon sounds of serenading cicadas in the distance are very different from one unexpectedly screeching in your ear.

On another day after making my deliveries, I decided to wander off into a big field of wheat. The wheat was much taller than I was and blocked my view. Soon I was so deep in the field that I had no idea where I was or how to get back home. I was feeling panicky and began going in circles. I was lost. When I felt the most helpless and stopped looking ahead, I looked up and spotted the red roof of the barn in the distance. I knew that if I stayed on a course, walking toward that roof, that I would eventually get out of the field. That's what I did. I rescued myself without anyone knowing I'd been lost.

The Aid Society managers would send out a social worker to the farm once in the fall and once in the spring to pick up Richard and me and take us into Philadelphia. The purposes of these trips were to have us examined by a dentist and a doctor and to outfit us with winter clothes in the fall and summer clothes in the spring.

During my first trip to Philadelphia, I was riding in the back seat of the car with Richard. It was hot. I was nervous. I had no idea about what was going to happen to us. The rocking back and forth and the stops and starts made me sick. I threw up, spraying my breakfast on the car floor and on the back of the social worker's seat. The social worker was very upset. She cleaned up the mess, but the car still smelled. Richard got to ride in the front seat. She told me to warn her the next time so that she could pull over. She drove us back home later that day in a different car.

The trip was a good one because we got new clothes and had graham crackers, milk, and peanut butter and jelly sandwiches for lunch. The doctor and the dentist were kind to us. The dentist gave us toothbrushes and tooth powder and told us that we should brush every day. Eventually, the trips to Philadelphia with the social workers were replaced by train rides, which we took alone. I enjoyed the freedom of those unsupervised trips, which afforded me the chance to deviate from the assigned transit plan.

Chapter 6
Old Kit-Bag

Before I went to school, every day I would see Richard read school books, Mr. McClelland read the newspaper, and Mom read the Bible. I wanted to read, too. I squinted, I looked at pages sideways or from other angles because I believed that reading happened when you did something mechanical or tricky with your eyes.

Mom saw me trying and said, "Roger, reading has to be learned. You have to learn your ABCs and how to spell. Then you can read words. That's what you'll learn to do in school."

Her comments excited me more about going to school. I wanted to be able to read the Bible, the newspaper, and books like everyone else, and the sooner, the better.

The one-room school for first and second grades was about two miles from our farm. It was named POS of A, which stood for National Patriotic Order Sons of America. We learned that the POS of A was an organization founded between two great wars, the American Revolution and the American Civil War. Its purpose was to preserve the public school system. We showed our respect every day to the men who had fought in those wars and for our country by reciting The Pledge of Allegiance. POS of A was another organization influencing and managing my life, similar to the Children's Aid Society of Pennsylvania.

Going to school introduced me to children who lived outside the foster care system. I learned that they came from real families who owned cars and trucks, who provided them with good clothes and gave them many gifts. I heard that families took "vacation trips" to the "shore" or to the Poconos, that babies were being born into their families instead of being delivered by social workers. Perhaps most importantly, I learned that these other kids had lots more toys and games than we did on the farm. I became aware for the first time that we were materially poor.

Our teacher had the unfortunate name of Miss Freking, which was pronounced, "freaking." The children made fun of her behind her back by calling her "Freaky Freking." I wanted to be like the others, so I made fun of her as well. She was very young compared to the McClellands and really cared for us children.

Since I could neither read any words nor write my ABCs like most of the other first graders, I was placed in a group with several others who seemed to lack intellectual promise. Likely the Aid Society's evaluation of me had been transmitted to the teacher. This small group in today's parlance might be called "children with special needs," but back then we were called "retards." Some of the children made fun of us, just like they made fun of Miss Freking, except that they didn't do it behind our backs. Name-calling hurt.

The school had a coal-fired furnace in the basement. When the furnace was used on cold days, ashes had to be cleaned out and fresh coal added to keep the fire going. Since I did it at our home as one of my chores, I knew how to do it and was eager to please. I volunteered. Miss Freking was relieved because the basement of the building was a messy place and tending the furnace might dirty her clothes. It was a perfect arrangement. She was always clean, and I got to play with fire twice a day.

I found some old toothbrushes in the basement that had probably been used for an art project since they had paint on them. I threw them into the fire and watched with fascination as they twisted and turned, melted, and then burst into colorful bright flames. The plastic toothbrushes burned with a terrible smell. The odor must have permeated the building because the door at the top of the stairs burst open. Suddenly, I heard the sound of Miss Freking's footsteps as she rushed down toward me.

She called out to me sternly, "Roger, what are you doing?" I turned, looked up, and saw fire in her eyes as bright as the furnace flames. I felt some relief because she didn't have a slat in her hand.

"I put some toothbrushes in the fire," I stammered.

She looked past me to be sure that nothing more was happening. "You're down here to take care of the furnace, not to play with fire. Do you understand?"

I nodded silently that I understood.

"Now finish cleaning up, close that furnace door, and come back upstairs." She turned, looking up to the ceiling while shaking her head, and went back up the stairs.

Her words were direct and had hit their mark. I knew that if I'd been home, I would have been spanked hard for doing something bad. I knew I had been caught doing something bad, but at the same time, I learned that plastic burns with a horrible smell. I would have to be careful not to burn toothbrushes again.

The furnace incident was soon forgotten and replaced by planning for the Halloween party. Miss Freking announced to the classes that we were in the Halloween season, and there was going to be a costume party. Everyone was to bring a costume to class on Halloween day and wear it for the party. There would be various prizes for costumes, but the grand prize would be for the child who was the most difficult one to identify. Everyone was excited about the party. The excitement increased each day as we drew scary pumpkin faces on orange paper, cut them out, put our names on them, and hung them up. Everyone talked about bobbing for apples. I had no idea what that was about, but no more than I knew anything about Halloween.

Because I wanted to learn about Halloween, after supper I talked to Mom about the costume party that was planned for us at school. She was sitting, bent over in her chair cleaning eggs as usual in the corner of the kitchen. She was either cleaning eggs or reading the Bible when she was in that chair. She seemed to enjoy some of my interruptions and would listen to me chatter while she worked.

She paused and said, "It is getting to be that time of year again, I guess. What do you want to know?"

"What is Halloween? What is trick-or-treating? Why do people wear costumes?" The questions spilled out of me.

She thoughtfully described the ancient tradition of Halloween much like a teacher would with kind patience. She told me about ghosts and goblins, and trick-or-treating. She said that we could carve a real pumpkin that we raised to feed our cows and put a candle in it. When I had said that I wanted to go trick-or-treating, she explained to me that we lived too far away from other people and that going to their houses would be out of the question. I don't think that I was too disappointed at the time because we really did live pretty far away from other houses and it seemed reasonable. However, I did need a costume for Halloween day at school.

The practical reality of that time in my life boiled down to the question: "What could I wear?"

We did not have a car or a truck. We never went shopping. People came to our farm and dropped food off and picked up our eggs and other produce, including hogs and chickens. We got clothing through mail-order catalogues, which would be too slow to be on hand for the big day, even if we had the money to buy a costume. I asked for help, but there was nothing that could be done. I expected not to have a store-bought costume, but I had an idea.

Halloween came. I went to school and watched all the other kids line up their boxes and bags with costumes in them. When it was time to dress in our costumes, I went down to the furnace room, my workplace, and took three of the large brown paper bags stored there for starting fires. I put one bag on each leg and pulled one over the top of my upper body. The bags were big enough that they completely covered me. I could see to walk by looking straight down to the floor through the tiny crack between the tops of the bags on my legs and the one on my upper body. Let the judging begin—I was ready.

When we returned to the classroom, we saw that Miss Freking had moved the desks and chairs into the middle of the room. She directed us to march around the room in a circle. She identified each student by calling out their names. She would say, "Look at Hopalong Cassidy, that must be Eddie Boyle," "There's pretty Cinderella, that must be Hope Star," or "That woodsman is Eugene Pone." As we marched around the room, the number of unidentified costumed children dwindled until I was the only one left marching. I was the winner of the grand prize.

I don't remember what the prize was, but I do know at the time that I believed that I'd fooled Miss Freking with my paper bags. I felt great.

She gave me a boost at a time when I needed it, in my young life that already felt to me lacking in promise. Her boost whetted my appetite to win again. That was my true grand prize.

After Halloween, Thanksgiving and Christmas came and went. After Christmas, I began to notice what the other children had gotten for gifts in contrast to the clothes that Richard and I had gotten. The other children brought red fire trucks, little cars, cap pistols, games, coloring books, and even new lunch pails to school. I could only imagine what they must have had back at home. I assumed that what they brought to school was their overflow stuff.

When I was home, I would talk about what others had and we did not. I was tagging along behind Mom, whining about how poor we were while she was gathering eggs, feeding the chickens, and doing other chores. She was not pleased.

She paused, looking up from her work and down at me. Then she said, "Pack up your troubles in your old kit-bag, and smile, smile, smile." She went back to her chores.

Her comment stopped me then and every time afterwards when she felt the need to repeat it to me. She was never mean in the way she said it, but she was clearly not sympathetic either and wanted me to stop. She was a stoic. I was told to accept things the way they were and keep on going. Although I eventually learned that she was quoting a World War One marching song for the soldiers, which may have helped her to get through her day, it was not helpful to me.

As the weather warmed up and spring came, school was fun. Recess was great, especially in the warm weather. The other kids would let me play with them, and they shared their toys with me. On one spring day just before the end of the school year, I was playing with Eddie Boyle. He was a nice boy, who loved Hopalong Cassidy. His parents had given him a Hopalong Cassidy vest, a white hat, and two matching pearl-handled cap pistols with holsters. The caps were circular instead of the typical long rolls, which meant that you would have to reload after six shots, just like real guns. They were special.

We played cowboys and Indians during recess. Since I had no guns, I was always one of the Indians. We would run around and hide in the tall grass or in the bushes along the road or behind trees in the pasture behind the school. We would ambush the cowboys, and they would shoot at us with their cap guns. The popping sound of cap guns and the smell of burnt paper filled the air and made our imaginary world real.

I was excited to tell Richard stories about school, especially recess and the ambushes. I always wanted to impress him. Usually, I either bored him or annoyed him.

As we were doing our evening chores—Richard would fill water buckets while I cleaned the feed troughs—we talked. On one particular evening, when I was telling him about the guns and Eddie Boyle, Richard abruptly stopped pouring water and looked down at me.

"Is Eddie Boyle's mom a teacher?" he asked.

"Yes, I think so."

"I never liked her. She caused me trouble more than once. The bitch even punished me for swearing." Richard was smart but did not apply himself in school and had developed a reputation for being a troublemaker.

"How big are the guns?" he asked with a gleam in his eye.

"Big and long."

"How far away from the school did you go when you played?"

I was all too eager to please him by answering his questions.

"Not too far. Just up to the telephone pole along the road in the front of the school. And maybe past the first few trees in the back in the pasture."

"Did you ever get to use the guns yourself?"

"I've touched them, but Eddie likes to keep them."

"Did you say white pearl handles?"

"Yup, carved pearl handles and long, shiny, silver barrels."

I could tell that Richard was putting together a plan. I felt important. After all, I had the information that he needed to complete his plan. I thought that there might be a part for me in the plan. There was.

"You said that he had two guns. Right?"

"Yes."

"Then if he lost one, he would still have one. Right?"

"Yes."

The logic was clear. But I knew it wasn't right. However, at that moment it was more important to me that I please Richard than it was to think about Eddie.

Richard's plan was simple. The next day during recess I was to get Eddie to let me have one of the guns to play with. Then I would run after the kids who were the Indians and lose the gun in the tall grass near a place where it could be found by Richard after school.

His plan for me to play and lose the gun worked. I hid the gun in the tall grass near the telephone pole when no one was looking. I told Eddie just as recess was ending that I'd lost the gun playing in the pasture. He was very upset. Miss Freking let us go out and search in the pasture. Eddie cried. I felt so bad that I wanted to cry, too, but I didn't.

The school was close enough to our farm that it was an easy trip for Richard after our chores were done to ride his bicycle to the school, find the gun, and ride home without being missed. When he came home, he had the gun in his waistband and a big grin. We went up into the hay barn and hid it in the loose hay. We were glad to have the gun, but we had no caps. Richard told me that he would get some caps for us.

The next day the kids at school and I spent all recess looking for Eddie's gun, but, of course, no one could find it. That evening when Richard and I were outside watering and feeding the chickens, a car came down the lane. Mrs. Boyle and Eddie were in the car. This was bad. I was scared.

Richard took me into the barn and said, "Stay out of sight. If they come and get you, don't squeal. Do you understand?"

I agreed but inside I was scared of the McClellands, Mrs. Boyle, and most of all, Richard. My stomach was turning as I watched through the cracks of the barn wall. I saw Mrs. Boyle march briskly up the walkway to the house with Eddie in tow.

The McClellands were already outside on the porch since it was unusual for a car to arrive in the evening.

Mrs. Boyle greeted them, saying, "Hi, I'm Mrs. Boyle, and this is my son, Eddie."

Mom immediately said, "Hello, how might we help you?" She sensed that this was not a social call because she did not invite them into the kitchen.

Mrs. Boyle went on by saying, "I think we've met before. Don't you have a son named Richard?"

"Yes, we do," Mom replied. "Does this have to do with him?"

"Not him. This has to do with Roger." She told them the story about how the gun was lost when it was in my possession. She even showed Mom the gun that was the match to the one that was lost.

"Have you seen Roger with a gun like this one?" she asked.

The McClellands were in their sixties and always working. They did not see everything that we did on the farm. Mom was very convincing when she said, "No, we've not seen any guns and certainly not a special one like that one." She pointed at the one Mrs. Boyle was holding. Mr. McClelland agreed very quickly.

Mrs. Boyle took another tack and asked, "Have you heard any caps go off around here in the past two days?"

I was glad that Richard hadn't gotten the caps yet. Mom went on and said, "Roger is a good boy. If he said he lost the gun, he must have lost it. And he must feel terrible about it." The more they stood there talking, the worse I felt. I was glad that Mrs. Boyle did not ask to see me and confront me directly.

They talked some more. I heard Mr. McClelland say that if he saw me with that gun, he would make me wish that I'd never taken it.

Finally, Mrs. Boyle left with Eddie still in tow. She seemed sure that I'd taken Eddie's gun. However, Mrs. McClelland promised to be on the lookout and would tell Mrs. Boyle if she saw me with the gun.

We waited in the barn for a long time after they left. Richard made me promise again that I would never tell what had happened. Overhearing the conversation and learning how much Mom trusted and believed in me, made me feel really bad.

Mrs. Boyle came to school the next day and asked me directly if I had taken the gun. I stuck to my story and lied again in front of her, Eddie, and Miss Freking.

We rarely played with the gun even after Richard had stolen caps for it. When we did play with it, we were sneaky. We never had much fun, if any, with that gun.

I was glad that school ended for the summer soon afterwards. Eddie and I were never friends again. Eddie was really hurt to lose the gun since it ruined his perfect set. The bad news for me was that I'd taken something that was not mine, lied about it, and gotten away with it.

Chapter 7
'Twixt the Cup and the Lip

I had some advantages compared to most foster children. I was born in the United States. I was male. I was white. I was placed on a farm that isolated me from many outside influences during several critical years. This allowed me to engage with the quietness of the natural world. In addition, I had a foster mother who had been a Normal School teacher as a young woman and approached me with a teacher's mindset. Furthermore, her age and workload allowed me to have many unattended hours where I could experiment and learn on my own.

Normal Schools were founded to teach high school graduates to become teachers. These schools eventually became "teacher colleges." Normal Schools were designed to teach behavioral norms and societal values. Mrs. McClelland, born as Maud Webster, was raised in Vermont where the first Normal School in the United States was founded. She was an educated woman whose relatives included the notables Nathaniel and Noah Webster. She took on raising foster children as a serious mission, which I believe significantly influenced my development.

In the early summer Richard and I could find wild cherries in the hedgerows. When we could, we would slip off from work and pick cherries on the edges of our fields. The best cherries always grew on the higher branches of the trees. We would climb up the trees to get them. Richard would climb higher, but because I weighed less, I could go farther out on the limbs than he could. On one such forage, when we were happily filling ourselves with cherries, the branch I was standing on unexpectedly snapped off.

I could hear Richard in the distance calling to me, "Roger, Roger, wake up!"

I could hear, but, at first, I couldn't move. My head began to clear. Richard was worried. I heard him say, "Oh, shit! I'm in trouble."

I came to and began to move. Apparently, I'd dropped to the ground and hit my head. I must have been briefly unconscious. I was surprised at how fast things happened when I fell. As I stood up holding my head, I felt a lump. "I'm okay," I mumbled, feeling a bit groggy.

"Maybe you should sit down for a few minutes," Richard said with relief. And then he added, "We won't tell anyone about this. Right?"

As I look back and try to explain how I went from being grouped with the slow learners in school to the better-than-normal group in one year, it may have been that fall and the blow to my head that did it. The analogy would be like bumping an incandescent light bulb and seeing its brightness suddenly increase.

My social worker noticed the disparity between her expectations and my performance. She decided that I should be retested. Sitting in the front seat of the car with the windows open to help avoid motion sickness, I rode to Philadelphia with her without getting sick.

I liked being the center of attention all day. While I was in the Aid Society building, a woman gave me puzzles to put together and showed me pictures of different shapes, which I had to draw. Everything was timed. There were number memory games and word games. The examination ended with a long conversation about stories and word definitions. The woman smiled a lot and was very positive. The experience was fun, and the results of that day impacted how I thought about my future.

About a week after I was tested, the social worker came out to the farm and gave her report to Mrs. McClelland. She stood on the porch while she spoke to Mrs. McClelland without really paying attention to me. What I remember from that conversation was her statement, "Roger is definitely college timber." I had no idea what the word "college" meant, but it seemed to be important and positive.

After the social worker left, I asked Mom, "What does the word 'college' mean?"

"Roger," she said with a smile and a hint of hopefulness, "College is where you could go after you graduate from high school. It is where you learn to be a professional."

"What is a professional?"

"A professional is a doctor, a minister, or veterinarian like Dr. Binswanger."

"I want to go to college and become a professional."

"Each of those professions will take many years of college education after high school. In order to get into college, you have to earn excellent grades every year from now on until you graduate from high school."

"I intend to get good grades, Mom."

She looked out past the barn and said quietly, "There are many a slip 'twixt the cup and the lip."

"What does that mean?" I asked. She had sayings for most situations.

"It means that good intentions don't always work out."

I decided at that moment that going to college was my long-term goal. I wanted to be a professional and be able to quote sayings. I wasn't worried about things not working out.

Mom had told me that reading was very important and that it was the best way to learn about the world, especially when you could not experience things directly. I liked to read. In fact, I liked to read so much that it got me in trouble with Mr. McClelland, who would catch me reading instead of working. He often told me that I was a daydreamer and lazy.

The first novel that I found and read in the third grade was a Western called *The Little Knight of the X Bar B* by Mary K. Maule. Based on what was written on the inside cover of the book, which I still have, that book was given to Maud Webster in 1921 as a Christmas gift. In fourth grade I read a history book called *The Founders of Our Nation*. In fifth and sixth grades I was obsessed with the biographies of famous Americans. These books were written from an idealized perspective, which helped frame images of success for me. There were no references to sexual dalliances, immoral or unethical behaviors, and other types of human frailties that populate current biographical sketches of today's famous men and women.

The idealized stories were about men including Benjamin Franklin, George Washington, Thomas Jefferson, George Washington Carver, Abraham Lincoln, Thomas Edison, and Theodore Roosevelt. Each was portrayed as smart, strong, and determined, with ethical traits like admitting to having chopped down a cherry tree and reputed to have never told a lie. I read the life stories of men like Nathan Hale and Lou Gehrig and was saddened by the way their lives ended. However, I admired the courage they showed when they were faced with death. All these men were heroic and their lives set high standards for me as a young boy trying my best to be good and attempting to find my way in life.

My fifth- and sixth-grade teacher, Miss Hanisch, was a great supporter of my reading addiction. She fed me a steady diet of books from the Doylestown Public Library. She would bring books to class in two boxes. The books in one box were for everyone else in the class; the other box of books was just for me. She required us to fill out a short report for each book we read. I won two dollars at the end of both my fifth and sixth grades for having read the most books each year.

Miss Hanisch was a special teacher to me. She taught both the fifth- and sixth-grade classes. She was very short in stature, but long on experience. Of German ancestry, she wore glasses, had black hair, and was a no-nonsense teacher. The fifth and sixth grade school was called Iron Hill School because it was on Iron Hill Road. The school was on the McClelland farm, which was named Iron Hill Farm. Mr. McClelland had given the school board a long-term property lease for the school.

The school was so close to my home that it was easy for me to do some chores at lunchtime. Being close also made it possible for Miss Hanisch to know Mrs. McClelland and her foster children. They had a mutual respect for each other probably because of their interest in children and teaching, but also because they were honest, hardworking women in a world dominated by men. Although she never said anything disparaging about Mr. McClelland, I got the feeling that she did not like the way he treated us.

When the other children were playing during lunch, I would often have to leave to do some chores. Several times during the lunch break, I saw her looking out the big school windows with a concerned expression when I passed by on my way to the farm.

Once she asked, "Tell me, Roger, exactly what is it that you have to do that is so important that you have to leave during the noon recess?"

I explained, "Sometimes I have to get the cows from the pasture or water the chickens. I just have to help out when Mr.

McClelland is plowing in the fields all day or sowing seed or hauling loads of corn."

"Wouldn't you rather be playing during lunch with the other boys and girls?"

"Oh, yes," I replied, "but that isn't possible when important work has to be done like planting."

She stood silently for a few moments, shrugged, and walked away.

She cared for me and took a genuine interest in my academic and social development. Academically, I earned the best grades of everyone for the two years I was in her classes. There were about fifteen to twenty students in each class. Socially, I did get some extra guidance, at one point in particular.

I knew what it was like to be bullied, and I didn't like it. I observed that Gerry Meyers was being pushed around by Howard Urbanchuk, who was much bigger. I warned Howard to stop. He did not. I swung my fist and knocked Howard to the ground with one punch. He was stunned, got up, and ran past me and went inside.

Miss Hanisch came out to the play area. "Roger, did you hit Howard?"

"Yes. He was picking on Gerry."

"The reason does not matter," she responded. "We don't settle anything by fighting. Come inside now."

Once inside and alone, she said, "I'm disappointed about what you did out there. The others look up to you and follow you. I don't want them to copy that kind of behavior."

I lowered my head and said, "I'm very sorry."

"You go to the Methodist Church, right?" she asked.

"Yes."

"I'm going to lend you a book on Quakerism, which will teach you to be persuasive without fighting. When you finish it, I want a report about it. I know you want to go to college. However, you need to know that it takes much more than good grades to go to college. You have to be a good citizen, too."

Chapter 8
Ocean of Mixed Feelings

Mom was a religious woman. She was a member of the Methodist Church in Chalfont and also a student of Christian Science. She read the Bible every day and took Richard and me to church with her every Sunday. Her brother and sister-in-law would pick us up on Sunday mornings and drive us to and from church. Mr. McClelland never went to church. His religious belief was centered around hating Catholics, which was probably a result of his Northern Ireland heritage. Mom had full rein over our spiritual development.

She sent me to Bible School for two weeks in the summer between first and second grades. Each session of Bible School lasted three hours. I liked going because I got out of work, and I knew some of the kids who had been in class with me at POS of A. Mom arranged for one of the Sunday school teachers to pick me up on her way to church.

All I had to do to prepare was finish some chores, wash, and be at the end of our lane on time. I was always there earlier than I needed to be for my ride. The weather was warm, and I would stand, listening to birds and looking at the sky, dressed in my church clothes. While waiting, I saw some brown, papery, cylindrically-shaped masses on the dried stems of weeds. I picked quite a few and stuck them in my pants pockets with the intention of looking at them more closely when I had a chance. My ride came, and I rode off to church and forgot about them.

When I returned home, I went to my bedroom and changed. My room was fairly sparse. Against one wall and away from the two windows was my big bed, a chair, and a well-worn white bureau with four drawers. A small picture with a woven wire frame hung on the wall opposite the head of my bed. The woven wire looked like rope. The picture was a painting of Jesus carrying a lamb in a pasture filled with many other sheep. The pasture stretched off into the hilly distance where white fluffy clouds floated in the sky. On the picture written in white script were the words, "In all thy ways acknowledge Him."

When I pulled off my pants, some of the little brown papery masses fell out of my pockets and onto the floor. I emptied my pockets and gathered the masses together. I hid the little treasures in one of the bureau drawers. I did not think about the brown masses again.

A few days later, I was surprised to see what looked at first like black ants all over my walls and bed. There were hundreds of them. They were crawling out of the drawer of my bureau. Looking closely, I saw that they were all tiny praying mantises. They were clinging thickly to the woven wire frame around the picture of Jesus. I realized that the innocent-looking brown papery cylinders were praying mantis egg capsules.

There were so many of them that I didn't know what to do, but I knew I'd be in trouble. I opened one of the windows and tried to brush them out, but they scattered and there were too many. Herding them made them spread out more. My noisy efforts attracted Mom.

She appeared and asked, "Roger, what's going on? What is all the fuss about?"

"There are all of these baby praying mantises crawling around in my room," I said as though it were an act of God.

She looked at me with a frown and said, "Roger! This didn't just happen. What have you been doing?"

I made a quick decision to tell the truth and told her what had happened. She mellowed and noticed all of the little praying mantises around the picture of Jesus.

She stood, fascinated by what she saw. She spoke thoughtfully, "Isn't it appropriate that the praying mantises would be drawn to a picture of Jesus? And look—their little legs are posing in prayer. Remarkable!"

I felt relief sweep over me. "Yes, amazing," I said. She seemed to be taking all of this as some sort of an omen; I was in the clear.

"Okay," she said, "let's open the other window and close the door. They'll find their way out."

By nighttime, there were still a few in my room, but most had left.

When Bible School ended, the Korean War started. Mr. McClelland had fought in World War One in the British army but now was a loyal American citizen. His younger brother, Tom, was a career army man and had fought in World War Two. His son-in-law, Ed Kulp, had been in the Navy during that war, too. This new war was on everyone's mind. Mr. McClelland read the Philadelphia Bulletin every day looking at troop movements as diagrammed on the maps. War suited his nature.

When I arrived on the farm, the McClellands were in their late-fifties. He was fifty-eight and she was fifty-six. The differences between them were remarkable. He was raised on a farm in Northern Ireland with dark memories of the Potato Famine and had emigrated to America about 1910. She taught Normal School in Montgomery County, Pennsylvania, until they were married. He had only an eighth-grade education because he had to leave school and work on his family's subsistence farm. He was smart, shrewd, and sometimes cunning. In reality, he was better informed and more knowledgeable than you would expect for a person with only an eighth-grade education.

She was a peace-loving, Bible-reading, teetotaling Christian.

He was a reformed alcoholic with occasional slippages. She'd been a spinster until they met. He was a widower who had lost his wife and a daughter in the 1918 Spanish influenza pandemic, and his son was killed in a truck accident. He also had a daughter named Betty who was raised by one of his sisters and her husband.

He was rough, had bad manners, and was ill-tempered. Mom was demure and kind. She suffered in silence. His crude behaviors gave her many opportunities to suffer. I saw her look away when he would pass gas at the table during meals. He also had the habit of blowing his nose in his hand and throwing his snot on the kitchen floor. Often, Mom would get up immediately and mop the floor where he had thrown his mucus.

He spent time during the evening studying war tactics employed by our troops who were led by General MacArthur. He would talk about MacArthur and compare him to the English General Montgomery who played a major role in World War Two. He favored Montgomery. By listening, I learned that summer that Mr. McClelland could be distracted by encouraging him to talk about wars. This was a useful ploy at times to slow down the pace of our work and get a little break.

In addition to the praying mantis encounter and the start of the Korean War that summer, there was a totally unexpected trip to the Jersey Shore. Uncle Hugh and his wife, Aunt Lizzie, who was Mr. McClelland's sister, arranged with other relatives to do the noon chores. This allowed us to get away and go to Asbury Park, New Jersey.

Mr. and Mrs. McClelland, Richard, and I all packed into Uncle Hugh's gray Buick with Aunt Lizzie. Uncle Hugh drove us to Asbury Park. The park was about eighty miles from the farm, and it took over two hours to get there. They chose a day in August to make the trip because August is when there is the least field work to do.

Uncle Hugh said, "You, boys, are going to love Asbury Park. The beach stretches for miles, and you can walk barefoot on the sand."

"I know," replied Richard, "I've been there before." He was excited about a day off and doing something other than work.

"Here's some money for each of you to spend on ice cream and soda and maybe an arcade game or two," said Aunt Lizzie as she turned in her seat and gave each of us a dollar.

Richard already had some money and added this dollar to it. Mom took mine, saying, "I'll hold this for you, Roger."

There was a lot of excitement among all of us, except for Mr. McClelland. He was willing to take the trip, but we could tell that he was not enthusiastic. He had no interest in the amusements or the rides that people talked about, and he certainly was not going to go swimming in the ocean.

When we got to Asbury Park, Uncle Hugh pointed to the boardwalk's stairs and said, "Remember those stairs and be back here no later than four o'clock sharp." Richard was gone in a flash. Mr. McClelland and Uncle Hugh drifted away. Mom, Aunt Lizzie, and I stayed together. For a while we walked on the boardwalk, which was lined with booths. Drinks, food, and cotton candy were sold in some of the booths. There were games to play, pennies to pitch, and a shooting gallery in others. The boardwalk was crowded with people. Mom and Aunt Lizzie bought some cotton candy for me, which stuck to my hands and face and made a mess.

The boardwalk had stairs that we used to go down to the beach that was also crowded. We sat on the sand. I felt out of place because we did not have bathing suits. Mom was enjoying herself anyway. This was one of the few times I ever saw her with a relaxed look as she viewed the ocean from under her hand and chatted easily with Aunt Lizzie. Aunt Lizzie and Mom were quite a pair. Mom was slender and on the tall side. Aunt Lizzie was heavyset and short. Both were good workers who were delighted on that afternoon to have had a chance to get away from work.

Richard appeared. "Let's hit the waves," he said as he kicked off his sneakers, tore off his shirt, and raced to the ocean.

I took off my sneakers and rolled up my pant legs. I was

willing to wade, but I was not going to go swimming. Richard was already tumbling in the water. I stood at the edge until Mom came and took my hand and walked close enough to the ocean that the waves washed over our feet. The water was cold and made frothy swirls up to our ankles. A bigger wave hit us and soaked the bottoms of both legs of my rolled-up dungarees.

Richard yelled over the sound of the waves, "Hey, sissy, come on in!"

I stayed where I was. The moment had overcome Mom; she stood there with a faint smile, taking everything in. She let go of my hand and walked away slowly up the beach, wading in the water. At that moment she wandered like a child in the water—free of every responsibility that governed her daily life. When she came back up the beach, she said, "Lizzie, thank you for this day," and sat down to brush the sand from her feet as they dried.

The day on the beach ended with a ride on the Ferris wheel with Richard. It was a little scary, especially when we crested the top and Richard rocked the seat back and forth. He grinned and laughed throughout the ride.

When the day ended, Mom still had my dollar from Aunt Lizzie. I wanted to give it back to her, but she said to keep it.

At four o'clock we were all standing by the car waiting for Mr. McClelland. He was late. The adults whispered among themselves, and Uncle Hugh was worried. When Mr. McClelland appeared, Uncle Hugh walked out to meet him. Their arms were animated as they talked. When everyone was back in the car, Mr. McClelland smelled and Mom stared past him out the window. It was a quiet ride home.

Chapter 9

The Octopus

On the last day of school each year, the New Britain Township School District would host a gathering for all of the elementary schools in the township. These gatherings happened at the Forest Park Amusement and Picnic Center, which was located almost adjacent to the POS of A School on the opposite side of Callow Hill Road. The center was located on the water at the intersection of the North Branch of Neshaminy and Pine Run Creeks.

The last-day-of-school picnic was a fun day for everyone. We brought our own lunches, and the district served each of us Dixie cups filled with Breyers ice cream in several flavors for free. The Forest Park Amusement and Picnic Center had several different rides that we paid for with our own money. Mom gave Richard and me two dollars each to spend on any rides or arcade games we wanted. The rides were either five cents or ten cents, depending on how sophisticated they were.

My favorite was bumper cars. We were supposed to drive the cars around in a circle in the same direction. However, it was a lot more fun to pick a target car with someone you knew in it and head across the circle and smash into them. Richard was really good at smashing into me and jamming me into the side of the arena, making it hard for me to get unstuck and retaliate. The older I got, the easier it was for me to reach the accelerator and steer the car, so I was able to ambush him more. That was the only amusement ride in which we could have fun attacking each other. We enjoyed most of our time in the picnic area playing baseball or other pick-up games.

Eugene Pone was a foster child from the Lutheran Home who lived with his brother on the Schaeffer farm across Iron Hill Road from us. We were friends and sometimes one of us was allowed to cross the road to play. His foster parents were even older than mine and were less attentive to how he spent his free time than mine. That meant that he usually came across to our farm. The Forest Park picnics were a great time for us to play together.

"Hey, let's go ride the train," Eugene would say and off we would go for a trip around the park. The train ride was a great way to see what was going on. We saw boats on the creek, the Ferris wheel, picnic tables everywhere, an arcade, a swimming pool, the ball field, and the Octopus ride. We used the train tours to decide what to do next. Eugene was attracted to the Octopus ride. "Let's ride the Octopus. I love the way the cars go up and down, and spin around," he said.

That ride cost ten cents. When it was our turn to board, we climbed into a car on one of the eight arms. At first, the motions were easy since it moved slowly from position to position to load passengers. After a few starts and stops, we were underway and the arms began to pick up speed. As we accelerated around the hub, our car began to rotate in a circle. The ups and downs and the spinning car started to impact my stomach. I felt cold and began to sweat. I pushed my head over the side of the car and threw up. My breakfast and other food shot out, forming a long trail in the air like a brown comet. The vomit rained down on a few of the kids waiting below, who then ran away, gagging with disgust. I was embarrassed. Eugene thought it was funny. I couldn't wait for the ride to be over.

When we got off the Octopus, the operator said, "Hey, kid, did you make a mess in the car? If you did, here's a rag. You clean it up." Luckily, there was nothing in the car except maybe some regrets that I'd ridden the Octopus.

"Let's go to the arcade," I suggested, trying to get away quickly.

"No, let's go to the swimming pool instead," Eugene replied.

I didn't have a swimsuit, and besides Mom had said to stay away from the pool because they don't let colored people swim in the pool. She did not want me to be around racists. "I can't go there," I said.

"Why not?"

"The pool owners are bad people." I did not fully understand who owned what, but it was clear that I was not to go near the pool.

We arrived at the arcade. Eugene said, "I can't play in there. I don't have any money."

"You can have some of mine," I offered. He smiled, and we went in.

There were rows of pinball machines. The one that I liked had a baseball field under glass. The object was to get hits by using a lever on the panel to swing a paddle at a ball, which was pitched by pressing a button. We pitched to each other and had fun scoring just like in a real baseball game. The time passed and we used up my nickels. On Thursdays you could play for nickels, but on all the other days you needed dimes. If you got a home run, you got a free game. We got one free three-inning game. It would not be the last time that I played baseball games in that arcade.

Although Forest Park was not far from home, I only went there for the end-of-year school picnics and two other times. The township stopped supporting the school picnics when I entered fourth grade. Unknown to the McClellands, I made two other short visits.

In order for Richard and me semiannually to see the doctor, the dentist, and get new clothes, a social worker had to make two round trips between Philadelphia and the farm. It meant a lot of driving in one day for the social worker. The Aid Society staff decided that it would be better for them if Richard and I took the train down and back. It was an adventure to walk the mile and a half to the New Britain Railroad Station, take the train to the Reading Terminal, and then walk the several blocks to the offices of the Aid Society. I liked the feeling of being on my own and the opportunity to avoid meaningless talk that always accompanied rides with a social worker. When I came back from Philadelphia in the late afternoons, I would buy an ice cream cone in the grocery store in New Britain regardless of whether or not it was hot or cold outside.

On one trip back, I decided to get off the train in Chalfont, which made a longer walk home and the walk led me past Forest Park and the arcade. I stopped at the park. I was amazed at how quiet the park and the arcade were. Maybe it was because it was late on a weekday in early summer. I had two dimes. I played the first dime and got my three innings but did not win a free game. The second dime was a miracle! I managed to develop a rhythm between the pitching button and the swing lever that produced home runs galore. I stood there for a long time blissfully hitting homers to the upper stands and winning free games. I had beaten the machine. I only left because it was getting so late that I had to get home and do my chores. I left twenty-seven free games on the board for the next player to enjoy. I was ecstatic, but since I had stopped without permission, I couldn't say anything about my success to anyone. I couldn't even tell Eugene since he'd been moved away by the time this happened.

There were a couple of big hurricanes when I was twelve that flooded many parts of southeastern Pennsylvania. Forest Park was hit hard by flooding because of its location on the two creeks. There was speculation that it would close for good, but they cleaned it up and repaired the damage.

A couple of years after the cleanup a friend of mine drove me to the park. We went swimming there because Mom was too sick to know what I was doing. I only splashed around in the water for a while because I had a "farmer's tan," which embarrassed me to reveal to others. That was the last time I visited the property. Not long after that visit, we heard that there had been a race riot at Forest Park, and it closed down for good. I assumed that the riot was because of the swimming pool segregation issue. Mom was right —racism was bad.

Chapter 10
No Unnecessary Strain

I looked forward to going back to the POS of A School and seeing my friends for our second year together. We had a new teacher, Miss Gebhardt, who was much older than Miss Freking. Miss Gebhardt was all business. She introduced herself and then read each of our names from a list. I noticed that Hope Starr's name was not read. Hope was a friend from first grade whom I had sat next to after I was moved from the slow group.

During the first recess I went up and asked, "Hope Starr's name was not called. Did she move?"

Miss Gebhardt looked at me and said, "I was told that she died in the summer."

I stood in front of Miss Gebhardt, not understanding. I knew that old people died, but Hope was just a young girl.

"Do you know how?" I queried.

"Not exactly. I think it was during surgery," she replied.

I remembered that Hope smiled a lot and was very friendly. I knew I was going to miss her. I thanked Miss Gebhardt and went outside and played. Later, I told some of my classmates and asked if they might know more about what happened to Hope. Everyone I talked to was surprised and couldn't add anything more and said that they would miss her, too. After a few days, I did not think about her again until the following spring.

That spring we were taken to Philadelphia by yet another social worker for our semiannual visit. When the doctor examined me, he was friendly until he asked me to lower my underpants. He made a low whistling sound and said, "What do we have here?"

He had discovered a sizeable inguinal hernia, which was unusual for someone my age. He told me that some of my intestines were pushing out and he showed me how to push them back in, but they would not stay in.

"Have you been lifting heavy objects?" he questioned.

"How heavy do you mean?" I asked back.

"Well, an object that made you strain to lift it?"

I didn't recall any one specific thing, so I said no.

"Have you jumped off something high like a branch of a tree?"

"No, not that I recall."

"Do you have trouble going to the bathroom and strain a lot?"

"No," I said, but there was no way I was going to discuss my bowel movements with anybody, let alone a stranger, even if he was a doctor.

He pushed it in and left the room. I could hear him talking to the social worker outside the door. He came back and told me to get dressed. Then, he invited her into the room and told both of us that I was not to do anything that involved lifting or jumping until the hernia was repaired.

He concluded the exam by telling the social worker, "Please make sure that his foster parents know that Roger is not to be active and that we will schedule a surgery appointment for him at the Abington Hospital as soon as possible."

I felt guilty. I must have done something wrong to have caused this hernia. This was serious. I recalled that Hope Starr died during surgery, which scared me. The benefit was that I might not have to work for a while.

When we went home, the social worker explained that I had a hernia. I felt relieved that someone in authority was telling them that I had to take it easy and be careful for a while. When Mr. McClelland heard about what was going on and my limitations, he showed me that he'd had a hernia for a long time and that he wore a truss to keep it in. The truss he had was a big tan and brown belt with shiny rivets. It looked ugly and awkward. He told me that I should get one, too.

Fortunately, within a couple of days the social worker came back and took me to the Abington Hospital for surgery. I had no idea what surgery entailed, but I knew it was supposed to fix my problem for good. It seemed better than wearing a truss for the rest of my life like Mr. McClelland. Besides, a truss would have meant no break from work.

On the way to the hospital, the social worker gave me a lot of reassurances. The hospital was a big brick building with many rooms, all of which had white walls. The halls were long and everyone wore white or blue clothes. It was very quiet. They put me in a big room with other children, a few of whom had already had operations. Some of the children's parents were there. Other children were crying. I was not going to cry. The beds were high and narrow, and the sheets were tight and clean.

I went to bed hungry that night because they said I could not eat before an operation, but after the operation I could eat lots. I fell asleep thinking about Hope Starr.

They woke me up early and took me to a small room. I was nervous until a nurse with bright red hair and a big smile came in. She told me that she was going to prepare me for the surgery. I liked her until she pulled down my underpants. I was totally exposed and felt embarrassed. My face must have turned red like her hair because she looked at me and with a knowing look adjusted my underpants to cover my privates. She shaved all the fuzz off of my lower stomach and the bulge where the hernia was. I was all set for surgery but not ready for what happened next.

She rolled my bed into a much larger room with bright lights and several other people. They placed something, which looked like a cloth tea strainer, over my face and asked me to breathe deeply. When I took the first deep breath, I felt like I was going to choke. I remember a twisting spiral in my mind's eye as I lay on the table, thrashing and feeling the pressure of people holding my arms and legs down. The next thing I remember was waking up and finding myself back in the children's ward. I was happy to be alive.

I stayed in the ward for exactly one week. While I was there, I talked to some of the other kids. One had had his tonsils taken out, and another had had an operation on his arm. There was a girl who had had her appendix removed a few days before my operation. She showed me the top of her incision, which was red with staples across the cut. A few days later the nurses came and took her away. When she came back, she told me that they had taken her staples out. I asked her if it hurt to remove the staples, and she said that it really didn't hurt at all. That day they let her go home. I never saw her again.

Although the Abington Hospital was about twenty miles from our farm, I was only visited once. Ed Kulp and his wife, Betty, who was Mr. McClelland's daughter, brought Mom on a Saturday afternoon to see me. They were glad that I was okay and that I liked the food. I told them that I had ice cream for dessert almost every day. Mom said a prayer of gratitude, and they all left.

My staples began to itch a lot. Since I did not want anyone poking around down there again, I began to wiggle the staples back and forth. I removed them before the nurses did. This caused a little stir when they saw what I had done. I had healed enough that the doctor let the social worker take me back to the farm.

It was not long before I was doing chores and other work again. After three or four weeks, the social worker returned and took me to see the doctor who did the surgery. He checked the incision area and looked at me with satisfaction because the healing was almost complete. He touched my arm while looking at the social worker and said, "He's doing fine." He stood up and said in a very professional voice to the social worker, "He can begin to play now and can even pick up a baseball bat." I cringed inside because I'd already been picking up buckets of water, carrying corn, and hoeing for the past couple of weeks. I was worried that I might get in trouble with the doctor if he found out that I was already doing unauthorized activities.

Chapter 11
Active Learning

Although the hernia operation created a momentary pause in the growing list of the kinds of jobs I was expected to do, an easy task and one that I liked to do was picking up the mail.

The farm was located on the top of a hill, which sloped towards Creek Road where the mailbox was. The mail typically arrived around noon each day. During the summer, it was fun to run down the hill with Rex to see what had arrived. The path went between one of the farm's cow pastures and the edges of two fields. The mail always consisted of a previous day's copy of the Philadelphia Bulletin and some other pieces of mail if we were lucky. The Bulletin was important because it contained the hog and egg prices; Mr. McClelland read it every day. In addition to the newspaper, there could be a magazine like The Farm Journal, a Sears and Roebuck catalog, or one or two letters for Mom.

There was another mailbox to the left of ours. It belonged to the Collins farm on the opposite side of Creek Road. They had a white fence around their property and a long lane like ours. They did not farm. I never met them, but I had heard that they were rich. Every once in a while, I would peek into their mailbox to see what they had gotten.

Once when I opened it, I saw a package inside. I wanted to see who it was from. I pulled it out and read the return address. It was from the state agricultural extension office. I thought to myself, "Why would they be getting something about agriculture when they aren't even farmers?" I shook it. I could hear something rattling inside. I gave in to temptation and took the package and headed back up the path toward home with it.

I slipped into the cow pasture because I could hide among the trees where it was easy to sit since the grazing cows kept the grass short. I tore off the brown wrapping paper and opened the package without any hesitation. Inside was a green box, which had hinges and a clasp and opened like a treasure chest. Inside I found several colored vials, two eye droppers, and some empty tubes along with an instruction booklet titled "Soil Test Kit," with colored charts and some numbered procedures. I read words like "potassium," "potash," and "nitrogen," and the initials "pH." The package contained nothing of value to me. I was very disappointed. It was getting late, and I did not want to have to explain what I was doing. I tossed the package and the contents under some bushes and went home.

That incident was my first contact with applied chemistry, which meant little to me at the time. I felt some guilt about stealing the Collins' package, but not too much because they were rich and we were poor. I did want to know what "pH" meant but did not dare to ask anyone because it might lead to more questions. I had to wait until the fall to find out what those initials stood for. No one came to the house asking about the missing package.

Another daily chore was to go to each of the seven chicken coops scattered around the house and barn and switch on the lights each evening and turn them off the following morning. Mr. McClelland had learned that chickens laid more eggs when exposed to light at night. This chore had important economic consequences since we sold hundreds of dozens of eggs weekly to wholesale buyers, and more eggs meant more money.

As part of my early morning routine and before I switched the lights off, I would have to pee. There was a little shrub called nightshade that grew at the corner of the house that bloomed with pretty purple and yellow flowers. I decided to see what would happen if I peed on that plant every morning. I was amazed to see the plant turn brown and die in less than a month. I was excited by my first chemical experiment until I realized that this little flowering plant was one of Mom's favorites.

"Has anyone noticed that the beautiful nightshade plant at the corner of the house has died?" Mom asked one night at dinner.

My head was down as I fumbled with the green beans on my plate. I could feel my face getting warm, and I was glad that the lights weren't on.

"Which corner?" Richard inquired.

"You know. The corner by the spring kitchen," Mom replied.

"Oh, yeah, I know. It's dead, huh," Richard acknowledged while helping himself to some meatloaf.

"What's one plant more or less when you have as many as you do, Maud?" Mr. McClelland joined the conversation.

"Roger, did you see it? You go by there a couple of times a day," she stated.

"Yeah, I did see it. I thought it might be dying, too. Is it really dead?" I feigned curiosity. My face had cooled down.

"I'm going to miss those purple flowers and the berries," she said with resignation. "Yes, I do have a lot of flowers, and I love them all. That was the only one with purple flowers that I had." She made the remark looking directly at Mr. McClelland. He kept eating.

"Maybe it will grow back," I offered hopefully.

"Maybe," she said.

I felt sad. Mom sounded like she had lost a friend. I hadn't told a total lie, but I hadn't been truthful either. I could have told the truth and cleared up the issue, but I had no idea what the consequences would have been for killing a plant that Mom loved. It felt at the time that the consequences would have been worse

than the crime once Mr. McClelland would step in. I'd learned
not to trust him and his anger since my arrival. Even when he
was not angry, I couldn't trust him.

When my first baby tooth was loose, he saw me wiggling it.
"Hey, son, are you losing a tooth?" he said.

"Yes."

"Let me take a look at it. I can tell you when it will
come out," he said.

Because he had a full set of false teeth, both uppers and
lowers, I assumed he had to know something about teeth. That
was my first loose one, and I wanted to know how long it was
going to take before it came out. I obediently went over to the
chair where he was sitting.

"Open up and let's take a look," he directed me.

I opened my mouth. "Now wiggle it around so that I can see
which one it is," he said.

I wiggled the tooth for him.

Next, he said, "Let me touch it to see how much it moves."

In an instant he put his two fingers in my mouth and
jerked the tooth out.

It hurt. I was afraid to cry out. I stepped away holding my
mouth and swallowed some blood. I was angry.

Chuckling, he looked at me and said, "Well, what's the
matter? I told you that I was going to tell you when it was going
to come out. Now you know—right now is when it came out."

"Some joke," I thought as I moved farther away from him.

That was the only tooth that I ever let him touch. I kept it a
secret when my other baby teeth loosened. There was no tooth
fairy in that house. When I told Richard what had happened, he
said, "That same thing happened to me when I was your age. You

have to learn that if you stand behind a mule, you're likely to be kicked. Be careful around him is all I've got to say."

Many other things on the farm scared me at one time or another. There were big animals like a bull, and small things like bees, wild dogs, an angry older foster brother, snakes, skunks, and so forth. One of my evening chores led to a very scary moment.

Just before the sun set, I routinely had to go to the cow pasture near the house to gather the ducks. The ducks had to be locked up in their coop overnight for their own protection. Alone in the pasture they could easily be eaten by a fox or weasel or even a hungry stray dog. One evening I had put off this chore until it was a little later than usual.

The muddy stream that flowed through the middle of the pasture was a great place for the ducks to forage for grubs and worms. Although the fence along the pasture was good at keeping cows and horses in, it didn't keep predators out. Any stray ducks could usually be found playing in the stream at the end of the long pasture at the edge of the big woods.

In order to be really sure that all the ducks were either home or headed home, I had to go all the way down to the far end of the pasture along the stream near the woods. My strategy of calling to the ducks by making quacking sounds helped to draw them up toward their coop and usually kept me from having to go too close to the woods.

This particular evening, I had to go further toward the woods than usual to be sure that I had all of the ducks. The trees in the woods created many different shadowy shapes at dusk, shapes that shifted around in the evening breezes as though they were alive. The tall trees had irregular tops; some even appeared to have heads and arms like you'd expect giant monsters to have. As I got closer to the woods, my quacking sounds became quieter and quieter because I didn't want to attract too much attention if something else were nearby.

The evening breezes were picking up, and I could hear the leaves rustling. I quit quacking entirely. I was sure that there were no ducks near the woods. I stood still to assess what was happening. Some of the branches appeared to move apart, independent of the wind that had replaced the light breeze. The moving branches and the late day sunlight created elongated shadows, which magnified the movement of the imagined heads and arms.

"No! Stop imagining things," I said softly to myself. "There's really nothing there!"

I tried hard to concentrate on searching for ducks, but my eyes and ears were drawn to the moving shadows and the sounds of the trees. I knew it was just the evening wind. I really knew it. Confidence in that belief was eroding. I turned away from the woods and even tried to whistle to reassure myself that everything was okay and I was safe. My lips couldn't whistle. They were dry. Worse, I now had my back turned to the shadows, which meant that I couldn't see if something was sneaking up on me from the woods.

A small creature of doubt had taken up residence in my mind. It began to whisper to me that I might be right about the wind, the trees, and the leaves, but some of those shadows might be from big animals. I'd heard adults talking about flying saucers. After all, it was the early 1950s and everyone was telling stories about strange lights in the skies. Some people even said that they'd seen little men come from the saucers. What if some of the sounds and movements were really from spacemen? I was alone and unprotected. I could be abducted.

I reassured myself that my job was done, and I could return to the house. The little creature of doubt was growing, nourished by my imagination. The sound of the wind in the trees had gotten louder. I began to walk back toward home with as much control as I could manage. I argued with myself about how safe I was. At some level I knew that I had to walk because if I started to run, I would want to run even faster. My pace quickened anyway.

The pasture seemed longer going back to the house. A particularly long shadow caught the corner of my eye. I tried to look away, but I knew that I had to be sure that there was nothing there. I could not let whatever it was surprise me and grab me. I looked quickly and saw the shadow moving toward me. I began to walk faster and faster. The doubt creature had grown and taken me over and was beginning to move my arms and legs faster.

The hairs on my neck stood out. I felt a chill run down my back. I began to run. I jumped over the stream on my way to the house. There were shadows everywhere. I had to get home. I ran faster. I was flying, hardly touching the ground. The creature in me was in full control. I was a goner.

The stone path was beneath me. Next the porch. Then the porch door. I tore through the screen and fell to the kitchen floor, flopping around like a fish in a net, gasping for breath.

I heard stunned adult noises. I was safe. Or was I? The voices were angry. I'd been so scared that I'd torn the screen. I was scared again. Only this time, it was not due to my imagination.

Chapter 12
Revenge

I attended the Newville Elementary School for the third and fourth grades. Newville Elementary was a bigger one-room school than POS of A. A large movable partition divided the big room in half and separated grades three and four from grades five and six. Each morning the partition was open so that all the students could hear the Bible reading and the announcements. After the students recited the Pledge of Allegiance, the partition was rolled into place so that each teacher had two grades to themselves.

My third-grade teacher was Mrs. Bond. She was an experienced teacher. Once we were settled into our seats and class had begun, I asked her a question. "Mrs. Bond, what do the letters P-H mean?"

She looked at me with a smile and asked me, "Do you know how to use a dictionary?"

"Sort of, I think."

"Well, now, come with me to the back of the class." As she said this, she looked around the room and added, "This is something that you all should pay attention to."

She went to a large brown book that sat on a small stand. "The first thing you should know is that P-H is not a word. It's a chemical abbreviation." She opened the dictionary and showed me that the words were in alphabetical order. She turned the pages to the Ps and pointed to "pH." She read the definition, which was something about hydrogen ion concentration, which meant nothing to me. She could see that I didn't understand.

"Where did you hear the term 'pH'?" she asked.

I mumbled something about the men on the farm talking about it.

"Farmers like to know if the soil is too acidic. A pH test tells them how acidic it is. Vinegar is an example of an acid, and plants won't grow in it," she said.

She gave us all a science lesson that didn't make much sense to me. What I learned and remembered was that dictionaries are the places to go when you want to know about words. I vowed to get one.

Mrs. Bond was strict. Everyone looked forward to recess to escape her strictness. Outside when the weather was warm, we talked and played games. Inside, we had to be quiet. She was well organized and helped us to plan for all of the major holidays. Christmas was one that we looked forward to celebrating, especially the gift exchange.

"Each student will please come forward one at a time and pick a name from a box," she announced about two weeks before Christmas. She went on to say, "Do not tell anyone the name that you pick. It will be a blind gift exchange."

I was not familiar with the process. "How will you know what the person wants," I asked, "if you can't talk to them?"

She looked at me, pursing her bright red lips as though she was going to punish me but thought better of it and smiled and said to the class, "I want you to spend less than two dollars, and I am sure that you can surprise someone with a nice gift for that amount." I did not say anything, but I thought that two dollars was a lot of money to spend on a classmate.

The name I pulled from the box was Joseph Spitalia, who arrived in third grade as a new member of our class. He'd moved during the summer from Philadelphia. He was smart and always scored well on arithmetic homework and tests. We could track our progress on math exercises by counting the number of stars pasted like ornaments on the green paper trees assigned to each of us hanging on the front wall. We got a colored star for each perfect homework paper. His tree and my tree had the most stars on them compared to others in the class.

He dressed exceptionally well and occasionally even wore a small bow tie. I had no idea what to get him since he was so proper. I wasn't interested in getting a gift for my competitor. I talked to Mom about it.

"Why don't you buy him some handkerchiefs?" she suggested.

"He probably has a lot of them at home already," I said. "If I get him something, I want it to be fun."

"Okay," she replied, "Uncle Ted is going to take Richard, you, and me to the Montgomeryville Mart this Saturday night so that we can shop for Christmas gifts. They have so many things there that I'm sure that you will find something that will be fun for him."

I knew that I had to find four gifts: for Mom, Mr. McClelland, and Richard, and now Joseph, too. The only person I was sure about was Mr. McClelland because I could get him another corncob pipe. I would have to wait and see what there was at the Mart for everyone else.

The Mart was very crowded. Christmas music was playing in the background, and everyone was happily shopping. I had some money in my pocket and wanted to get good gifts. I saw small flashlights on key chains on one of the countertops. Since it was very crowded and busy, I believed that no one would notice me when I picked up a flashlight and pretended to test it. I looked to be sure that no one saw me and slipped it into my pocket. The problem of Joseph's gift was solved. I had more money to spend on each of the other gifts. It was like a math problem in which you subtracted a zero amount from the money you had and the total amount stayed the same. It occurred to me that Joseph didn't seem like the kind of kid who would appreciate getting something stolen. He need never know.

The name of the recipient was on each gift without any indication of who had given it. Mom had wrapped the gift and put Joseph's name on it. I placed it under the small tree in the classroom and tried to see what there was for me without success.

Some of the presents looked substantially larger than others. My gift for Joseph was one of the smaller ones.

I watched as I waited for my name to be called as others got their packages and opened them. One girl got a doll, another got a hand mirror, and a boy got an airplane. I began to squirm because my gift was pretty small and not as valuable as the ones the other kids were getting. When my name was called, I went up and Mrs. Bond gave me a thin rectangular package. I went back to my desk and opened it slowly. It was a set of three white handkerchiefs. I looked at them and wondered what I was going to do with them. I noticed that Doug Rice was looking at me. He started to cry. He came over.

"My mother insisted that I give you handkerchiefs," Doug said apologetically. "She got them anyway even though I told her that you wouldn't want them."

"Doug, thank you. I need them for church," I said. He looked relieved and went back to his desk.

In the meantime, Joseph Spitalia had opened his gift and did not seem very pleased with the flashlight.

"Doug, do you know who would like these? Joseph. Besides, I need a flashlight. I'll tell you what. If I trade him these handkerchiefs for his flashlight, it would be just like you had given me the flashlight. How does that sound?"

His expression changed into a little smile. He saw the logic. The exchange worked, and each of us was happy with his gift.

The rest of the year after the Christmas party was uneventful except for the last day of school.

The Newville School teachers had a tradition of a picnic and a baseball game to mix the students and parents at Newville with those at Iron Hill School on the last day before summer. The sixth graders at Newville were graduating to become seventh graders at Iron Hill and join the eighth graders already there. The teachers gathered all the students and some parents together at Newville School in the afternoon to have a picnic and play softball. The softball game was always between the Iron Hill students (the seventh and eighth graders) and the best of the Newville students (the third through sixth graders). The older students always won the game. Since I was just a third grader, I didn't play in the game. However, I was there supporting the Newville boys. After the game, which the older boys won, some of us who hadn't played gathered together and started our own game.

Richard, who attended Iron Hill at the time, had left with a few of the older boys to get something to eat. He was going into ninth grade in the fall and probably had no interest in anything we were doing. Richard was called "Heifer" because of his last name, Heffentrager. I think they called him that behind his back because he was bigger than they were, and he'd developed a reputation as someone to avoid. Even if he picked on or hassled someone, they weren't going to fight him. Most of the parents and children had gone away from the playfield and were down at the school when I heard someone yell, "Hey, there's Heifer's little brother!"

I became the unfortunate center of attention, more like a "target." These boys saw me as an opportunity to take out some revenge on Richard. They wanted to pick on me like they'd been picked on by him. I was blindsided. Some of the boys in the small group became disinterested and left. They probably didn't want to be part of a possible retaliation from Richard. The two boys who remained began to intensify their harassment.

"You're not so tough when your brother isn't around, are you?" one boy said while the other nodded in agreement.

"Leave me alone," I pleaded.

"Are you some sort of coward?" one taunted.

The other spoke up chanting, "You farm kids are all alike. You smell like shit. You look like shit. And you're worthless as shit."

"Stop it! Leave me alone," I repeated.

There was some shoving back and forth and more words. One left.

The one who stayed was named Jeff Keller. I'd thought he was Richard's friend. I was wrong.

He kept repeating, "Little shit, little shit," as he thumped me on the chest. He was excited and angry about something. His pushing became harder.

"I haven't done anything to you!" I yelled at him as I tried to get away.

He tackled me. He was bigger and stronger. We were on the ground, swinging at each other. He hit me hard in the face with his fist several times. I tried to protect myself. Dirt got in my mouth. I gasped and tried to slide away. I was being hurt, and I was scared. No one came to help. As we were rolling around on the ground, swinging and kicking, I suddenly found my head just below his belt. I stuck my face into his crotch and bit down just as hard as I could. In that instant I could sense that I had clamped onto more than his trousers. Jeff stopped fighting. He untangled himself, got up as fast as he could, and ran away, screaming. It was a dirty move, but it stopped the fight.

Later I discovered that he'd given me two black eyes. There was nothing to brag about. I walked the two miles that last day of third grade filled with anger and worrying about how to explain what had happened. When I got home, my eyes had gotten very black and swollen. My face was bruised. I was greeted by Mrs. McClelland, who tried to comfort me by washing my face and cleaning me up. Mr. McClelland looked at me and accepted that I'd been in a fight and lost. Richard just stood there and teased me for being a loser. My emotional memory of the fight was so strong that the fact that Jeff Keller was much older than me didn't matter. My pride was hurt, and I felt alone and defeated.

That summer was hot. We pitched hay, hoed corn, did our chores, carried rocks from the fields, and hauled manure. Just like the plants we cared for, I grew, too. It was a pretty typical summer of hard work, but a summer during which I never forgot how I'd lost that fight on the last day of school. The memory of that fight was refreshed by the periodic teasing from Richard about being a loser. It stuck in my stomach like bad food.

The first day of school arrived, and I was able to break away from the long workdays on the farm and get some easy time in school. The routine for me was to walk up to Iron Hill School and wait for the bus, which would come by to drop off the seventh and eighth graders, pick up several of us in the Iron Hill School area, and take us to Newville School. As I stood there waiting for the seventh and eighth graders to get off the bus, I was surprised to see Jeff Keller coming down the steps of the bus. Pure reflex describes what happened next.

All in one motion, I threw my lunch pail into his leg, grabbed him, and pulled him to the ground. He tried to shield himself defensively, but to no avail since I was in full anger release mode. I beat him until his nose began to bleed, and the bus driver pulled me off him. I was shaking, Jeff was crying, the bus driver was looking between us in order to decide whether he should take care of Jeff or punish me for starting the fight. I guess the bus driver saw a little fourth grader fighting an eighth grader who must have done something to start it. He couldn't figure out what was going on. In the moment of confusion, Jeff got up and ran toward the school, holding his bleeding nose. The score was settled. We were even.

The bus driver helped me pick up my lunch pail and ushered me up the steps and into the bus. Riding to school that day, I was filled with satisfaction, and, although I didn't know it at the time, I was to learn later that the size of people in a fight mattered less than the size of the anger inside them. And, I had plenty of that.

Chapter 13

Combat

Corn governed our lives. Our tasks were focused on getting the highest possible corn yields and feeding our livestock. This was an annual cycle supported without regard to human effort, inconvenience, or boredom.

Much of the acreage was used to grow corn. We plowed the land in the spring and planted corn as soon as the threat of frost had passed. We cultivated the rows of corn until the stalks grew so tall that they would be damaged by the machinery. After we could no longer mechanically cultivate the corn, we hoed the rows of corn by hand. We hired a man with a mechanical corn picker to harvest part of the crop of corn in the fall. We hand cut the remainder and stacked it, stalk by stalk, making teepees in the fields. The corn stood there until it dried. Once the corn was dried, we husked the ears by hand, threw them in a wagon, and hauled the wagonloads of corn to one of our four long corncribs and unloaded it. All year long we fed corn to the pigs, chickens, and cows. We even used the dried corn stalks to insulate the farm buildings in the winter. Nothing was wasted.

I'm sure that little was expected of me when I arrived at the farm as a four-year-old. Although I don't recall any specific duties upon arrival, I do know that by the time I was in first grade that I had one daily responsibility involving corn. I would come home from school and sit on an upside-down basket at the side of a large tub filled with corncobs. I would take the cobs one by one and rub the kernels off. This had to be done because the new, bright-green John Deere corn sheller didn't shell all the kernels off the cobs and Mr. McClelland did not tolerate waste.

At first, I was too small to turn the crank on the sheller, which had a wooden crank handle and a flywheel mechanism to give needed momentum when the handle was turned. The momentum enabled the ear of corn to pass through the sheller smoothly as the ear was stripped of its kernels. I was given other corn-related jobs as I grew. There seemed to be an endless hierarchy of jobs that required more skill, strength, and judgment.

Mr. McClelland, whom I'd eventually call "Daddy," came to me one day and said, "Here, son, is a hoe designed just for you. You can come to the fields with Richard and me and join us hoeing corn."

He'd sawed off part of the handle, which made it the right length for me. He spared no effort to put us to work. Hoeing corn defined many weeks of my summer life after that.

The fields were hot and dusty. The corn rows seemed endlessly long. I was cursed at if I accidentally missed the weeds and cut down one of the precious cornstalks.

"Son, do you realize that each time you cut down a stalk of corn there will be two less ears of corn to feed the pigs?" Hoeing accuracy was a high priority.

"I know. I'm sorry," I would say with my head down. I was a cog in the economic system of the farm. My inaccuracies negatively impacted the farm finances.

The cornstalks in each row were usually further apart than the width of the hoe. Cornstalks were easier to cut down than weeds because cornstalks had more turgor than weeds. I was challenged to learn how to hit only weeds. I learned quickly from Richard that when you did cut off a cornstalk it was best to hide the mistake. I would bury it in the dirt if it was small. Or

I could take the decapitated corn and throw it across rows that had already been hoed and hope that Mr. McClelland wouldn't find it. The corn had just enough weight that you could throw it; once thrown, it would sail gracefully and land many rows away and be out of sight.

There were places where the weeds would be really thick, and the going would be slow. The chopping rhythm of the hoes would be broken since we would have to bend down and pull the weeds that were so close to the corn stems that there was a risk of hitting the stalk if we used a hoe. There were other places where there would be very few weeds and we could go faster. After a while, I learned to keep an eye out for the rows of corn ahead to see which ones had the fewest weeds. I would try to pick one of those easier rows to hoe on my return back up the field.

The hot summer sun made us sweat. We conserved energy, which reduced sweating, by developing a rhythm. The rhythm could be hypnotic. I'm sure that I reached a meditative state many times over the days and weeks during those summers of hoeing. I learned to pray for a thunderstorm. Rain meant that we could go home. The heavier the rain, the more time before we had to get back into the fields because of the mud. Reprieves were rare because the summers were usually dry. I studied the skies, watching for certain cloud types and formations. I listened to older farmers who told me how to predict storms. I would amuse myself by wishfully thinking about anything other than hoeing. I did a lot of dreaming while I hoed. It was a good time to detach myself from the work at hand and imagine anything but those green stalks, the weeds, and the dusty fields.

Occasionally in the fields we talked. I would try to get Mr. McClelland to tell us about World War One and where he'd fought and how he'd gotten wounded. If I was lucky, he would stop and tell a story or two about his time in France in the trenches. He described how the Germans would wrap themselves in white blankets during snowstorms and roll toward the English trenches. He never spoke about being scared, but I could tell that talking about the war was painful to him. He was in the infantry and lost many friends. He even touched on the use of gas, which killed and maimed many of his fellow troops. He never romanticized anything about the war except to say that he'd helped to defeat those "Jerry bastards." When I asked him why the Germans were called "Jerries," he said it was because the helmets the Germans wore reminded the Irish and the British of chamber pots, which were called "jerries." Then, he would smile a far-off reminiscent type of smile as though he were thinking of other jokes long lost in the past. The reprieves from work didn't last very long, and soon we were silently hoeing again.

We were at war with weeds. Each field was a war zone. Our mission was to save the corn. The only way to escape a row was to defeat each weed. We were engaged in real hand-to-hand combat. The war was not over until all the zones were liberated from weeds.

When I went back to school in the fall, I learned that while I was in combat with the weeds, my classmates had been swimming, playing sports, going to beaches, or taking interesting trips. Our teacher in fourth grade made us tell stories about how we spent our summers. I listened to the stories of the other kids, wishing I'd been able to do what they'd done. I knew that telling everyone about working on the farm, hoeing, and praying for rain would not be very interesting. I wanted to be like everyone else in the class, but I was not.

The dreaded moment of my turn to talk came. As I stood up, an idea popped into my mind.

I spoke enthusiastically about my summer trip to France. "While I was there, I saw the trenches from World War One and even met some old soldiers who had fought in the Great War, as it was named. One of them had been wounded, and they all had lost many friends in the war. The winter was the worst time and the Germans, who were called 'Jerries,' would wrap themselves in white blankets and roll toward the English trenches, using those white blankets as camouflage in order to ambush the Allied soldiers."

I continued without hesitation. The story took on a life of its own as my classmates listened with amazement. Their interest excited me, and I felt that I was like them and finally belonged.

Mrs. Monahan, who'd been standing at the front of the class, walked toward me with a questioning frown on her face.

"Roger, how did you get to France?" she asked. "Where did you stay? What did you eat?"

I stood at my desk silently. I couldn't think fast enough.

She looked at me with a mixture of puzzlement and frustration, and sternly asked me to sit down. "Roger, stay after class. I want to talk to you." She called on someone else to talk about their summer.

This was the first time that I'd had Mrs. Monahan as a teacher. She didn't know me, but I'd heard about her from other students who'd had her. She had a reputation for being strict. I sat there waiting while my insides turned over. I'd gone from excitement to panic.

After everyone had left for the day, she came over to my desk. "Roger, why did you make up a story like that?" she asked.

I looked at my desk and nodded, saying, "I don't know."

"I don't know what you are up to, young man, but if it ever happens again, you will learn that telling lies in my class is not acceptable. Do you understand?"

"Yes," I mumbled.

"Say it louder."

"Yes, yes, I understand that I must not lie," I said loudly with enough conviction to fill the room.

"Okay! We have an understanding. Now, get out of here and go home."

I left quickly.

Making believe that I was like everyone else did not work. I wasn't like everyone else.

Fourth grade had started badly. Deep down I was worried that I might flunk and never be able to go to college.

That fall was particularly cold and harsh. Because of the early snows, we weren't able to husk all of the corn before Thanksgiving. Since you cannot husk corn wearing gloves, I used bare hands to strip the cornhusks while kneeling. My bare hands were cold and became chapped and raw and bled at times. We husked corn every day through the Thanksgiving break.

When I returned to school, I took my usual seat near the back of the classroom. Mrs. Monahan was very particular about cleanliness. She noticed me and saw how dirty my hands appeared. "Roger, would you please go to the boys' room and wash your dirty hands?"

I got up and went to the boys' room. I washed them using the Borax soap from the dispenser. When I finished, I went back to my seat.

As I passed her, she glanced down and saw that my hands still appeared dirty. "Roger, I told you to wash your hands until they were clean. Now go back and do it right," she ordered.

I went back to the bathroom and washed really hard. My hands were sore and the soap stung and I scrubbed until my knuckles began to bleed.

This time Mrs. Monahan met me outside the classroom door and grabbed my hands to inspect them. She started saying, "Why do you make things so difficult for—" and stopped. She saw that both of my small hands were bleeding and that they were not dirty but badly chapped.

"What have you been doing?" she asked.

"We husk corn by hand, and the weather was cold over Thanksgiving," I said. "We need the corn for the animals."

"Oh my, over Thanksgiving," she said softly. She looked up and away from me as she stroked my back. I thought she might cry.

She recovered and said, "I'm sorry. I didn't know about your farm work. It must be hard."

Chapter 14
Suckers

Motion sickness was a persistent problem for me. I tried my best to avoid riding in vehicles, including school buses. Because buses stopped and started frequently and swayed back and forth going around curves on bumpy dirt roads, they frequently made me sick. So, I walked to and from school as often as I could. I liked the quiet time and the opportunities to observe seasonal changes in the natural world along the roads.

In first and second grades, we learned the words to the song "Happy Wanderer." Since I was known not to be able to carry a tune, I amused myself on the walks by singing and humming the song without fear of criticism. Creek Road led directly from our farm to Newville School. Each day I got to cross the North Branch of Neshaminy Creek on a concrete bridge. If I had time, I would stand on the bridge and watch the water passing underneath.

The creek was moody. Sometimes it was quiet and flowed smoothly. Other times it was turbulent and raced by, impatiently carrying debris. I saw a tree being dragged along in the angry current until it got snagged on one of the supports of the bridge. Other debris became entangled in the branches of the tree and a dam formed. Eventually the rushing water tore the whole mass away from the bridge support, and the giant leafy barge floated away downstream. The next stop would be the bridge in Chalfont adjacent to Forest Park.

When the water was clear and the creek was flowing smoothly, I could see a school of fish. I noted that each fish in the school was pointed upstream and worked its gills to allow water in and out. I imagined what it would be like to catch it and take it home for dinner. I knew that Mr. McClelland liked fish and would be pleased to have fish for dinner.

One evening when I was cleaning the cow barn with Richard, I said to him, "Have you ever seen the fish in the stream on the way to Newville School?"

"Sure have," he replied.

"What kind of fish are they?"

"Suckers," he replied.

"Do you think we could catch some for dinner?" I asked.

"We don't have anything to catch them with," he said with finality.

I was intrigued by the idea of catching some fish and had one more question, "Are they good to eat?"

He paused, looked at me, and said, "I dunno. Those fish are suckers and so are you if you think you are going to catch one." The conversation ended, and he returned to shoveling manure.

I decided to keep my fishing thoughts to myself. Although he was probably right that my idea was foolish, I had no fishing experience and nothing to fish with. I knew that Mr. McClelland had told stories about catching fish in the "old country," using horsehair loops. Our horses had tails with long hairs on them, but it seemed too complicated to cut enough hairs and wind them together to make a loop long enough to snag a fish from the high bridge. I thought that there had to be another way.

I made a plan to fashion my own fishing gear. I knew that I needed hooks, bait, fishing line, a pole, and a reel. I would use worms for bait; we had all sorts of worms. I took a string that was used to tie the chicken feed bags and made it into a fishing line. I wrapped the fishing line around four nails hammered into a square piece of two-by-four and had a reel. I had seen a picture of treble hooks, which had three barbs, which I duplicated by bending three nails and wiring them together. I decided that I did not need a pole since I could throw the baited treble hooks into the water without a pole. I was all set to go fishing.

The time to go fishing was Sunday afternoon. We usually didn't work between the noon chores and the evening chores on Sundays. I waited for Mr. McClelland to take a nap, and when he did, off I went to the bridge with Rex trotting beside me on a grand adventure. I was filled with optimism that my cobbled fishing gear would catch fish for dinner. I'd learned part of the John Greenleaf Whittier poem "The Barefoot Boy" and happily kept repeating the lines I knew:

Blessings on thee, little man,
Barefoot boy, with cheek of tan!
With thy turned-up pantaloons,
And thy merry whistled tunes;

The world was perfect for me at that moment as I arrived at the bridge ready to engage nature.

There were three positions from which to fish: the bridge, the steep shore side, or the sloping sandy bank. The bridge position was too high, and because the sun was so hot, the fish were hiding underneath the bridge in the shade, which made them inaccessible. The steep bank side put me directly above the fish, and every movement I made scared the fish away. The best approach was to wade into the water slowly from the sandy side, which had the gentle slope.

I attached a worm and threw out the line—splash! The fish scattered. I repeated this process over and over, and each time the fish moved away. I realized that the hook assembly with the worm was too bulky and made too much noise going into the water. My optimism faded with each futile toss. It was getting late. The time for me to go home was coming, and I hadn't had a nibble. A blessing came in the form of an idea. What if I threw the makeshift hooks and bait over to the steep side of the creek and slowly drew it into the water without making a big splash? I tossed the end of the line to the other bank and dragged the bait without a splash into the middle of the school and waited.

Still no nibbles. Frustrated, I began to pull the line toward me; it unexpectedly became taut. I'd hooked a fish. I felt a surge of excitement rush through me. This was the first fish I'd ever caught! What a feeling. When I grabbed the blue-gray fish, I saw what had happened. The nail-hooks had dug into the side of the fish— I'd snagged it. But a catch was a catch. I went fishing and caught a fish. I gathered together my gear, put my prize in the burlap bag, called to Rex, and went home a winner.

Mom said, "That's a good-sized one."

"Looks like we'll have fish for supper tonight," Mr. McClelland acknowledged. "Mum, help him clean it up. I can't wait."

"You didn't really catch the fish. You foul-hooked it," Richard pointed out.

"Ignore him," Mom directed. "Let me show you how to take the scales off and fillet it."

The fish had a lot of bones, but the white meat was tasty. What I remember most was not the taste, but the smiles during that supper. It was a complete treat. I bathed in the stream of compliments, which nourished me, like the waters supported the fish.

Another new social worker, Miss Burns, came the next day and took Richard and me to Philadelphia for our semiannual examinations. New social workers meant introductory small talk. Richard answered her questions. I listened and stared out the window.

"How are you both doing?" Miss Burns asked.

"Fine."

"When will school be out?"

"In two weeks."

"What will you do this summer?"

"Work."

"What kind of work?"

"Chores and stuff."

"How are you two getting along?"

"Okay."

"Roger, are you usually this quiet?"

Richard answered for me, "He usually talks too much."

"Really?"

"I caught a fish," I interjected.

"He only thinks he caught a fish," Richard said. "The dumb fish got snagged on the hooks. It was all an accident."

"I went to the creek and caught a fish, a big one," I stated stubbornly.

"Still dumb luck," Richard responded.

"You couldn't do it," I said.

"Oh, yeah. I wouldn't waste all afternoon for one lousy fish," he pushed back.

"Stop it! Boys. That's not the way brothers should be talking to each other," the social worker said diplomatically.

"He's not my brother. That's for sure," said Richard.

I knew Richard was right. It was just luck. The fun of that afternoon was beginning to fade. Richard had made it seem like I'd wasted a lot of time to catch just one fish. He always knew how to say things that hurt.

The social worker glanced over at me and inquired, "You went to the creek by yourself?"

"Yes."

"Do you do that very often?"

"No, not really."

"You could have fallen in and drowned."

"I wouldn't be that lucky," Richard spoke up.

"How far away from the farm is the place you went fishing?"

"About a mile or two," I said.

"That far from home? And you were alone?"

"That's because no one else would waste their time with him," Richard blurted out.

"That's enough," she said.

She was fishing with her questions, and I did not want to be caught. I remembered that Richard had warned me about social workers. He'd said, "Be careful what you say to them. They really don't know what happens on the farm or any farm. They probably don't want to know. If we tell them too much, the word gets back to the old man and the old lady and then we get in trouble." I decided to stop talking about fishing. I believed Richard.

The streets of Philadelphia were congested and noisy. She parked the car, and we entered the Aid Society building together. I was glad to be inside and away from the noise. I liked riding the old brass and glass elevator, which had a big door and a smiling elevator man who said pleasantly, "Welcome, Miss Burns. All aboard to the third floor."

On the third floor we walked down a hall and into an area with three rooms all opened to each other. One space had a dining area with tables and chairs, a refrigerator that was humming away in the corner, a water cooler with a big bottle of water on top, and a storage closet that had graham crackers and cereal on one shelf and office supplies on the others. Adjacent to that was a play area with toys, several open windows with vertical bars that were painted white, several bookshelves, and two red overstuffed chairs and a red sofa. The other open room had a desk and a staff worker who was busy typing away using a headset that was feeding her messages. There were several black cylinders on her desk waiting to be processed.

We were given graham crackers and a container of orange juice and one of milk. Both were refreshing drinks after the drive. The cold whole milk was very tasty in sharp contrast to our unpasteurized farm milk. The graham crackers were a real treat and when we could, we would sneak extras from the food cabinet.

When we finished getting our snacks, we waited in the play area for someone to come and take us to the doctor's office or the dentist's office, which were in the same building on different floors. I remember sitting in the waiting area of one office and seeing women bulging with their pregnancies and wondering if that was what my mother had done when she was about to have me. After the exams, I was escorted back to the play area to wait my turn for clothes. Richard was already back from his exam.

When we were alone in the play area, he said, "Look at what I found." He held up a rifle, which appeared to be a genuine military one from World War Two. He shouldered it, "presented arms," and pointed it at make-believe targets around the room. He went over to the open window and looked down on the narrow alley below.

He poked the rifle barrel out through the bars and pointed it at a man in the alley and yelled down, "Hey, you! Yeah, you! I'm going to shoot you!" The man looked up, apparently saw the gun, and ducked under a stairway for cover in the alley.

"Now, there's a real sucker for you," Richard laughed.

We waited and watched, but the man never came out. No one caught Richard doing this; however, there were no guns in the room the next time I visited the Aid Society.

Another person came and got both of us and took us to the clothing floor. They gave each of us tooth powder, a toothbrush, underclothes, a pair of sneakers, a pair of dungarees after we tried them on, a belt, and two striped polo shirts. They put all of our stuff in paper bags, and we went back upstairs to the eating area and had milk and peanut butter and jelly sandwiches. Miss Burns came and took us back to the car.

On the way home, she said, "I have some news for you. You boys are big enough now that you can take the train from the New Britain station to the Reading Terminal here in town. I won't have to come and get you and then take you back home."

"You know that the train stops in Chalfont, too, right?" Richard said. "Can't we take the train from there instead of New Britain?"

"Of course, you can."

"Will we still have to go down twice a year?" Richard asked.

"Maybe not," said Miss Burns. "They're thinking that they are going to give your parents a clothing allowance and maybe have your local doctor and dentist do the checkups."

I liked the idea of not riding in a car. When we got back to the farm, Richard and I went to our rooms to change into our work clothes. I overheard talking in the living room.

I heard Miss Burns say, "He is only ten years old. My supervisor says that it is too dangerous for him to go down to the creek by himself."

"He was only fishing," Mom said.

"It's not only about fish. I'm told that there are lead mines nearby and that boys have drowned there. What if he fell in? He was two miles away."

Mom replied, "The lead mines are in the opposite direction toward New Galena. He was fishing near the bridge on Creek Road, a road he walks on every day going to Newville School."

Mom was defending me and her judgment to let me go fishing. Miss Burns was insistent about restricting me. I felt bad for Mom.

"I understand that Roger was placed here after the unfortunate death of Phillip, which I know was an accident. Roger has already had surgery for a hernia. We just want you to be careful with the boys in your care."

I went quietly down the stairs and slipped out the kitchen door, bypassing the parlor. I didn't want to be supervised more. This woman didn't know anything about the way we lived.

Chapter 15
Partners in Pranks

The older I got, the more work I could do. As I did more work and shared responsibilities with Richard, the more we began doing things together. The summer between my fourth and fifth grades was the time when I could do enough work that he no longer considered me to be only a pest and a burden. We were never peers since he was the clear leader; however, I was no longer just a target. There were ways in which he served as a parent since the McClellands were often out of touch with the realities of young boys growing up. Richard was making his way on his own and letting me see the world through his eyes. We worked together, got into mischief together, and even played together when we found the time.

I began pitching hay instead of just tramping it down on the wagon like I used to do. I was glad to be pitching because I had been stabbed in the hand the previous summer by Mr. McClelland's pitchfork when he threw some hay onto the wagon without seeing me. Loading and unloading hay was hard work. We used Belgian Draft horses named Kit and Bill to haul the hay from the fields and into the barn. Mr. McClelland preferred to have them go into the barn versus the tractor since there was no danger of a spark flying from them and setting a fire like there was with a tractor. Each time we unloaded the hay and drank some water, we backed the horses and the empty wagon out of the barn and down the hill. Richard and I were supposed to drive the horses back to the hayfield while Mr. McClelland took a breather in the house and drank some coffee.

Richard would ask me to keep an eye out to make sure Mr. McClelland was not around. Feeling safe and unseen, he would slap the reins on the horses' backs and say, "Giddy-up!" Off we went racing back to the field. It was like a wild stagecoach ride. The horses galloped in the hot weather and got lathered up. Once in the field we waited in the shade for at least fifteen minutes until Mr. McClelland joined us.

He would examine the horses and say, "What have you boys been doing with these animals?"

"It's very hot out," Richard would answer convincingly. We would have our fun without getting caught.

Another prank we shared was helping ourselves to bakery treats. Our farm was on the route of two bakery trucks. Both Bond Bread and Freihofer's Bakery made deliveries to our farm. One driver came on Tuesdays, and the other came on Fridays. They delivered sliced bread, pies, and other sorts of bakery treats like glazed cinnamon buns with nuts buried in the toppings. Mom rarely bought treats like that unless they were one or two days old.

When Richard and I were alone, cleaning stables or throwing down hay, it was ideal planning time. He had a plan to get some cinnamon buns. He stopped working and said, "Have you noticed that sometimes the bakery guys stop their trucks in the driveway where their view is blocked by one of the maple trees in front of the house? Besides, they turn their backs to the door when the old lady is buying bread."

"They do turn their backs," I acknowledged. "What are you thinking?"

"Well, I know that you really like those cinnamon buns they sell," he said.

"So do you," I replied.

"I think there's a way that we can get some for free."

"Really?"

"Yes. All we have to do is watch for the trucks when we're doing chores around the house. Then, if you go and sit on the porch, you can watch to see if the drivers turn their backs or if the drivers' trucks are partially blocked by the tree."

"Yes."

"If you think everything is okay, wave to me, and I'll hop into the truck on the other side and grab some cinnamon buns or cookies."

The plan worked perfectly each time we were around on delivery days and the drivers' backs were turned. We had all the treats we wanted for a while. The truck driver from Bond Bread caught on first that we were helping ourselves to his inventory and would not turn his back. A few weeks later even the Freihofer's driver no longer turned his back. They were on to us, but they never mentioned it to Mom. We got away with stealing without any penalty.

We were not as blessed in another activity we engaged in for entertainment. Our barn had lots of pigeons. The pigeons were a nuisance, and their droppings made a mess throughout the barn, including on the hay. Richard had another idea.

"Do you see the big barn window near the roof with the beam underneath?" he asked.

"Yes."

"The pigeons like to sit on the rafters near the ceiling at the other end of the barn away from the window," he said. "If you climbed up on the beams at the other end of the haymow near the wall, you could make noises and scare them and they would fly out the big window."

"I know I can scare them out because I've done that many times," I said. "So, what?"

"If I stood on the beam near the window with a baseball bat, I should be able to hit the pigeons when they try to fly out the window," he replied.

"That might work." I said, believing that we might get some credit for getting rid of the pigeons.

We both climbed up our designated walls and took our positions. I made noise, and the pigeons took off for the exit window. Richard connected with an unfortunate pigeon with his first swing. The stunned and dying pigeon spiraled down toward the ground and landed full force on Mr. McClelland's straw hat.

He reached up and grabbed the pigeon, swearing, "What the hell is going on? What are you boys doing up there when you're supposed to be working? I was wondering what was taking you so long. Get your goddamn asses down here and finish your chores."

No credit.

I came away with several observations. Richard was smart, and his plans usually worked to perfection. Pigeons may be protected by some deity since the precision of that pigeon landing on Mr. McClelland's head had spared the lives of many other pigeons that evening. Mr. McClelland was unconcerned about the dead pigeon but very upset that we would be fooling around instead of doing our chores. Once again, he made it clear that work output was his priority.

When our chores were done in the summer evenings and we had supper, we had some free time. When the moon was full and the sky was clear, it was bright enough at night to play catch with a football. The memories of playing with Richard in the empty hayfields after dark on those bright nights are my best with him. The sweetness of the dew-dampened grass hung in the air around the fields where we had been working in the day; the night air was fresh and energizing. The sounds of crickets and katydids could be heard all around us and mixed with our calls to one another of "Here it comes" and "I got it." On those few nights when we played—work faded from our minds and we were just kids.

On some Friday nights, the McClellands would walk with us across several fields to the Perry's house in order to socialize and be entertained, too. The Perrys had one of the first televisions in the neighborhood. Mr. McClelland loved the Friday night fights sponsored by the Gillette Safety Razor Company. We would sit around eating potato chips while Mom talked to Mrs. Perry and Mr. McClelland and Mr. Perry would watch the fights. Richard and I watched the television with awe. We'd never seen anything like it. At ten o'clock the fights were over. We got up, thanked Mr. and Mrs. Perry, and trooped back through the fields to home. I would repeat, "Look sharp! Feel sharp! Be sharp!" until told to stop.

After a few Friday nights of making the trips back and forth to the Perrys, Mr. McClelland bought an RCA Victor black-and-white television. Richard's reaction was, "Where did the old man find the money for that? He won't buy an old pickup, but he can buy a television."

I didn't have any idea where the money came from. I chimed in, "I think it'll be fun to have."

Richard was a doer, not a watcher. He couldn't have cared less about any form of staged entertainment, including the fights. "The old man is Scotch-Irish and probably has money hidden around this place somewhere," he concluded.

I was intrigued by the thought of finding his money, but I was mostly interested in thoughts of what we could see on the TV. The set was installed on a strong black buffet-cupboard in the kitchen near one of the windows. There was discipline about watching the TV. The only shows we watched at first were the news, the fights, and Milton Berle. Next, it was turned on during breakfast to "catch the weather" presented during the Dave Garroway show. Eventually, it became part of our evening lives, which included a diet of regular shows but nothing late into the night because we all had to get up early the next morning. Sometimes I would sneak into the kitchen on Saturdays and catch a cartoon, but it was always done with apprehension. I had to keep one eye on the paths around the house to avoid being found wasting time.

The relationship between Richard and me evolved rapidly that summer. It got to a point that I believed him and depended on him more and more for good advice. Just when I thought he knew enough to be really trusted, I learned otherwise.

We had a small spring-fed creek, really just a ditch, that crossed Iron Hill Road and ran through the farm and into the woods at the foot of the pasture. It carried a lot of water during storms and had noticeable banks and a small footbridge over it so that we could service one of the chicken houses. One summer evening we discovered that bumblebees had built a hive in the ground on one of the banks. We decided to torment them. Richard got a shovel.

"This will fix them," he said as he began to dig them out.

They came streaming out of their overturned hive. Richard sprang backwards yelling at me, "Don't move and they won't sting you."

I stood still like a post. I became their target. They stung me, and I raced away with the bumblebees chasing me and stinging me more. Richard was laughing.

Chapter 16
Defenseless

Farming was tough. The McClellands were economically borderline subsistence farmers. They depended on pigs and chickens for income, and, of course, the money they received for housing foster children, who were also expected to work. A system supported each revenue source, but there were risks.

The system for raising pigs was fairly straightforward. The combination of a boar and a sow would produce about two piglet litters per year. The number of babies per litter ranged between eight to fifteen. Once the babies were weaned, they were fed corn, which we grew, and some commercial hog feed mixed with milk or water. When they were several weeks old, the males were castrated. Castration was performed by our veterinarian; the process always made me cringe. The helpless pig's legs were spread open while his testicles were cut out, and the pig screamed loudly. The openings made to remove the testicles were doused with a blue antiseptic and the victimized pig was released. Some farmers prepared the testicles and served them as "mountain oysters." Thankfully, we did not do that.

The time from farrowing until the pigs reached a market weight of about two hundred thirty-five pounds was about six to eight months. Mr. McClelland sold the pigs to a Mr. Foley, who hauled the pigs to market in his big livestock truck. We helped to load the squealing pigs onto his truck using an electric prod. When Richard was older, he was able to pick up the most stubborn pigs and bodily put them on the truck.

When the loading was done, Mr. Foley would reach into

his pocket and pull out a big wad of bills; he always paid on the spot in cash. I was amazed by the amount of money he carried in his pocket and often wondered just how much money he had. He was rich.

Raising chickens was a more complicated process. We raised Long Island Reds, a breed known for good egg production and calmness compared to other breeds. Mr. McClelland preferred them. "Don't know why the Schaeffers like those damn Leghorns," he would say. "Hell, those chickens would pile up in a corner at the slightest scare and kill themselves. You could lose them all."

Chickens were not so important to the Schaeffers. They were dairy farmers, not chicken farmers. They had about fifteen to twenty Jersey milking cows and one henhouse. We had two or three Holstein cows and about a thousand laying hens scattered in multiple henhouses around the farm.

Three-day-old chicks would arrive in boxes. When we took the lids off the boxes, the little yellow furry balls with orange legs and bright eyes were cute. We would slowly tilt boxes into brooder pens, and the chicks would pour out in yellow waves onto the peat moss-covered floor and scramble toward the warmth of the heat lamps. I thought it was strange, at first, that we only got chicks that grew into hens. Logically, eggs would hatch into either baby roosters or baby hens. They must have been sorted in some way.

"How do they tell the difference between baby roosters and baby hens?" I asked.

"You can see the difference between the hens and roosters when they are just hatched by looking at their wings," Mom told me.

"How?"

"The baby chicks that grow into hens have double rows of tiny wing feathers, whereas the rooster chicks have only one row of tiny feathers," she said.

"What happens to the baby roosters that nobody wants?" I asked. Early on, I was thinking that maybe they became "foster roosters."

She just nodded her head and said, "I don't know."

Richard told me later with a certain satisfaction, "The baby roosters are ground up and made into chicken feed."

There was little waste in farming even if it meant, in this instance, that the chickens unknowingly became cannibals and may have eaten their unfortunate male siblings.

Once the chicks left the brooder house, they were put into large outside coops where they were fed and watered until they reached egg-laying age, usually at six months of age. When the chickens started to lay eggs, they were moved to larger chicken houses, which had nests for them to lay their eggs. Simultaneously, as they were moved, they were individually vaccinated to prevent coccidiosis.

Moving the chickens and vaccinating them was a time-consuming process. The chickens had to be individually caught. We used "poultry hooks," which were about three feet long with a curved hook at the end to catch chickens by the leg as they tried to race away. Hooking the chickens was a form of sport for Richard and me because there was something comical about a chicken being snagged by the leg and dragged away unexpectedly from its neighbors. One moment they were standing quietly with their friends, and then—whoosh—they were gone.

Once the chickens were moved to the poultry houses, we all had our tasks to care for them. Richard and I watered them every day. Mom fed them and collected the eggs twice a day; twice daily avoided breakage. Richard and I put straw in the chicken houses every few weeks to help absorb the manure, which chickens produced in abundance. Mr. McClelland, Richard, and I dug out the chicken manure-straw mix every four to six months. Cleaning the chicken houses and hauling the manure away was hard and smelly work, which was worse in the summer than in the winter because the summer heat made the smell worse.

Mr. McClelland was not a scientist, but he knew that to get the maximum egg production chickens needed artificial light, especially in the winter when there were fewer daylight hours. This meant that someone had to go from henhouse to henhouse every evening and turn on the lights and then turn the lights off in the morning. That was one of my chores. Sometimes when I switched the lights on, I would see rats eating the chicken feed. I devised ways to surprise them and to kill them. When I got older, I would quietly approach the hen houses at dusk and try to shoot them with my .22 rifle. I did manage to kill a few. The best rat and mouse population control on our farm were cats. We had more than a dozen cats roaming the various buildings on the farm. The cats who hunted the rodents were well fed.

When the chickens got older, their egg-laying production slowly declined. I was never aware of egg-laying records being kept; however, Mr. McClelland seemed to know when it was time to sell the chickens. He had a different buyer for the chickens than Mr. Foley. The buyer was Harry Henderson, a wholesale poultry man who lived in Fountainville about five miles away. Once when he came, he brought his two sons, who were fraternal twins and were older than Richard by several years. It was clear that they didn't enjoy the dirty work of hooking chickens and stuffing them into chicken crates. Mostly, they stood at a distance and watched.

Richard, Mr. McClelland, and I would help Mr. Henderson clear the selected henhouse filled with less productive chickens, which took about thirty minutes or so. When the truck was filled with crates of cackling and clucking chickens, the twins and Mr.

Henderson would climb into the truck and drive off to the market. The dogs would chase after the truck, going up the lane, barking as if trying to quiet the noisy chickens. It was very still after the chickens were gone.

We would set about the tasks of cleaning the henhouse and preparing it for the next batch of new hens. Mr. Henderson returned a few days later and paid Mr. McClelland in cash. He was more discreet than Mr. Foley since he just handed over an envelope filled with money and a receipt for the chickens without showing a big wad of bills. I noticed the difference between those two buyers and thought that dealing in pigs seemed less refined in some way compared to chickens. The refinement did not rub off on Mr. Henderson's boys.

I hardly knew the Henderson twins since they were about seven years older than I was and I had only seen them on those times when Mr. Henderson picked up chickens. I encountered them one day when I was about eleven years old. I was walking down Iron Hill Road; they were standing beside their car. They saw me, and I heard them say, "Hey, there's Heifer's kid brother." They motioned to me and one of them said, "Hey, kid. Your name is Roger, right?"

Since I'd already met them and knew who they were and I wanted to see their shiny red car, I went over. I was relaxed and leaned my hand against the car, feeling its smooth surface. They seemed to be talking to me and about Richard at the same time. It felt cool to be around them.

I was startled when one of them said, "Hey, kid, get your chickenshit hands off our new car."

I stepped back, apologizing but sensing that something had shifted.

They were standing on either side of me like two tall towers.

Next, I heard, "What do you think we should do with him?"

"Let's teach him a lesson."

I turned to run, but just as swiftly as I'd turned, one of them stuck out his foot and hooked my legs like I was a chicken. I fell to the ground. They were big, and they were on top of me. They dragged me by my feet over to the hedgerow. I had no idea what offense I could have committed to warrant this treatment. I was used to being pushed around by Richard, but this felt different. I was scared. I started to yell, but one of them covered my mouth with his big hand. "Shut your fat mouth," one of them said.

"This farm kid stinks," one said. "I wonder if he has a load in his pants?"

As that was said, they began to pull at my trousers. I grabbed at my pants, trying to hold them up.

"Let's depants this little son of a bitch. It'll teach him to mind his own business and to stay away from our car."

They rolled me onto my back and yanked my pants and underpants down to my shoes. I could feel the cool grass and the rough ground under my back. I was squirming and twisting frantically to escape from their grip, but they managed to grab my legs and push them back over my head. I was totally exposed and felt helpless like the pigs when we castrated them. I was terrified. It flashed through my head that they were going to grab my testicles.

I heard them say, "Oh, look at that little thing. The little prick has a little prick."

One of them grabbed a green weed stalk. They were laughing. I was sobbing. I was helpless. They took the stalk and stuck it into my bottom.

"There, his shit should make that plant grow big," one said.

They stood up laughing and let my legs go. I felt the stalk go deeper into me when my legs came down. I cried out and rolled over onto my stomach. I reached back and pulled the green stalk out and lay there crying. I heard them drive away. It was over. What did I do? What could I do? I pulled up my underpants and my dungarees. I was dazed by what had just happened.

I got up and tried to walk. At first, all I could do was wobble. I was trembling. I was hurt. I didn't know what to do. I'd been humiliated and was embarrassed. I thought that I must have done something really bad to have had this happen to me.

I went to the barn and just stood in the safety of the shadows. My underpants were bloody. I scrubbed them in the watering trough. I wanted to throw them away but couldn't. There was no one to tell. I'd heard about depantsing boys, and I knew that it had just happened to me. However, I didn't want anyone to know what they did. It wasn't a joke. They'd had power over me for that short time just like we had power over the pigs and the chickens.

I vowed not to be a victim ever again.

I never saw the Henderson twins after that day. However, their father arrived months later with a tape recorder. He came into our kitchen and sat down and played a message from one of the boys who had apparently joined the Army. He'd been sent to South Korea after the war was over. Mr. Henderson wanted to record a message from us to him that he would send. I made a bad face. Mr. McClelland said, "What's so upsetting to you? Why aren't you talking?"

Chapter 17
A Greek Tragedy

From the Bible I knew that Daniel had been forced into the lion's den for praying to God, but he had been protected by an angel and was not eaten. Joseph had been sold into slavery by his half-brothers but eventually rose to great power. These Biblical stories inspired me to have faith that I would heal and grow and somehow escape the life I was living. There had to be a reason why I was abandoned by my real parents and eventually ended up on this farm. I vowed to pray and use whatever power I had to do good for others. If I did that, I believed that I would be saved.

The McClelland farm, like all farms, was abundantly filled with the many phases of life. We witnessed breeding and birthing, growing and declining, flourishing and suffering, and, ultimately, dying. Each of these processes was part of the natural order of the world for me. Sometimes I got drawn into one or more of these cycles, and as often as not, I was deeply impacted by just how helpless I was to make a truly lasting difference.

Mr. McClelland spoke to me at noon one summer day, saying, "Son, the potato bugs have to be picked off the potatoes down near the pullet houses. Richard and I are going to hoe tomatoes this afternoon. You need to pick the potato bugs."

"Okay," I said. I actually liked working alone without direct supervision. I knew that if I worked fast, I could get the job done and have some free time with Rex.

When baby chicks grew enough to become classified as pullets, we would move them from the brooder houses to pullet sheds where they would remain until they reached their egg-laying stage. The pullet sheds were ramshackle outbuildings built with fencing and slats, and tongue and groove walls. Over time as the sheds aged and became weathered, cracks would appear in the walls. Sometimes the cracks would begin at the roof as wide openings that gradually tapered forming V-shaped cracks. We had three of these pullet sheds facing one of the cow pastures with a path running along behind. The path led to the potato field, where I was headed that day.

When I passed one of the pullet sheds, I noticed that a sparrow was flapping its wings, struggling to free itself from a V-shaped crack in the wall of one of the sheds. The poor sparrow was accidentally hanging itself. I dropped my potato bug pail and went to the wall and freed the struggling bird. It was already limp.

I ran back to our house with the bird cupped in my hands. In the kitchen I turned the faucet on and poured water onto its head to see if I could revive it. I stroked the poor wet little bird; it started to recover. The little sparrow had been about to die from hanging itself in that crack in the boards, and I'd managed to save it. I was elated.

After a couple of minutes, it was struggling to get out of my hands. I went to the kitchen door, which opened onto the porch, in order to give the bird its freedom and a second chance at life. I stood in the door looking at my little bird, which was quickly drying, said goodbye, and released it.

The porch roof sloped down. The bird started to fly away but alertly ducked just a bit to clear the porch ceiling. Just as the bird dropped down, one of the cats sprang into the air and snatched the bird into its mouth. In that instant, my joy turned into horror.

The cat ran from the porch with the sparrow in its mouth. I raced after the cat. I caught the cat in the yard and choked it until it released the bird. I was too late. The bird was dead. I felt horrible. The bird that I had saved from hanging to death had been killed by the cat.

As I grew older, that incident stuck in my mind, especially when I read Greek and Roman stories. They basically taught that when it is your time to die, there is nothing that can be done about it. What could I have expected to have done to interfere with the power of that bird's fate on that day?

Chapter 18
Half Full or Half Empty?

The news that I had a mother was a seismic event. The aftershocks of implications and possibilities rippled through all of us on the farm. When we were back in the field, Richard asked questions nonstop, which was unusual for him. I didn't have answers to his questions, nor did I want to share my thoughts.

I wondered why Miss Fleming hadn't taken me aside to talk to me privately. She'd delivered the news to the McClellands first, and only after they'd had a chance to discuss it, did they talk to me. Afterwards, she excused me so that they could talk some more. What else could they have been talking about? Were there other letters that they hadn't shared? What did "fallen woman" mean?

That night at supper there was more conversation. They talked as if I weren't there.

Mr. McClelland was puzzled and angry, asking, "What kind of woman would leave her son and then years later come after him?"

"She did not come after him, John. She just wrote him a letter," Mom clarified.

"Then, what's all this talk about a brother and a sister and making it sound like there's a family out there for him?" Mr. McClelland questioned.

He paused and then added, "What does she expect to accomplish by disturbing us and him now anyway?"

"Maybe she just wants to know that her son is okay and that she is thinking of him. Some women are like that, especially if they have regrets, John," Mom said.

"Yes, and we know what kind of woman does that," Mr.

McClelland replied. "The kind that don't make suitable mothers."

"Maybe she just made a mistake," Mom suggested. "Perhaps, she couldn't afford to take care of a child then, and maybe she can now."

"That might be all well and good, but she went on and had another one, a girl. Right? She was unfit then, and she's unfit now to be a mother. She's probably a Catholic," he said with a sense of satisfaction. His prejudice and her behavior coincided perfectly.

"John, not in front of the boys. Let's talk about this later," Mom spoke slowly and quietly to keep Mr. McClelland in check.

He could not help himself, "Did you notice that Miss Fleming never mentioned anything about a father? His mother never mentioned anything about a father in the letter either. I wonder what went on back then?"

Richard had been listening and watching the exchanges throughout dinner. "If she is a Catholic, maybe there are more brothers and sisters out there somewhere?" Richard suggested.

"Yeah! And maybe she has them scattered around in other foster homes," Mr. McClelland added, summing the situation up.

"That's enough, John!" Mom had spoken with finality.

I was done listening and done with supper. "Where's the letter?" I asked.

"There on the buffet table behind you with the other mail," Mom answered.

I reached back and took the letter and stuck it in my pocket.

"What are you doing, boy?" asked Mr. McClelland.

"I want to go outside and read the letter again," I said.

"Okay," Mom said, "but before you go, please clean up your place and put the dishes in the sink."

I wanted to get away from the house and the conversation as quickly as possible. Besides, I thought I would share this new information with two of my friends, Doris and Carl Weik. They lived about two miles away in Chalfont, and I knew I could run over and back before dark and still turn the chicken lights on in the hen houses without getting caught. Even though Doris was two years older and was going to be a seventh grader, I liked her, and I was especially eager to get her reaction to my amazing news.

I knocked at their door and they came out. I told them about what had happened that day. They looked puzzled. Doris said, "I thought you told us that you were adopted?"

"I never told you that," I said. "Here, read the letter."

They took turns reading the letter. "What does this mean? Does it mean that you'll be moving away?" Carl asked.

"No, it means I have a mother, a sister, and a brother."

"So what?" Doris said. "You ran all the way over here and got all sweaty just to tell us that?"

I was confused. I thought that they would be excited for me. They didn't get that I never knew I had living relatives. It was important to me. It meant nothing to them.

Doris said, "It's getting late. We have to go inside now. If you move, let us know." I was dismissed.

They were neither interested nor excited for me. I thought that they were friends and would be curious and happy for me, but they weren't. I wanted to talk about it with someone. I was disappointed. I was alone in the world. A world so foreign to others who had real families that they couldn't understand the significance of suddenly knowing that my real mother had contacted me. I was sad. I stopped and looked down at the stream below the Newville Bridge. The idea crossed my mind to jump. I didn't want to go on feeling different and unwanted. Richard was right—no one would understand about us. We should just be quiet.

I had to get home before dark. While I trotted along the dirt road, I began to think about whom I could talk to. There were foster kids living at the Schaeffers. They took in foster kids from the Lutheran Home affiliated with Tabor Home. The Schaeffers were even older than the McClellands. They had a car, burned wood, and had no indoor plumbing. Various boys were placed there; however, the boys usually did not stay there very long. The boys worked hard. None of them were good students, and some even quit school after they were in ninth grade.

When I was a first grader, two Pone brothers lived there. Eugene was my age. Sometimes we played together, but those boys moved before we got to know each other. The Still brothers, Frank, Bill, and George, came next, but they moved before too long, also. They were older than I was. George had a car and liked to play hardball. One time he took me to Chalfont to play in a pickup game. I was pitching to him, and he hit a line drive into my stomach, which knocked me down and hurt me. The Stills were nice guys but too big for me to play sports with. The more I thought about it, the more I realized that they wouldn't care about my letter either. We never discussed anything about our personal family situations.

Richard was not a conversationalist and had already expressed himself when he had said that I shouldn't leave the farm. The idea of leaving the farm might have been implied, but it wasn't mentioned by Miss Fleming or in the letter. The letter was just an introduction to the idea that I had relatives. If I were going to talk to anyone, it would have to be Mom, as in Mrs. McClelland. How would I start the conversation? I wasn't going to tell her I had any ideas about leaving. I just wanted to share the news and get some advice from someone that would see this as important to me, instead of either treating it with indifference or seeing it as a threat.

The next day was a Saturday. While Mr. McClelland was taking a nap and Mom was cleaning eggs sitting in her chair, I approached her.

"What did you think of the letter?" I asked.

She stopped cleaning, gave me her full attention, and said, "Roger, that letter was a surprise for all of us. I know it must be confusing to you."

"I'm excited to know that I have living relatives. Can my mother just take me back?"

"Maybe, but I think there are a lot of steps to go through before she can just take you back," Mom answered. "You are a ward of the Children's Aid Society and that makes them responsible for you. They have to consider what's best for you and not just move you carelessly from one place to another."

"I would like to know more about all three of them," I said.

"Miss Fleming said that they might make it possible for you to meet your sister."

"I want to do that," I said.

"I think meeting her depends on whether or not she wants to meet you. I believe that the Aid Society has to discuss a possible meeting with her foster parents and with her, and then they will get back to us."

"What do you think is going to happen with my mother and brother?"

"I have no idea. Why don't you sit down and write her a letter? You have her address on that envelope."

"I could ask her about my father," I said.

"You may want to ask her some other questions first. That kind of question could be asked in a second or third letter."

I felt impatient. Letter exchanges would be slow and drag things out. I wanted to be able to play more like other kids. I didn't want to work. I couldn't mention how exciting it would be to not have to work so much because it would make me seem lazy. It would mean more work for Mom and everyone else. It would be too selfish. I had to be careful what I said about what I was thinking around anyone in the family.

Chapter 19
The Great Cherry Caper

Over the next few days, I started several letters to my real mother and finished none of them. I didn't know the woman. I didn't even know how to address her. I'd already had three so-called "Moms" that I could remember and several before that. Starting a letter with "Dear Mom" may have been biologically accurate, but it didn't feel right. What was I going to say anyway? I had a lot of questions tangled up in my mind. There was anger, too, since she was the one who'd let this happen to me.

Richard saw me trying to write and asked, "What are you trying to do? Make friends with her?"

"No. I just want to say something to her in response to her letter."

"Why don't you say, 'Dear Mom, having fun on the farm, wish you were here. PS I'll send some pig shit in my next letter'?"

I chuckled and realized that in reality there wasn't much I could say that would be honest.

I heard nothing from Miss Fleming over the next few days. Hearing from her might have motivated me to write. No one else mentioned my attempts at letter writing or my blood relatives. The McClellands and Richard were my real family. The fact that I had a relative out there who'd reached out to me started to be less important. And, I began to feel guiltier about even the far-fetched thought of leaving the farm. I knew how hard Mom worked every day making meals, collecting and cleaning eggs, feeding chickens, doing laundry, and generally taking care of everyone. I couldn't imagine that my natural mother could work harder and deserve help more than Mom. Besides, nature had ways of distracting young boys.

In the early spring, fresh asparagus grew in the hedgerows waiting to be found, picked, and taken home for dinner. Then came the hunt for fresh dandelion greens to be cooked like spinach and eaten as "spring tonic." Not long after dandelion greens, in coveted secret patches in the pastures there appeared wild strawberries suitable for strawberry shortcake with rich cream followed by the inevitable stuffed stomachs.

We had an abundance of fruit-bearing trees in our hedgerows. In the late spring, the farm borders would be bright with the blossoms of pear, apple, peach, and cherry trees. All we had to do was remember where we saw the telltale flowers, and we would find fruit in those places in the summer. The apples and the peaches would be riddled with worms and were seldom good to eat. Pears didn't have worms but were only okay to eat. Cherries were the best fruit to find and eat. Unfortunately, the wild cherries had lots of worms, too.

There were several types of cherries around the farm. Oxheart and Bing cherries were the most abundant. You could pick the cherries by the handful, but you had to look closely before eating them because many had insect larvae growing in them. Since we never sprayed the fruit trees, this meant that insects were undeterred and would lay their eggs in the flowers. Their larvae would hatch as small worms and eat the fruit. Once, when I picked a pailful of cherries, hoping that I would be rewarded with a cherry pie, I was very disappointed. The pail with the cherries was set aside until the next day. When we started to sort the cherries, we saw the pail was crawling with white larvae and had to be thrown away.

Other farmers did spray their fruit trees. Mr. Mason, the

gentleman farmer who lived down the hill from us, sprayed. He was a particular man who, we were told, was a singer from New York City. He and his wife had the uppity-sounding first names of Helfenstein and Sindonnia. She was a piano teacher. Richard and I never called them by their first names except when we were alone. Sometimes he hired Richard and me to mow his lawn, weed his garden, pick strawberries at ten cents a quart, or do some work around his chicken house.

The Mason farm was located on the corner of Iron Hill and Ferry Roads. That corner was our bus stop. This gave us a strategic position to gather intelligence about what was happening on the Mason farm. They had a large Bing cherry tree growing alongside the road adjacent to their house. We saw when the tree was filled with blossoms and watched him spray the blossoms to prevent insects from laying their eggs. We saw smaller branches bend toward the ground as the fruit grew. We saw the tree waving bright-red, marble-like fruit as the limbs bounced in the breeze. What a lovely sight!

Our eyes grew large and our stomachs ached for the sweet taste of those cherries. Just as a bull gets excited and charges when it sees red, there had to have been a similar chemistry at work inside us when we saw those dancing cherries. Our matador was Mr. Mason. We feared him as would any young boys with mischief in their hearts.

However, that fear didn't deter us. Richard had a straightforward plan.

"Look," he said, "we know since we worked there that he takes afternoon naps just like the old man does."

I thought that it was a lucky coincidence that Mr. McClelland and Mr. Mason napped at about the same time after lunch.

Richard described his plan. "All we have to do is go down the road on a Sunday afternoon when they're both napping, climb up into the tree, and have a cherry feast. The Masons will never miss a few from that tree, which is so loaded."

Iron Hill Road was a road with banks high enough that I could walk down the road and not be visible from the sides. When we got near the tree, I crawled up the bank and climbed the tree. Richard was much taller and stood on the ground picking cherries from the low-hanging branches. We had hardly started treating ourselves when the door to the Mason's house opened and out strode Mr. Mason directly toward the tree.

Richard slid down the embankment out of sight. I was stuck in the tree. All I could do was to wrap my arms around a big branch and pray that I would not be seen. Mr. Mason stood proudly looking up at the tree. Suddenly, he looked straight at me. I was really scared. My heart was pounding and my forehead beaded up with sweat. I was frozen and tried to melt into the bark. He stood there for a long time staring up before he finally walked away and went back into the house.

I slid down from that tree so fast that I skinned my arms. Richard was already running back up the road keeping his head down, and I followed as fast as I could. Once we got out of sight, we stopped and caught our breath. We both knew that it would have been a disaster to have been caught. Mr. McClelland's belt for sure.

My heart was still beating hard. I was scared and excited by our escape.

"What made him come out?" I asked.

"He must have heard something," Richard said. "He probably heard you talking too much."

"We were both talking," I said defensively.

"Why didn't he see me?" I asked.

"I think the sun was in his eyes," Richard answered.

"I was wondering if he saw me and deliberately didn't say anything because he knew I would get whipped if Mr. McClelland found out," I said.

"Two things I know for sure," replied Richard. "You would've been strapped if the old man found out. And, there's no way that anyone out there gives enough of a shit about us to let either of us off."

"You're probably right."

"I have another idea," said Richard with enthusiasm. "We can treat today like a scouting mission. We pretty much know where the branches are with the most cherries. Let's come back after dark."

"Okay. How late? Do you mean tonight?" I said with renewed interest.

"Yes, tonight."

We knew that the ripe cherries wouldn't be around very long before either the birds would eat them or they'd fall to the ground. It was possible that the Masons would pick all of the cherries within easy reach, too. It meant that we had to act fast.

Richard's next plan was a little more complex but a sure winner. After we went to bed that night, I waited for Richard to come to my room since he had the alarm clock and would know when it was late enough. He came and got me. We went to his room and slid out on the porch roof and let ourselves down to the ground using the downspout.

I followed Richard to the toolshed. There he said, "I was thinking that it would be best to cut a branch down that was loaded with cherries and take it away to eat the cherries somewhere else."

"Good idea," I said softly and nodded in agreement. I thought that the less time in the tree the better. I believed that a big branch loaded with cherries would even give us plenty for later.

Richard selected a small bow saw and off we went to the cherry tree. It was a clear night filled with choruses of insects, the flashes of lightning bugs, and a bright moon. Again, I climbed the tree while Richard waited below. I picked a good-sized branch and anchored myself so that I could see without falling. I was surprised at how loud the sawing sound was in the quiet of the night. It echoed back and forth—*see-zaw, see-zaw.*

Suddenly, the Mason's pole light came on, lighting up the whole area around the tree. Mr. Mason came out onto the porch. He called out, "Who's out there? Who's out there?"

I froze. I thought he might hear my pounding heart; it was pumping so loudly. He waited and listened. We waited and watched. He called out again, "If anyone is out there, I have a gun. I'm not afraid to shoot it at trespassers." He cocked his head as if to listen more intently. Eventually, he gave up, went back inside, and turned off the light.

We waited a while longer. "Finish cutting the damn branch and let's get out of here," Richard whispered.

I took the chance and sawed quickly through the limb and dropped it down through the other tree limbs to the ground. I was afraid the loud rustling sound falling to the ground would wake the Masons again. The pole light was not switched on. We made it.

The branch was too big to carry, so we dragged it back up the road to our barn. We turned on the inside barn light and prepared for a feast. There were no cherries to eat. There were some green ones but no ripe ones. The ripe cherries had fallen off when the branch had dropped to the ground, or they'd been shaken off as we dragged it home.

"I'll be damned," Richard said. "What the hell!"

I stood staring at the empty branch wondering how it could

have happened after all of our work. We threw the empty branch on the brush pile in the pasture. Completely discouraged, we climbed back up onto the porch roof, through the window, and into our beds.

The next morning, I got up early and ran to the road to see if we'd left a trail. Sure enough, there was clear evidence that a branch had been dragged along the dirt road leaving grooves in the dust and some cherries scattered here and there. When I did my morning chores, I was worried that Mr. Mason would be coming down our lane to report us, but he never came.

I think that there might have been more understanding and kindness in him than we knew.

Chapter 20
Road to Perdition

The McClellands worked most of the time and expected Richard and me to do the same. However, Saturday afternoons, Sundays after church, and rainy days offered us opportunities to be on our own. Since the McClellands were in their sixties, they couldn't keep track of us like younger parents might have. One Saturday while I was still waiting to hear from Miss Fleming about the possibility of meeting my sister, Richard and I wandered off the property.

There was a farm located about a half mile away, which was owned by an absentee "city person" named Mr. Wolfe. Richard and I divided people into two classes: city people and farmers. We applied the term "city person" to anyone who didn't farm. This meant that they didn't do hard manual work, they didn't have animals, and they weren't serious about caring for their land like real farmers. Mr. Wolfe owned about seventy-five acres of land, some of which he rented out to others to grow hay and soybeans. He was an unknown to us. We never met him, but it was general knowledge that he lived somewhere in or around Philadelphia. His property had several old buildings on it that attracted us.

The McClelland farm was situated on a "country block," which was roughly rectangular in shape and had a small creek running through it. The creek flowed past the farm buildings, through one of the pastures, and into the woods and beyond. By following the creek, we could get to Mr. Wolfe's property without being observed by other farmers. There was a lane to his property leading from Callowhill Road, which formed the western border of the McClelland farm block.

The Wolfe farm was hilly and had an abandoned orchard with apple trees, many of which had fallen down, rusting equipment, an open wooden shed, and an old farmhouse. We liked to sneak onto the property and slip into the house. On this day we had to climb into the house through one of the broken windows because there was a new padlock on the door.

Richard climbed in first. He tested the stability of the floors and said softly, "Okay to climb in. Watch out for the broken glass."

I entered the house through the window with more difficulty than Richard since my legs didn't clear the sill as easily.

When I got in, I called out, "Where are you?" Several birds flew out an upper window.

"Keep it down," Richard whispered to me from upstairs.

I climbed the shaky stairs after him to a hallway that led to several rooms. The rooms were draped with cobwebs, and the floors were covered with bird and mouse droppings.

"Be careful. The floors are rotten in several places, and I don't want to carry your sorry ass home because you got hurt," Richard said.

I ignored his comment, but I could see that he was right about the floors. In one of the rooms a bed was leaning down because one of the legs had gone through the floor. He came back down the hall toward the stairs where I was standing, saying, "There's nothing here worthwhile. Let's check out the shed."

He went downstairs, and instead of climbing out the window, he went into the kitchen and pushed on the front door. It didn't yield.

"I don't think we should bust it open," I said. "They would see that someone was here."

Richard grunted, gave it one more hard push, turned, went

past me, and exited through the window.

The last time I was on the farm, I saw that the shed, like the house, was falling apart. There was a door that could be pulled open and a window on one side. There was nothing in it, just junk. This time we discovered that a new door and a lock had been installed. The window had been replaced with cinder blocks.

"What's going on here?" Richard asked as he stood back to assess the changes.

"This looks like a garage now," I said. "Maybe there's something valuable inside?"

Richard tried to lift the garage door, which wouldn't budge. "I wonder if they have a car or truck inside?" he said. "That would be something valuable."

I was actually thinking about treasures, not some old vehicles, but I kept it to myself.

Richard inspected the building to assure himself that there was no easy way in. "We have to get home before the old man gets up," he said. "Let's get out of here for now. When we come back, we'll bring some tools with us and get in."

I knew that we would be back and get in. No city person was going to keep us out.

Our chance to go back to the Wolfe property came a couple of weeks later on a Sunday afternoon. Mr. McClelland was napping and Mom was visiting with several churchwomen, who had her full attention talking about redemption. Our focus was on a path that led away from the church and toward perdition.

Richard decided that the best tools to take would be a sledgehammer and a crowbar. We grabbed them from the tool shed and ducked along the creek back to the Wolfe farm. Our minds were not burdened by thoughts of risk, punishment, or wrongdoing. We were on a mission to discover what secrets that garage held and what bounty we could find in it. We didn't see ourselves as being bad. We only saw the challenge of getting into a building on a vacant piece of property and wanted to confront the challenge and overcome it.

We arrived at the farm, which was still and quiet, and saw no evidence that anyone was around. We went to the shed and looked again for weaknesses in the structure. Finding none, we decided to pry the door open with the crowbar. The door flexed in its tracks but didn't yield enough to crawl under it. Richard disappeared with the sledgehammer while I poked at the door with the crowbar. I was still fumbling at the door when I heard several deep-sounding thuds coming from his side of the building.

I looked around the corner and saw Richard pounding on the concrete blocks where the window used to be with the sledgehammer. He was big and strong, and the blocks sealing the old window collapsed under the sledgehammer blows. The newly created window-sized hole in the east side of the garage was big enough for us to enter easily.

At first, we couldn't see what was in the garage since it was dark. When our eyes adjusted to the light, which was filtering in through the hole in the wall, we could see objects on the floor of the building and an outline of light around the garage door. We worked our way toward the highlighted door and found the latch, which unlocked the door. When we raised the door, daylight flooded in and we saw what was inside.

The garage had a new concrete floor, and scattered about were empty wooden crates, some implements, a gas can, and a new orange Jacobsen brush mower.

"There's nothing to drive in here," he said in a tone of complete disappointment.

I motioned toward the mower and said, "This has an engine.

Maybe we could have some fun with it?"

The brush mower had two big rubber wheels and was outfitted with a horizontal mower blade exactly like the one we used to mow fields. It had an engine and a starter that needed a key. We wanted to start it but couldn't find the key. We were frustrated that there was nothing of any value for us in the garage and that we couldn't even start the mower. We had gone to all of the trouble to break into the building and had found nothing worthwhile. At this point the Devil may have whispered to us both. Wherever the idea came from, it was not about doing good.

Richard took the gasoline can and poured some gasoline on the rubber tires. They became sticky and almost seemed to dissolve. Richard found some matches, lit one, and ignited the gasoline-soaked tires. A cloud of black smoke rose out of the open garage door. The smoke smelled like rotten eggs and dead bodies combined, a smell even worse than that which I recalled from the plastic toothbrushes burning in the furnace in the POS of A basement. We knew that it wouldn't be long before someone would see the smoke and either come to see what had happened or call the fire company or, worse, the police. We grabbed the tools, hurriedly scrambled out of the shed, and ran back to our place.

When we got home, we listened for the fire alarm or the screaming of a police siren. There were no alarms. We waited, but no one came to our house days later to ask if we knew anything.

Chapter 21

More Means Less

Next to the excitement of the comings and goings of vehicles to the farm, were phone calls. Phone calls were rare. We had a party line shared with four of our neighbors. Since we were outside most of the time during the day in the summers, Mr. McClelland had The Bell Telephone Company install a large loud ringer on the outside of the house so that we could hear the rare calls when they came. When the call was for us, it would signal us by two rings—a long and a short.

We were loading manure in front of the barn when the phone signaled us. I was about to run into the house to answer the phone when Mr. McClelland stopped me by saying, "Never mind. Mum's in the house. She'll get it."

We finished filling the manure spreader. Richard drove the tractor, pulling the load out to the field. Although I was curious about the call, I knew that I had to clean up the area so that Richard could get closer to the pile when he returned. Mr. McClelland stuck his fork into the manure pile and went into the house. Richard returned, backed up the spreader, and parked.

"Where's the old man?" he asked.

"He went inside. I think he went in to find out who called," I replied.

"Seems to be taking a long time. I wonder what that call was about?" Richard said as he pitched a fork load of manure into the spreader.

We finished another load and Richard left. I used my thirst as an excuse to go to the house to get a drink and maybe learn about the call.

I passed Mr. McClelland on my way into the kitchen. He paused and said, "Mum wants to talk to you. Go on in."

She was standing at the kitchen sink scrubbing a pot. She heard me and turned around. "You got here fast," she said.

"I was on my way in when Mr. McClelland told me you wanted to speak to me."

"Yes, sit down at the table. Give me a minute to finish cleaning this pot."

I sat down and as I did, I noticed that she had scribbled some notes on the back of an envelope. "Who was on the phone?" I asked.

"That was Miss Fleming finally getting back to us about your sister and some other things."

"What other things?" I wondered.

She sat down next to me and took the envelope in her hands to make sure that she told me exactly what Miss Fleming had said. Mom was always careful to be one hundred percent accurate and honest about anything she said.

"Miss Fleming has spoken to your sister Karen's parents. Although they think it is important that Karen knows about you and your mother, now is not a good time to meet. Apparently, Karen has exceptional musical talent and has an important recital coming up soon. They think, and the Aid Society people agree, that learning about you would affect her emotionally in unpredictable ways. They believe that at a minimum it would negatively impact her upcoming performance."

I thought that our mother must not have sent a letter to her like she did to me. I was disappointed. I was eager to meet her in order to see what she was like. I didn't show any reaction because I knew that Mom would tell me less if I showed too much disappointment.

"Did they say when we could meet?"

"No, they want to wait and see how Karen reacts before setting a date."

"When is the performance?"

"Apparently, it is in early September."

Early September didn't seem that far away. But, I knew that I had something important to do, too, picking potatoes, which we always did after the first day of school each year. It would have to be after that. Maybe we could meet around the middle of September. It would have to be before we started husking corn in October. "Well, maybe we could plan on late September," I offered.

"It isn't up to me, but I'll suggest that to Miss Fleming when we talk again. There's something else that I'd like to discuss."

"What's that?" I asked.

"How would you feel about having two new foster brothers?"

"You mean living here with us?" I asked with complete surprise.

"Yes."

"It's not definite yet, but Miss Fleming says that one would be older than Richard and one would be younger than you."

I immediately thought it would be interesting to see Richard around someone older than he was. Before I could think more about it, my thoughts were interrupted by Mom saying, "I know that Richard picks on you a lot. Would you be nice to a younger brother?"

"Sure, I would," I said. I figured it would mean less work for Richard and me. "Where would they sleep?"

"You and Richard would stay in your rooms and the younger one would sleep in Richard's old room next to us and the older one would probably sleep on the third floor in one of the rooms where the Puerto Ricans used to sleep. It's not certain yet that either of them will come, but, if they do, it will happen before the school year starts," Mom added.

This was big news to me. Since I'd arrived, no other foster children had been placed on the farm. The Schaeffers often had different boys living with them to help out on their farm, but here it had always been just Richard and me.

Mom went on, "There's something else, too. Daddy and I have been discussing giving you and Richard an allowance."

"An allowance?" The words jumped out of me. The McClellands were always careful about money. Sometimes for our birthdays they would give us a few dollars or give us money to buy gifts at Christmas but never a steady allowance. We had earned money helping out at the Schaeffers. Mr. Mason paid us to mow his lawn and pick strawberries. I'd even earned enough and combined it with gifts of money to buy two savings bonds valued at twenty-five dollars each.

"How much?" I asked.

"We thought that we would give you one dollar a week and give Richard two dollars a week since he is bigger and does more of the harder work. What do you think of that?" she asked.

"That's great," I said without hesitation. "When will you tell Richard?"

"Daddy's telling him now."

That was a lot of news to digest. I could hardly wait to talk to Richard about it and get his opinion.

"That's all for now, Roger. I have more work to do here before lunch, and you should get out there and help out."

That afternoon when Mr. McClelland was taking his nap, I asked Richard what he thought about all the stuff that was happening.

"The way I see it is this. The old man is thinking you may be leaving in the next few months. If you go, he'll need someone to do your work. They probably asked if the Aid Society could place another boy here just in case."

"If that's so, why two boys?" I asked.

"Maybe they're brothers like Bill, George, and Harry are across the road—a package deal."

"Possible," I had to agree with him.

"What about the allowance?" I asked.

"Maybe Miss Fleming told them that they had to pay us something for the work we do. After all, the allowances don't amount to that much. Besides, the Aid Society pays them money to take care of us. If they get two more boys, that means that they'll be getting twice as much money."

I always felt uncomfortable when I was reminded that the McClellands were paid money to be our parents. It connected to what Mr. McClelland said sometimes when he was angry, that no one else wanted us and we should be thankful that they took us into their home. I wondered what Karen's foster parents were like and how she felt about them being paid. Did she have to do work, too?

Mom was a generous person. I remembered in first and second grades when she would put together "care packages" for the German children suffering after the War. She gathered together cans of soup, chocolate candy, soap, toothpaste, toothbrushes, and some other things that a child would like and put them into special boxes. Before closing the boxes, she would write a short note as well as a prayer for the children and include my name and address. I would take the boxes to school and they would be included with boxes that others had brought and sent to Germany. One time we even got a thank-you letter back, which included a picture of the little girl who got our package. The girl was dressed in a long coat and looked sad. It was hard for me to believe that a kind person like Mom had us on the farm just for the money.

When I went to bed that night, I knew I would meet my sister, and when I did, I would ask her how her parents treated her.

Chapter 22
A Real Country Bumpkin

In the summer, lunch was usually rushed because it was squeezed in between outside work and chores. On this day we slowed down to listen and speculate about the loud pounding noise in the distance mixed in with the sound of a big engine.

"That sounds to me like work going on in the Shillings' field," Mr. McClelland said.

"I think the noise is coming from farther away than his field," Richard added.

I thought that it might have something to do with the Wolff place. It was best not to say anything if that were the source of the disturbance. I decided that after lunch during Mr. McClelland's nap I would take Rex and investigate. I finished the potato salad and hot baked beans, grabbed my chicken, tomato, and lettuce sandwich, and went to the door.

"Roger, where are you headed so fast?" Mr. McClelland asked.

"I want to finish watering the chickens. Then, I thought I would duck over to see what's making the noise," I answered.

"Oh, okay, but don't take too long."

I was surprised that he'd agreed so quickly. "I'll be fast."

When I finished the watering chore, I called to Rex and headed toward the field next to ours. The noise was louder and sounded like it was in the field beyond the Shillings'. Rex and I trotted over to that field. When we got there, we saw a man driving a big orange bulldozer. He'd cleared a road through the woods and was pushing dirt aside, creating a big hole in the ground in the middle of the field. I walked toward the hole to get a better look. Then I saw another man wearing a baseball cap and holding several sheets of paper. He saw me. Before I could do anything, he yelled over the sound of the bulldozer, "Hey, boy, what are you doing?" He walked toward me.

I stood quietly, not knowing what to do. Rex barked. I kneeled in order to calm Rex since the man was smiling and didn't look like a threat.

"Do you live around here?"

"Yes, a couple of fields over," I answered, pointing toward the McClelland farm.

"What's your name?" he said. "My name is John VanAlstyne." He offered me his hand.

I took it and noticed how rough it was. I shook it and said, "My name is Roger. What are you doing here?"

"I'm building a house. We're going to be neighbors." He looked at Rex and said, "Is he a Cocker Spaniel?"

"Yeah, he's a Toy Cocker," I clarified and relaxed.

"We used to own a pedigreed Springer Spaniel," he said. "What's your dog's name?"

"Rex."

"That's a big name for a little dog. How old is he?"

I liked the man. He was friendly. Those calloused hands told me he was not a city person. "About six years old. I guess you're moving here, right?" I asked.

"Yes, my wife and I hope to be moved in before Thanksgiving."

"Where are you coming from?" I asked.

"Bensalem Township. You'll like this, we live on a road that used to be called Pig Turd Lane," he said with a smile.

I grinned back. He had a sense of humor. I could see that he was bald around the edges of his cap and his face was wrinkled and sunburned. I judged that he was old but not as old as the McClellands. I had the information I needed and felt I should get home.

"I have to go now," I said.

"I'll bet you and Rex are going fishing or playing ball," he said.

"Nope. I have work to do."

"Well, stop by again. You can help me out by keeping an eye on this project when I'm not here."

I'd found an adult friend. I liked him. I wondered how he and the McClellands would get along. When I got back and shared the information, Mr. McClelland wondered how many acres he'd bought, what his work was, and what kind of house they were building. Since I didn't have the answers, I knew I would have to go back. The realization pleased me.

Not long after that day, school started. I was enrolled in Iron Hill School, which housed the fifth and sixth graders from our area and was situated on the corner of our property. Miss Hanisch knew I was a foster child and was understanding when I had to take a day off to go to Philadelphia to meet my sister.

I dressed up like it was a Sunday. I walked to the train station in New Britain, bought a round trip ticket, and rode the Reading Railroad train into Philadelphia. I arrived at the terminal station earlier than the appointment to meet my sister. Because I had extra time, I decided to explore the Reading Terminal Market, which is where Mr. Moyer sold our eggs. I wandered around the market and saw booths where men sold whole chickens, parts of pigs, scrapple, all sorts of meats, cheeses, vegetables, fruit, ducks, and different prepared foods like salads, pies, and sandwiches.

Eventually, I found a sign that said, "Alvin F. Moyer, Chalfont." There he was. He was delighted to see me and made a fuss over our eggs, which were on display. He had a special place for our duck eggs, which were more than twice the price of our chicken eggs. He had a lot of other food items for sale like fresh garden vegetables, chickens, pork chops, and steaks. He spoke to me, "Roger, have you ever asked John or Maud if you could raise some vegetables? I would buy them from you and sell them here."

"No, I hadn't thought of doing that. You mean that you would pay me just like you pay them for the eggs?"

"Sure would," he said. "Maud has told me that you'd like to go to college. This would be a way for you to earn some money. I know that college is expensive."

"You mean I could raise tomatoes, string beans, and lima beans, and you'd sell them here?" I was amazed at the possibility.

"Yes, exactly. I'd take beets and carrots, too."

"I'm not sure that Mr. McClelland would let me."

"Let me talk to him. Maybe I can get him to think it was his idea," Mr. Moyer said with a knowing wink.

Mr. Moyer was a kind and gentle man. He was a Mennonite, which to me equated to being honest and hardworking. Those characteristics helped him to be a prominent leader in the Chalfont area. He had two children, a son and a daughter. His son, Alvin Junior, followed in Mr. Moyer's footsteps and became a local leader as well. I never met his daughter, Ana. I was happy to learn that he thought I had possibilities beyond high school and that he would help me earn money that I'd need for college.

"That would be great," I said.

I knew that asking Mr. McClelland for anything made me feel uncomfortable. If I did ask and he granted me something, he would want me to promise to do more work in exchange. He often just said no.

"What time is it getting to be?" I couldn't be late for the meeting with Karen.

"Quarter to eleven," he answered.

It was getting late and I had to go.

"Thank you, Mr. Moyer. I really appreciate your idea."

My thoughts turned to getting to 311 South Juniper Street, which was a few blocks away, and meeting my sister for the first time. When I arrived at the building, the elevator man took me to the third floor where the waiting room was. I glanced at my reflection to be sure I looked okay. I was beginning to feel nervous.

As I got off the elevator, the man said, "You look great. Have a fine day, young man."

I smiled and said, "Thank you, it's been great so far."

The door to the Aid Society waiting room had an opaque frosted glass on top and a wooden bottom. I wanted to be able to see in before entering so that I'd know what to expect, but I couldn't. I opened the door, and, as I entered, I experienced a burst of lightheadedness. There were two ladies and a girl seated around a table. Miss Fleming wasn't there.

Everyone stood up. "Hello, you must be Roger," one of the women said.

"Yes. And you must be Karen," I said, looking at the girl.

There was an awkward moment before one of the ladies said, "Let's all sit down."

Karen hadn't spoken. I could see that she was pretty with dark wavy hair and a big smile. She looked like she could be a famous actress. Even though I was dressed in my best clothes, she looked better dressed than I did. Her black skirt and white blouse were nicely ironed and fit her perfectly. The ladies introduced themselves.

"Where's Miss Fleming?" I asked.

"She's no longer with us. I'm your new caseworker. I'm pleased to meet you at this exciting moment," one of the women said as she introduced herself and gave me her name, which I immediately forgot.

The other woman spoke up and gave me her name as well and said, "This is a special moment. I've been Karen's caseworker for years. She has some very special musical talents." I noticed the situational difference between us. Her caseworker had stayed with her for years.

Karen spoke for the first time, "I'm so glad to finally meet you, Roger. I never knew I had a brother, and now here we are, brother and sister."

Her voice was theatrical. She was very poised and not like the girls I knew from school. I experienced her as sophisticated. The social workers politely excused themselves and said that they would be back in an hour or so.

"Have you met our mother?" I asked as soon as we were alone.

"No, I haven't met her, but I got a letter."

"I did, too. Did you write back?"

"Yes," she said. "She hasn't written back yet."

"I thought about writing her, but I didn't know what to say, so I didn't."

Then, she asked, "Do you know anything about our father?"

"Nothing. Do you know anything?"

"No. I was hoping you knew something," she said with disappointment in her voice.

"I guess we'll find out more when we meet her," I said.

"Do you really live on a farm?" she asked.

"Sure do."

"What kind of farm is it?"

"It is the kind of farm that has chickens, pigs, and cows. I might even raise vegetables to sell next year."

"Really. What kind of music do you like?" she asked.

"I don't know much about music."

"You must have heard Frank Sinatra, Ella Fitzgerald, or even Perry Como sing?"

"No, not really," I answered.

"Don't you watch *American Bandstand?*"

"No, I don't. I know that you're musical. What's that like?" Karen paused and looked around to see if anyone was listening before she spoke, "Miss Judd is one of the higher-ups here in the Aid Society, and she thinks that I could be an opera singer one day."

"Do you want to be one?" I asked.

"Oh, yes. I have voice lessons and take music lessons every week."

"That's great for you," I said. "I can't sing at all. In fact, my music teacher tells me to move my mouth and be sure not to let anything come out."

She started to say something and then stopped.

Hoping to change the subject, I said, "Let's go outside and take a walk."

"Okay. Where do you want to go?"

"How about we go where we can get a Coke and maybe some ice cream? I have a few dollars," I said.

We didn't go very far before we found a drugstore with a soda fountain. It was like the one Mr. Perry-Ferry used to go to. We went in and sat beside each other at the counter. We only ordered Cokes with ice since she did not want any ice cream.

"Roger, do the pigs on your farm smell?" she asked suddenly.

"Yes, pigs always smell," I answered.

"I thought maybe they did," she said.

That question, which came from out of the blue, didn't make sense to me until several years later. My new social worker at the time, Mr. Molitor, was talking to me about my relationship with Karen. He told me that after our first meeting she'd told her caseworker that I was a real "country bumpkin." She probably noticed that I smelled like a farm boy that day at the counter when we were drinking our Cokes. She was polite and didn't tell me directly what she was thinking about when she spoke to me.

"Where do you get your hair cut?" she asked.

"My foster father cut it. Who takes care of your hair?"

"I go to a beauty parlor," she said.

I replied, "Oh, wow! That's why it looks so good." She smiled.

On the way back to the Aid Society building she asked me if I played sports. I told her that I played baseball and football at school. She told me that she was a good runner and could run faster than the rest of the boys in her class at school.

When we got back to the office, the caseworkers were waiting for us. They asked where we'd gone and what we'd talked about. We both made pleasant remarks about our meeting and the conversations. Our responses pleased the social workers.

When we parted, we promised to keep in touch. I was glad to get back on the train and go home. I got home in time to do the evening chores before dinner. At dinner there were a lot of questions about Karen.

Richard asked, "Did she sing for you or play the piano?"

"No," I said. "I couldn't ask her to do that."

"Why not?" Mom said. "If she performs a lot, she would've been flattered to sing or play."

Based on that comment, I felt I'd had an opportunity to be polite to my sister and missed it.

"I was afraid to ask because she might have asked me to sing."

Richard said, "Smart move! Your voice would have caused the paint to peel in that office."

Mom interrupted, saying, "That's enough. Don't get started making wisecracks back and forth at the supper table."

Chapter 23
No School!

Although it was exciting to meet my blood sister and make comparisons, overall, it was disappointing. Her musical talent, combined with the encouragement of others, had already set her on a trajectory to become a professional singer. I knew that I lacked a core talent. I wanted to get away from all the farm work and go to college. However, in contrast to Karen, I lacked a specific career goal. Without a core talent, I believed that the only thing I could do was to try and be a better person every day. My fifth- and sixth-grade teacher, Miss Hanisch, served as the catalyst for my personal improvement.

I learned after my first few days with her as my teacher that she had high expectations for me. She'd expected me to be more like Richard and was surprised that I was eager to participate in class and be a student. Her expectations excited me and made me want to impress her. I volunteered to wash the blackboards, clean erasers, and take out the trash, which was burned on-site. I liked to watch paper trash burn, just like I had in first and second grades. In addition, I paid attention in class, did my classroom work on time, and spoke up often. I was also on the lookout for things to bring to class that might be interesting to Miss Hanisch and the students.

Late fall was the easiest time of the year on the farm. There was no planting, no hoeing, no harvesting, no need to put cows in pastures, and no snow to shovel. The ground was too soft to haul manure since big freezes had not yet arrived. Our work was mostly chores. It was cold but not cold enough to keep us inside. It was fun to walk through the fields and go into the woods with Rex. We could smell the pungency of dead leaves while we looked for burrows and nests, which the rich summer foliage had hidden. Sometimes we would find a blue jay's bright blue and white feather, a colorful tail feather of a pheasant, or even the bright red feather of a cardinal. I took each feather to class for Miss Hanisch to pass around to my classmates, and afterwards it would be placed on display on a deep windowsill. I wished that one day I would find something truly unusual. One afternoon on the Thursday before our Christmas break, my wish was answered.

I spotted two large grey masses hanging from branches in adjacent trees. They were about the size of balloons but shaped more like large lanterns. They appeared to be feathery and fragile. I had never seen anything like them before. The thought occurred to me that they might be nests of some sort. However, they were not flat and open like most bird nests. Also, there was a hole about the size of a half-dollar in the bottom of each one, which wouldn't be how a bird would enter its nest. I wanted them for class. They were too high to reach, and I didn't want to damage them by trying to knock them down with stones or poke at them with a long stick.

My eleven-year-old mind went into overdrive. I could climb the tree, but they were too far out on the branch for me to reach them. I could try to shake them down, but if they fell on the ground, they might break apart. They would only be valuable to Miss Hanisch and the class if intact.

A plan came to me. I would climb each tree, tie some twine around the branches, cut off the branches, and lower the branches gently to the ground without damaging the nest-like things attached to them. Filled with excitement, I ran back to the barn and the tool room where I grabbed a handsaw, a pair of large pruning shears, and some twine and hurried back to the woods equipped to get the prizes.

Climbing the first tree was easy, and cutting off the branch and lowering it to the ground worked out as planned. When I came down the tree and inspected the first papery nest, I saw that it was almost perfectly round and that it weighed more than I thought it would. I did the same thing in the second tree. These nests would be great to show Miss Hanisch and my classmates. After all, I thought that it was like having a ready-made science project. We could take one apart and place the other one on display. I was sure to get Miss Hanisch's approval.

I hid them in a ditch next to the path where I walked to school. I was afraid that if Richard saw them, he might take them just to tease me and then maybe damage one or both by accident. It was late and getting colder. I left them and did my chores quickly, filled with anticipation.

When Friday's morning chores were done and it was time to go to school, Richard said, "Hey! I'll walk up the hill with you today."

"Why?" I asked. My heart slowed.

"I am being picked up and driven to school is all," he said.

"Okay," I said meekly. My heart sank because it meant that I would have to walk by the nests without picking them up. I decided that I could come back after lunch and get them.

When I got to school, I spoke softly to Miss Hanisch, "Guess what I found yesterday in the woods?"

"What?" she said, reflecting my excitement.

"I found two great big papery nests of some sort."

"Really, what kind of nests?"

"I don't know, but maybe we can figure it out in class. We could make a guessing game out of it," I said hopefully.

I could see that she was very interested. She agreed that

I could get the nests after lunch and bring them to class for a discussion. When the time came late in the day, I was excused to get the special surprise for everyone.

When I brought them into the classroom, Miss Hanisch was really surprised by how big they were. I beamed when she said, "Look at what Roger found in the woods yesterday."

"What are they?" one of the girls asked. A murmur rippled through the classroom. Everyone was curious.

Miss Hanisch stepped to the front of the classroom. "Roger, please give me one, and I will pass it down this row, and you take the other and pass it down the row on the other side. I want everyone to handle them gently and guess what they might be while Roger tells us exactly what he did to find them."

Miss Hanisch and I started passing them down the rows, and I told everyone what I'd done.

I think Miss Hanisch knew what they were but asked each person to make a guess about what they thought they were. There was a lot of chatter.

"I think they are giant seed pods," one student guessed.

"No, no, they are butterfly houses," another said.

One of the boys said, "I bet they're from outer space."

Everyone laughed. Just then, the two school buses arrived and Miss Hanisch said, "We'll stop here today and finish this exercise on Monday. You should all take some time to think over the weekend about what you've seen. I'll put them in the windows."

I was elated to have caused so much excitement and interest. I marveled at my good fortune to have found them and went home glowing, all the while thinking that there could never be more excitement than that afternoon. How wrong I was.

On Monday morning I did my chores and left for school as usual. When I got to school, I saw the two school buses parked and still filled with children. Miss Hanisch was standing at the door holding the classroom bell. I thought that she was there to greet me.

"Good morning, Miss Hanisch," I said.

She wasn't smiling. "Roger, there's a problem."

"What?"

"Did you know that those nests you brought to class were hornet nests?" she asked.

"No," I said slowly.

"Did Richard put you up to it?"

"No, Richard had nothing to do with those nests."

"The school is filled with hornets. They have to be killed before the children can go in," she said with the strangest look on her face. She wanted to be angry, but there seemed to be a slight smile around the edges of her mouth.

She continued, "All the children are being sent home. There will be no school here today. I've called the head janitor, and he's coming to smoke them."

"What happened?" I asked.

"Those papery lantern-shaped things were indeed nests. The heat of the building over the weekend brought the hornets out of hibernation," she replied.

"Miss Hanisch, I didn't know there were hornets inside those nests."

"I believe you. Your curiosity helped us both to learn," she said in a tone filled with understanding.

I suddenly realized why the nests felt heavy; there were many hibernating hornets inside.

Miss Hanisch was lucky that she hadn't been stung. The children were lucky to get a day off from school. I was lucky that I wasn't punished. I was even luckier that I hadn't taken the nests to my bedroom like I'd done with the praying mantis egg cases.

The two loaded buses pulled away. Miss Hanisch looked at me and said, "Roger, I have a book that I want you to read during the Christmas break. It is called *The Yearling* by a woman author Marjorie Kinnan Rawlings. I'll give it to you Monday."

"What's it about?"

"When you read it, you'll find out and you can tell me."

Our conversation was interrupted by two men in an old truck pulling into the schoolyard. When they got out of their truck, I saw that they were wearing white beekeeping suits and were carrying netted hats. I was embarrassed and left while they were talking to Miss Hanisch.

She borrowed a copy of *The Yearling* from the Doylestown Public Library. This book was the first of many she signed out for me during her two-year tenure as my teacher. After I read the book, Miss Hanisch asked, "Roger, what are your thoughts about the book?"

"Growing up hurts," I said.

She urged me to tell her more.

"The people in the book were poor. They were poorer than we are. Jody's dad was more sympathetic toward him than his mother, which is the reverse in my situation where Mrs. McClelland is more sympathetic toward me than Mr. McClelland." I didn't tell her that I'd thought about running away just like Jody.

"Why did you want me to read it?" I asked.

"You have a free spirit like Jody, and when you aren't working, you and your dog, Rex, like to wander to wherever your curiosity takes you. I thought the hornet nests you brought to school exemplified an effort on your part to be appreciated for something other than work."

I could feel tears in the corner of my eyes, and I turned away.

Chapter 24
Ropes and Ladders and Red Paint

School and Miss Hanisch were predictable during fifth and sixth grades; whereas, my home situation was not. When I came home one day in the fall of fifth grade, Mom met me on the walkway to the house. Rex was jumping up and down on me enthusiastically as usual.

"Roger, a Miss Turner of the Children's Aid Society was here today," she said with some excitement. "We have a new foster child, a foster brother for you. His name is Paul Graiser. I want you to be nice to him like you promised."

"I know that you said that two new boys might be coming, but someone coming today is a surprise," I spoke as I bent over to quiet Rex.

"Yes, well, something happened that involved Paul, and they had to place him here suddenly," she said.

"Is he from the city? A city kid?" I asked.

"Yes, he is. He got into trouble there." She was about to say more but got interrupted when Paul came out of the house and stood on the porch.

He waited a moment or two, and then he spoke. "You must be Roger. I'm Paul. I know about you."

"Hi, what do you know about me?" I asked as I looked him over. He was short and skinny. His eyes were dark and didn't show any enthusiasm. I thought that he wasn't going to be much help around the farm.

"That dog almost bit me when I got here. He's your pet. You like to read. You have been here for about seven years." The statements came out like the drumming of a woodpecker. His monotone was robotic.

"Roger, get changed and take Paul around and show him the farm," urged Mom. That was exactly what I did.

Over the ensuing months I learned a lot about Paul. There was no doubt he was a city kid. He didn't like the smells in the barn, the pigpens, or the chicken coops. He didn't have a lot of strength, which limited his work assignments to collecting eggs, turning on lights, and shelling corn. He couldn't milk cows.

While I was learning about him, the VanAlstynes were learning about me. Mr. VanAlstyne had completed the building of his house during the summer and early fall, and he and his wife had moved in before Thanksgiving. They liked me. They'd lost a son to spinal meningitis twenty years earlier when he was about seven years old. They wanted to consider me part of their family and asked me to call them Uncle Jack and Aunt Margaret. Every Thursday evening after dinner I would carry a dozen eggs across the three fields to their house. I looked forward to their company and Aunt Margaret's homemade ice cream and cookies. They would set up a TV tray in front of the television so that we could watch the Wyatt Earp weekly show together. The weather never prevented me from going to their house, and they were always pleased to see me. I felt like I was in a real home when I visited them.

One Saturday afternoon, I took Paul to meet them. They were polite to him and Aunt Margaret gave us both cookies but no ice cream. The next Thursday when I took eggs to them, Aunt Margaret said, "What do you know about Paul?"

"I don't know much about him except that he swears a lot," I said. "He doesn't do very well in school."

"What happened to his parents?"

"I don't know. He won't talk about them. He came from

another foster home, I do know that," I volunteered.

"What does Mrs. McClelland say about him?" Uncle Jack asked.

"She says nice things about everyone," I said. "I do know that she doesn't like the way he behaves in church and scolds him afterwards."

"Devils are always uncomfortable in churches," said Aunt Margaret only half-jokingly.

"We think it might be best for you to come alone to our house from now on. Let Paul stay at home so that we can enjoy your company," said Aunt Margaret.

I got the message that they didn't like him and didn't trust him. He never went to the VanAlstynes with me again.

Eventually, I learned that Paul had been the youngest member of a gang of boys in the city. He had been placed in several foster homes that hadn't worked out for one reason or another. Some members of the gang, including Paul, had been caught by the police a few times. There was talk of putting him into some form of severe detention, maybe a reform school. Placing him with the McClellands was considered to be a "last chance" even at the age of nine.

Richard tended to ignore him because he was too small to do any meaningful work, even if he wanted to work. Richard stuck to himself more than usual and left me to deal with Paul. Then Bill Strauss arrived unexpectedly.

Bill Strauss was another city kid. He was older than Richard and very slick. Bill was more interested in the latest hit songs than doing anything around the farm. He had a radio and played it a lot. He and Paul got along with each other. I overheard Mom say to Daddy, "They're like two peas in a pod." Bill didn't stay on the farm very long. The one impression that he left with me was the fact that he gave himself a middle name. I didn't know you could do that.

One day Bill abruptly announced, "From now on I want you to call me 'Leon' as in Bill Leon Strauss." Paul was the only one who called him Leon. Two factions began to develop on the farm: the Leon-Paul faction and the Richard-Roger faction. The idea of two-person gangs appealed to Paul. I think that we never came to blows because they knew that Richard and I, and especially Richard, would've crushed them like gnats. About the time that things might have gotten out of hand, an Aid Society social worker came and picked up Bill Leon Strauss and took him away. I imagine that Mom had placed a call or two to the Aid Society suggesting that conflicts were developing among us. I'm sure that Mr. McClelland supported getting rid of one or both of them since they weren't good workers.

Paul, however, remained on the farm until late summer after my sixth grade. He was very frustrating to live with. He took my money and then denied it, he talked a lot about how great the city was, and he often used my bike without permission and even broke it once. The bike was a birthday gift from the McClellands, who had bought it from Mr. Moyer and painted it red. It was Mr. Moyer's daughter's bike, which was too big for me and certainly too big for Paul. He had to ride it standing up and couldn't steer it. He hit a fence post and drove the fender into the tire. He lied to Mom when I complained. I tried to be a good older foster brother to him, but he was hard to be around. Eventually, he left the farm but not before he took part in two things that made lasting impressions. One was funny and very lucky for Richard and me, and the other was horrible for Mom.

The lucky thing first—it was August and hot. The hay and wheat had been harvested. It was a perfect time for maintenance work around the farm. Fences could be repaired; drainage ditches could be inspected and cleared to improve the flow in heavy rains;

and roofs could be checked and painted or tarred as appropriate. The chicken coops and hogpens all had tarpaper roofs, which were low and flat. We coated them with fresh tar each summer to prevent leaks. Although the tar was smelly, it was an easy job compared to painting the barn roof.

The barn roof was high and steeply pitched. The metal part of the roof was red and needed to be painted to prevent rusting. Although we called it a "tin roof," I think it was some cheaper metal alloy.

Farmers are resourceful and inventive when faced with obstacles. Mr. McClelland was no exception. The way he arranged for us to paint the tin roof was a perfect example. First of all, since he was in his seventies, he wasn't going to be one of the painters on that high roof. That left Richard and me to paint.

"How can we paint that roof without sliding down?" asked Richard.

"First, we'll park the old horse cultivator on the manure pile in front of the barn," Mr. McClelland said confidently. "Then we're going to get three ladders and tie a rope to one of them."

We did as we were told and moved the cultivator into place in front of the barn. Next, we got the ladders and placed them against the opposite side of the barn.

"Take the extension ladder apart and lean one ladder against the barn roof," he instructed.

Mr. McClelland barked out more instructions. "Paul, go get a hammer and an old feed sack. Roger, go get a long rope. Richard, help me take the extension ladder apart."

We did as we were told.

Mr. McClelland took the hammer, placed it in the sack, wrapped part of the rope around the sack, and tied it.

"What are you going to do with the hammer in the sack?" I asked.

"Richard is going to climb the ladder and throw the sack with the hammer over the roof to the other side while we hold one end of the rope. That's what," he answered.

"Why is the hammer in the sack?" I asked.

"If Richard misses and the bundle doesn't go over the roof ridgepole, the sack protects the hammer from doing any damage to the roof."

Richard's first throw cleared the roof. Mr. McClelland went around to the front of the barn with Paul and me and untied the bag. "You two boys hold this end of the rope until I yell to you to start pulling to lift the ladder from the other side."

He went back to the side of the barn where Richard was and tied the loose end of the rope to one of the ladders. He yelled to us to start pulling the rope slowly. We pulled until he told us to stop. We stopped while Richard tied another ladder to the first one with another piece of rope. Mr. McClelland came back to our side and pulled with us until Richard yelled that the topmost end of the linked ladders had reached the ridgepole of the roof. The rope was tied securely to the cultivator. The big counterweight was in place. At this point we had a rope extending up the front of the barn and connected to the top rung of the first ladder. The connected ladders created just enough length to reach from the bottom edge of the roof to the top. The arrangement allowed us to go up and paint.

We took cans of red paint and brushes and climbed up onto the roof. By mid-morning, we were painting the roof starting at the top. Painting was easy work and satisfying. The roof sparkled brightly, and we could see our progress. In addition, when we paused, we had a good view of the countryside and the valley below. We talked and told jokes and enjoyed ourselves. The non-OSHA approved system worked like a charm. By noon we'd painted several yards of corrugated panels from top to bottom.

We only had to go down for paint twice and each time we did, we got a drink of water that Paul delivered.

When we came down for lunch, we felt like heroes.

Mom came out and looked up and said, "You boys have made great progress. What a fine job."

Even Mr. McClelland complimented us by saying, "I never thought you could paint so fast and do such a fine job."

I liked painting because we were hot but not sweaty; we weren't covered by chaff from haying or dust from hoeing. Life was pretty good. We had a refreshing lunch after which we did some noon chores and were ready to go back to work on the roof. If we maintained our morning pace, we were sure that we would finish long before evening.

We filled our paint cans, grabbed our brushes, and climbed up the ladder from the ground to the roof, Richard first. We got onto the first ladder on the slope of the roof and climbed along it toward the second ladder because we always started painting from the top to avoid dripping on the newly painted surfaces. Richard was just about to go onto the second ladder when we felt the first ladder start to slide down the roof.

"What's happening?" I shouted.

I looked past Richard toward the other ladder. The rope holding the two ladders together was unraveling and twisting like a snake as it came apart. Our slide down the roof was accelerating. There was no way to stop. I turned and saw I was gaining speed toward the ground below. I was very scared. There was no time to think, only time to grab.

In the few seconds from the moment I saw the rope coming apart until I was grabbing the top of the ladder, which had been leaning against the roof, everything was instinct. My momentum coming down the roof was so great that the ladder I grabbed went backward away from the roof. In an instant I became an unwilling and frightened pole vaulter. I landed on the hard ground, not in a soft cushion-filled box. Richard came down behind me without grabbing a ladder. However, the ladder that he had ridden on down the roof hit the ground before he did, and one of the poles of the ladder went up his pant leg. Luckily his very old dungarees tore apart, which prevented his leg from breaking.

We must have yelled out or screamed because Paul came running around the corner of the barn. He stopped, looked at us, and ran away yelling, "They're down! They're down! They're covered with blood."

We were down all right. But the blood was red paint from the cans that we must have tossed in the air in our frantic attempts to free our hands and grab something. I was on my back, lying there scared, wondering if I had broken any bones. Richard was on his stomach with his head propped on his hands, looking over at me and grinning as though he'd just been on an amusement ride. Luckily, none of our bones were broken. There were no major bruises except for Richard's thigh where the ladder had struck him.

Within a short while, Richard was back on the roof painting. I was so scared that it was a long time before I climbed onto the barn roof or the house roof to paint again, and, when I did several years later, I was still afraid. The image of that rope unraveling was unnerving and unforgettable. Paul shouting that we were down and covered with blood was often repeated to friends. Why we weren't injured or worse remains one of my life's great mysteries. We were very lucky and many said that we were blessed.

What happened next with Paul was really horrible. Although Paul's chores were easier than ours, he didn't do them reliably. Mom had been frustrated by Paul's unwillingness to be pleasant about helping her out. She was very slow to anger, but when she did become angry, she was very forceful.

I was sitting on the porch when I heard her say loudly, "Paul, when I ask you pleasantly to do something, I don't want to hear you swear at me."

I heard his reply. "You're always asking me to do this or that. If I listened to you, I would be working all the time. Just leave me alone, bitch."

"What did you call me?" she shouted.

When I heard what Paul said, I knew there was going to be trouble. I stepped into the kitchen quickly and saw him grab a paring knife and thrust it at her.

Mom was shocked. I was shocked. He lunged at her again. When she put up her hand to defend herself, his thrusted knife cut into it. She screamed. He let go of the knife. I grabbed him by the throat. I was protecting Mom and enraged by what Paul had done. In that instant, all of my anger toward him poured into my grip around his neck. I lifted him off the floor by the neck and began to choke him. He turned purplish-black. I dropped to the floor, still holding his neck. Mom was over me, yelling at me to stop. She pulled me off of him.

Her hand was bleeding. I was breathing hard. Paul was gasping for breath on the floor.

I took Mom to the sink and helped her wash her hand. She wrapped it in a towel. I turned to see what Paul was doing. Paul had run outside. He stayed away from the house until it got dark. When he came in, Mr. McClelland grabbed him and took him back outside and kept swatting him until he cried and begged to be let go. It was an awful night.

Two days later the social worker arrived and took him away.

Chapter 25

High Flying and Real Down Low

Although the arrivals and departures of Paul Graiser and Bill Strauss had complicated our lives on the farm during fifth and sixth grades, my real mother complicated things even more. She wrote to the Aid Society several times to insist that she meet me. She sent me a Christmas card and a birthday card and signed them "Love, Mom," which ruffled Mr. McClelland's feathers. In addition, I learned that they knew more about what was going to happen to me than I did.

I had to stay abreast with what was happening in our household by listening surreptitiously to the McClellands' private conversations. There was a hole in the floor of their bedroom through which heat escaped from the kitchen to heat their bedroom in the winter. The hole had a grate over it. If I went quietly from my room to theirs when I was supposed to be sleeping, I could listen to their conversations. In this way, I heard them talking about my mother.

I heard Mr. McClelland say, "What's she up to anyway? Why can't she just leave the boy alone?"

Mom said softly, "John, just let it be. She has a legal right to be in touch with him."

"Notes and cards are one thing. Now she wants to come here and see him."

I was startled. My mother is coming to the farm? My mother coming here? When? I listened silently in order not to miss a word.

"I don't care about legal rights," Mr. McClelland continued. "Can't you see that it distracts him from what he's supposed to be doing?"

"You mean his work?"

"Yes, I mean his work. Sometimes I think that he daydreams about leaving."

"He has a good imagination. He could be daydreaming about anything."

"Well, if you ask me, I would tell that Aid Society woman to stop this nonsense right now. They should tell that mother of his to stay away. She's tormenting him."

"You're the one being tormented, John."

"Maybe so." His voice was growing louder as he became more agitated. "But those two other boys are worthless as far as work is concerned. If they take him away, what do they expect us to do when Richard leaves?"

"Shush, John. They might hear you."

"Holy cow!" I thought. "My mother is coming here." I crept silently back to my room and into bed. All my thoughts were on when they were going to tell me. When was she coming? I couldn't let on that I knew. I didn't have to wait long.

The following morning, I was told that a social worker was coming to see me and that I should come in from the field and be cleaned up by eleven o'clock. I did as I was told and waited in the parlor. Promptly at eleven, I heard a car. I went to the window to see who it was. I was surprised to see who it was. It was Miss Fleming coming to our door, the one leading to the parlor, not the one leading to the kitchen. Mrs. McClelland greeted her and brought her into the parlor.

"Hello, Roger. It's been a while. How have you been?"

"Good. Why are you back here?" I asked. "I thought you were gone."

"Wow! He's straight to the point," she said, looking directly at Mom.

Mom smiled. "Would you like some water or lemonade after your long drive?"

"Yes, lemonade would be great," said Miss Fleming. "I have rejoined Children's Aid after I completed my degree work. They sent me out here to follow up with you about your mother since I was familiar with the situation. Your case, I mean."

Mom returned with three glasses of lemonade on a tray. She passed them out. Lemonade was a special treat that I liked a lot.

"Your mother wants to meet you and your family here," continued Miss Fleming.

"When?" I asked.

"She's visiting in the area now. She has a brother and his family in Ambler. We met with her the day before yesterday."

"That means I have an uncle nearby—right?"

"Yes, you do. And, as far as I can tell, you have a cousin, too."

Suddenly I felt swamped with relatives. Based on their relevance to my life until now, they may as well have been on the moon. The conversation continued about the meeting. They decided that my birth mother would meet me on the farm on Saturday afternoon. When Saturday afternoon came, Mr. McClelland took the boys away from the house to work in the fields and not be in the way during the meeting. Intellectually, I was curious and excited to learn firsthand about my mother but lacked any other emotions about the visit.

When Mom and I saw her car coming down the lane, we walked out to meet her. I was amazed when she got out of the car that she was so short and so young-looking. Mom and my mother shook hands.

"My name is Ruth," said my mother.

"I am Maud McClelland."

"Roger, I'm so glad to see you. You were just an infant when I last saw you. Now look at you. You are practically a man." As she spoke, she stepped toward me. I stepped back because I was afraid that she was going to try and hug me or maybe even kiss me with her bright red lipstick-covered lips.

"Hello," I stammered.

The awkwardness was palpable. Mom stepped in and said, "Let's go into the house and sit down and have something to drink."

We went into the kitchen, and Mom served lemonade. I didn't know what to say and didn't look directly at my mother. Mom diplomatically said that she had work to do outside and left the two of us alone.

My mother started the conversation by saying, "Rory, your brother, is very interested in meeting you."

"Is he in the area, too?"

"Oh, no, he's still in Miami Beach. You met Karen, right?" she said.

"Yes."

"I hope to meet her soon, too."

"I know you'll like her. She's pretty."

"Do you know what coincidences are?" she asked.

"Yes."

"What do you think of this as a coincidence?" She told me that she used to live in the same area of Philadelphia that Karen lived in and attended the same schools as Karen. As she got older, her father moved to Doylestown, and she graduated from the same high school that I would eventually graduate from.

I listened but didn't care. What I knew was that she'd abandoned us both when she put us in foster care.

"Where's my father?" I asked.

There was a long pause before she answered. "He's no longer in the country."

"He's alive, then?" I asked.

"Yes, he may still be alive, but he's not a very good man. You shouldn't be thinking about him."

"My father isn't Mr. Saillant, right?"

I'd heard Mr. McClelland talking about my mother and had learned what the phrase "fallen woman" meant.

"Let's talk about all of that at some other time, Roger. I'm here to meet you and see where you're living and to find out what interests you have. Besides, I have things to tell you about Rory and Miami and what I'm doing."

She wasn't going to talk about him.

For the next hour or so, she spent most of the time telling me about Miami, her jobs, and Rory. I listened and she talked. It was easy since she asked me very few questions. She told me that she wanted me to come to Miami to see where she lived and to meet Rory. She thought that maybe I could come down next summer. After the time was up, we stood and went outside. When she got to the car, she patted me on the back, got into her car, and drove away after thanking Mom for taking care of me.

My practical mind thought that going to Miami would be an interesting vacation. I kept that thought to myself because it would sound lazy and would irritate those who had to stay behind and do my work. My emotional mind was really not very interested in her except to get more information about my real blood relatives so that I might understand what possibilities could lie ahead for me. Maybe I was related to someone famous like a baseball player and they could help me. It would be nice to know that there were other types of talent in the family besides a singer and an artist. I was unwilling to share my emotions about all of this with anyone, especially Miss Fleming.

In the end, I did take two trips to Miami Beach while I was on the farm, one in the summer of 1955 and the other in the summer of 1957. I don't know why the Aid Society facilitated the trips. Maybe there was a legal requirement to let a mother see her son. Whatever the reasons, I know that my mother had lobbied for it because I wasn't pushing for it and the McClellands were against it. She was so eager for me to go to Miami that she bought the airline tickets.

Before the first trip, Mom bought a suitcase from the Sears and Roebuck catalog for my articles of clothing. It was about the size of a lady's makeup kit and held just enough underclothes and outer garments for the trip. I still have the small case. I may have held onto it like I did the ginger ale bottles when I moved to the farm. It was a connection to my past. I've used it to hold items like report cards, a few photographs, some letters, and a couple of newspaper articles. Those items remain the only solid evidence of my childhood.

Other people might have heard stories about their childhoods from their real parents and built memories based on those stories. Their parents might even have saved tokens of their childhoods for them. Since I didn't have the benefit of oral stories about my past, I've always been fearful that I might exaggerate my past and make it appear better, more interesting, or worse than it was. However, I have this belief that painful emotional experiences from childhood are so etched in our brains that we can't forget them. The trips to Miami were etched in my brain.

A social worker, not Miss Fleming, picked me up on the day of my trip and drove me to the Philadelphia Airport. We walked together down a long corridor to the Eastern Airlines gate. I was amazed at how many big planes I saw parked outside on the tarmac. The flight attendant at the gate greeted me, took me down a few stairs, through a door, across the tarmac, up the ramp to the plane, and pointed toward a window seat.

"Roger, the flight will last over four hours. If you sit in the window seat, you can put your head on this pillow, lean against the window, and take a nap," she said.

"Thank you," I said. In reality, I was too excited about flying to think about falling asleep.

"Is this your first airplane trip?"

"Yes."

"Enjoy yourself. If you need anything, you can push this button." She leaned over me and pointed to a white button on the ceiling over my head.

"After the plane takes off, I'll be back with some food and drinks."

Her smile and polite manner comforted me as I headed into the unknown. She reminded me of the nurse who'd shaved my lower stomach before my hernia operation. The good news was that I wasn't going to be put to sleep with ether this time.

I sat staring out the window of the air submarine that allowed me to breathe where I normally wouldn't be able to, were it not for the slender fuselage carried by the shiny wings and pushed forward by the noisy engines. Seeing so many farm fields and woods far below caused me to daydream about the number of people working those fields, how many were boys, how many pets there were, and how many real families there were.

My mother had talked a lot about Rory. He was four years older than I was. She said that he'd named me. Since I was born during the War, I assumed that his choice of names was influenced by all the military talk like "Roger and out!" She had said that we had the same initials, RBS, which would have made hand-me-downs easier if our initials were monogrammed on our clothes. She also had the same initials, but I didn't understand what she had that I would want to wear. Girls liked Rory because he was good-looking and had a great sense of humor. Supposedly, he was interested in meeting his kid brother. I really didn't know how I could think of him as a brother since I didn't know him. Besides, my foster brother, Richard, was all I knew about older brothers, and based on that experience, I knew that an older brother could offer a lot of challenges.

When the trip started, I could see a few scattered snowy white clouds off in the distance. They looked like soft cotton more so than when I saw them from the ground. As we got closer to Miami, the sky filled up with thick dark clouds. At one point, we entered the clouds and emerged between two layers of them. The clouds were thick and dark above and below us. I saw giant cumulus clouds far away, standing like Grecian columns as if they held up a ceiling of clouds. Flashes of lightning danced between the pillars, but I couldn't hear the thunder because of the engine noise. The sky had become ominous and threatening the closer we got to Miami.

The plane began to bounce in the stormy weather as we approached the airport. The bumpiness affected my stomach. I became worried that I might throw up. I must have attracted the flight attendant's attention because she came back and sat down next to me. She told me about the bag in the pocket on the seat in front of me and how I could use it. By the time we landed, I felt cold and sweaty, but I didn't throw up.

I walked down the stairs toward the terminal. My biological mother called out, "Roger, here I am. I'm so glad that you got through that storm okay."

"He was a real trooper for a first-time flyer," the flight attendant spoke up as she handed me over.

"Thank you so much," I said to the flight attendant.

Mrs. Saillant took my small suitcase and walked me to the parking lot. I was unsteady walking at first, but by the time we got to the car I was okay. The car was a cream-colored Plymouth built about a decade before seat belts. She was talking and driving fast in order to make up for my late arrival. Suddenly, she stood on the brakes, which launched me forward toward the dashboard.

Before I could hit my head, I felt her hand grab my chest and hold me back. That instinctive move to save me was the only time I ever felt her presence in my life to protect me from harm.

Miami and Miami Beach were hot and noisy cities. I didn't like cities. The lack of open space, the traffic noise, and so many people crowded around me made me anxious. There was no place to just relax. My mother and Rory, basically strangers, tried hard to entertain me and make me feel at home, but they choked me with their questions and the way in which they watched my every move. I was not at home.

Soon after I arrived, I had to go to the bathroom so badly that I felt like I would explode. I went into the tiny bathroom of their apartment and took a while to do my business. After I finished, I joined them in the living room area and sat down. Right away, they started to laugh and make jokes about the smell I'd made. I was so embarrassed that I wanted to shrink into my chair and disappear. These strangers were making fun of me. I wished that I'd stayed on the farm where I could be alone when I did my business. I vowed never to go to the bathroom in that apartment again. I kept my vow by going outside. Who knows how many dogs found my deposits around the neighborhood on the mornings following my nightly trips? There were other embarrassing moments ahead.

Rory was really a very good swimmer; he was on his school's swim team. The day after I arrived, he took me to the pool in the nearby park. We changed into our swimming trunks in the boys' locker room. Rory was deeply tanned. His complexion was darker than mine, which intensified his tan. I had a farmer's tan. I looked like a ghost with tan arms. I was freaky looking compared to Rory and the others around the pool. My embarrassment increased when it became obvious that I couldn't swim. The only thing I could do easily was sink. My one strength in the pool was that I could hold my breath for an impressive length of time. I focused on holding my breath and swimming underwater. Rory was patient with me. He tried to teach me how to move my arms and turn my head to breathe. I was a slow learner. In the end, he had more fun hanging out with the girls than trying to teach me to swim.

Once on the weekend when my mother sat poolside talking to her friends, I decided that I was going to jump off the high dive. I'm sure that it was set at a regulation height, but the more I climbed to the top, the higher it seemed to be. There were others who were climbing up the ladder and taking turns diving and jumping off the board. When I got to the top, I saw how far down the water was. I stood aside and let other divers pass me while I pretended to study the board and watch their technique. Eventually, I was alone. I had to do something. I walked out onto the board, bounced carefully, and looked down. The board seemed narrow, and I had to be careful not to fall. I saw my mother looking up at me, expecting me to do something dramatic. Others began to watch, too. I stood there for what seemed like a very long time. I was too scared to jump. Finally, I carefully backed off the board, climbed down the ladder, and went to the boys' dressing room, feeling ashamed that I couldn't make myself jump. I didn't have the guts to jump, and everyone there knew it. No one there knew what it was like to have fallen off the barn roof. My mother never comforted me about my failure to jump. I was alone.

Rory had a part-time job designing windows for Burdines department store. In the mornings, he would go to work at Burdines, and my mother, who was an official with the Hotel Employees Union, which was in the middle of a strike, had to spend a lot of time at work. This meant I was alone. I wandered around the area near the apartment and eventually found a drugstore. I may have had a little money, but I was pretty skilled at not spending it. On one occasion, I carefully selected three comic books that I liked, slipped them into my pants, walked out of the store, and ran back to the apartment. I really liked Tarzan, Superman, and Popeye comics. On the farm, Uncle Ted would bring us old comics. The comics I stole were brand new. I read them, relished their newness, and then hid them in the bottom of my suitcase to take home to Richard.

In addition to the occasional drugstore visit, I had time to snoop around the apartment. I found Rory's typewriter. I took it out and typed a letter without asking permission. When I finished, I realized that I had typed the current date on the letter, which meant that if he saw the letter, he would know that I had used the typewriter without permission. I found scissors and cut off the top of the letter because I was going to tell Rory that I had typed it on a typewriter at school and brought the letter with me on the trip. When he saw the letter, I am sure that he knew what I'd done but said nothing about my lie.

Rory liked to fish and so did I. One day very early in the morning, he made some sandwiches, gathered his fishing gear, and led me off into the darkness. I learned one of his theories about sleep as we were walking.

"Here," he said. "Eat this sandwich."

I was tired and not hungry.

"Go ahead and eat it," he urged. "Eating is one way to offset being tired."

"I don't see how eating offsets a lack of sleep," I replied.

"Eat and you'll see."

I ate a sandwich and felt refreshed. I didn't understand why it seemed to work, but I didn't object again.

He picked a spot on a causeway illuminated by a streetlight, and we began to fish. We could see the dark shadows of large fish in the water below that were much larger than the suckers back home, but they didn't seem interested in our bait. Rory said that the big fish were snook, which I'd never heard of, and wondered if he were pulling my leg. He said that they were tough to catch; we didn't catch any. We caught several small fish called moonfish that were actually bigger than the sucker. Rory cut them up and used them for bait.

The freshly cut bait attracted bites. Suddenly his reel started whirring steadily as yard after yard of his line disappeared into the ocean. I was really impressed by how the line just raced through the guides and into the water as though some giant had been hooked and hardly noticed the attempts to slow it down, turn it around, or stop it. Rory cut the line in order to save his gear because he said that what he'd caught was probably a shark. Whatever it was underscored the expression: the big one got away. When dawn came, we went back to the apartment. I learned that Rory could tell stories and that there were monster fish in the ocean.

I took a second trip to Miami a year or two later. My mother had upgraded to an Alfa Romeo convertible. All three of us rode in it down to Marathon Key. The causeways over the ocean linking the keys were long, and I wondered how they could have been built. We crossed one called Seven Mile Bridge, which was unimaginably long for a bridge. In all directions the bright blue sea sparkled and danced in the bright sun.

We stayed a few days in a motel on Marathon Key. The motel had a pool and several shuffleboard courts. Rory went scuba diving and spearfishing once or twice; neither of those activities included me. We played some shuffleboard games, which I never won.

During my stays, it was clear that Rory and my mother tried to entertain me and make things fun for me. However, I never settled in and relaxed. We lived in very different worlds, and the gaps between us were not going to close easily, if at all. My home was on the farm with the McClellands. My mother was Mrs.

McClelland, not Mrs. Saillant. Richard was my brother. The idea of a blood relationship didn't make up for the differences in the ways we grew up and lived together.

I never went back to Florida as a foster child.

Chapter 26
Making the Grades

The day I graduated from sixth grade Miss Hanisch awarded me two dollars for being helpful, two dollars for having the best grades in my class, and advice for a lifetime. She knew I was going to go to Central Bucks, the new regional high school, in the fall.

"Roger, Central Bucks will have over one thousand five hundred students and probably more than three hundred students in your class," she said. "You were a good student here in a small class. However, in a big class composed of students from all over the area, including children from families of professionals, you'll meet many strong students. Don't be discouraged if you meet others who are better students than you."

I was concerned that she thought I would disappoint her. "I'll study hard," I said to reassure her.

"I know you will, Roger. Studying will be important, but there will be some who will study hard, too."

"You mean that they'll be smarter than I am?"

"Some probably will be, yes," she replied.

She paused to let that thought settle in and continued, "You have other positive strengths. Build on them."

"What do you mean by 'build on them'?" I asked. "And what are they?"

"When you're happy, your smile fills the room," she said. "You protect others from bullies. You are fair with others and you're honest."

Her compliments about my character made me uneasy. She didn't know that I'd broken into buildings, stolen Eddie Boyle's gun, set fire to Wolff's mower, and taken things from stores. I had to do better if I were ever to live up to her assessment.

"You should focus on improving as a person every day and still continue to be a good student. You'll learn that success and happiness in life are about working hard and treating others honestly and fairly. People will respond positively to you if you're a good person. You'll be a success."

I nodded.

I was basking in her full attention. She was the first person to have spoken to me that way. Although she'd given me several dollars earlier that day, I felt that she'd given me advice worth a lot more. I didn't want to let her down.

She continued, "Be positive. Use your smile. You have already faced more challenges in your life than most do in a lifetime. You know how to overcome adversity. Your experiences can help you be very successful in life."

I already knew from Mom that smiling was important. She'd told me many times to "pack up your troubles in your old kit-bag and smile, smile, smile." I'd witnessed other foster children fail because they displayed their anger and unhappiness.

I was tingling with optimism and eager to get on with my life.

I'd already learned that honesty with customers and smiles were important in selling. The farm setting was an excellent place to learn about selling. I grew up watching buyers come to the farm to purchase eggs, chickens, and hogs. I learned that customers were happy when their expectations were met. The eggs had to be clean and uncracked. The chickens had to be plump and healthy looking. The pigs had to weigh more than two hundred twenty pounds to fetch a good price. I liked watching the money go from buyers to sellers. Most importantly, I observed that each transaction was accompanied by personal conversations that built trust and earned respect.

I became commercially active between fourth and fifth grades. Mr. McClelland gave me a small plot of land to cultivate so that I could raise vegetables, mostly string beans and tomatoes, to sell. I sold them to Helrick's Store and to Mr. Moyer. Although Mr. Moyer was my volume buyer, my most memorable single sale was a five-eighths basket of very early-season tomatoes sold to the Helrick's man. He delivered store-bought goods to us each Friday year-round. He paid me five dollars for those large, bright-red, polished tomatoes. I loved the feeling of selling and getting money.

Mr. Moyer would combine my vegetables with the crates of eggs from the McClellands and take them to the Farmers Market in Philadelphia and sell them. He bought all the vegetables I could raise and never returned any of them. Sometimes I would visit him and see his booth when I had to travel to Philadelphia for visits to the Aid Society. It was exciting to see my vegetables for sale in his booth just like he'd promised. I appreciated seeing the full cycle: when the season warmed and the soil was ready, the land was plowed; when the plowing was done, the dirt was prepared; when the dirt was just right, the planting was done whether by seed or by sets; when the plants grew, there was weeding and hoeing; when the vegetables were ready, they were picked and cleaned; when they were sold to merchants like Mr. Moyer, they would be transported to market and sold. It all made sense, and I was part of the system.

I liked growing plants from seeds. I had read about a special offer in a magazine whereby you could sell seeds offered by the American Seed Company and earn credits for rewards. I had my eye on two rewards: a fishing rod and a bow and arrow. I don't remember how many points it took to get those items, but I do remember trudging up and down roads in my spare time trying to sell seeds. Of course, I bought a lot of seeds for myself, which helped to earn points. Since the houses and farms were spread out in our area, it took a lot of time to go door to door. I probably canvassed about a square mile, which was an area big enough to cover about twenty families, some of whom bought seeds. Eventually, I earned enough points to get both the fishing rod and the bow and arrow. The benefit of this process was that the people in my area got to know me and I got to know them. That experience paid off in seventh grade.

Central Bucks was a big school and very different from the one-room schoolhouses I'd experienced. The student body was large, which supported a diversity of activities.

One of the activities that attracted me was a selling challenge. The school supported businesses that helped students to learn about different vocations. Curtis Publishing was one of the companies. They engaged students to sell magazines. It was a simple process. The students were to go out into their communities and sell magazines and earn credits toward prizes. I thought it was fairly easy to do since you would show lists of magazines to potential subscribers, and, if they were interested, you wrote their names and addresses next to the magazines they wanted, collected their money, and turned the money into the sponsor at school. We were given three weeks to finish canvassing. Whoever sold the most subscriptions based on dollar amounts would get a special prize in addition to the rewards based on points earned.

I was all set. All I had to do was go from home to home, and farm to farm like I'd done when selling seeds. I knew that the people would buy from me, or so I'd thought. However, in our area seeds were a necessity to grow food, whereas magazines were considered a luxury and no amount of smiling could win the potential customers over. The farmers and the rural neighbors were poor and very practical about spending their hard-earned money.

Each evening and on weekend days, when I could, I went from door to door over the course of about two and a half weeks.

Each school day we reported our sales. I had almost no sales even though I'd spent a lot of time. Fortunately, I was able to sell several subscriptions to *The Farm Journal,* which kept me from being totally "skunked." Some of the kids were selling to relatives and that really helped them, but no one in my family was interested in magazine subscriptions. So, I watched as the selling graphs for some of the students kept growing and mine barely moved.

The end of the selling period was close. I had one last house to go to: the Irwins. Since Mrs. Irwin's husband was an invalid, I'd thought she would be unlikely to subscribe to anything. I'd gone to their house on several occasions to help move plants and clean up the areas around their buildings. I thought that they couldn't afford to buy much. Boy, was I wrong! Mrs. Irwin sat me down at her table and picked out magazine after magazine to subscribe to. She wanted *The Saturday Evening Post, Hot Rod Magazine, Popular Mechanics, The Atlantic Monthly,* and several others that I'd never heard of. Just like that, I hit the jackpot. I was so excited after all those frustrating stops to have hit the mother lode. Walking up their lane on the way home, it occurred to me that invalids had a lot of time to read and that her purchases were very practical for her husband and his interests.

When I went to school the next day and handed in her check, I could hardly believe my eyes when my little bar suddenly jumped past all of the others except one. When the magazine subscription drive was over, I found out that I'd won first place in the Curtis sales drive. My reward was another "grand prize," a big watch, which didn't fit my wrist and was so dressy that I never wore it. However, I had a certificate that gave me recognition for "outstanding selling ability." There was even mention of my achievement in the school newspaper along with Sally Bitting. I felt a lot of gratitude toward Mrs. Irwin.

Miss Hanisch had alerted me to the possibility that I was

going to meet students who would be smarter than I was and others who had other skills better than mine. She was right.

I met a number of very smart students and benefited from being around them. Knowing them at an early age really helped me to have no misgivings about my own academic abilities. Ed Satterthwaite, Ruth Carwithen, Jane Phillips, and Phelps Freeborn all became gold standards for academic excellence. They were clearly beyond my reach intellectually.

I met gifted athletes whose skills exceeded mine by large margins. Nathaniel Duckett, who went to the same one-room school in sixth grade as I did, Barbara Bechtel, and Joe Arcade were real athletes. Although I was strong, I lacked their skills and athletic finesse.

Music and art were entirely outside of my skill set. I couldn't understand why my sister was such a good singer, and I was such a dud. Ruth Carwithen and Bonnie Swartley were friends who stood out musically. Art was another creative desert for me. I didn't know who the best artist in our class was, but I lagged far behind in art, too.

I had a history teacher, Miss Meyers, in seventh grade who gave me the only failing grade in my entire academic career, an E, on my report card for my first quarter. Apparently, there was a bit of a communication problem between her and me over coloring maps of the Middle East and Asia. Since I didn't have crayons or colored pencils, I handed in maps that were uncolored. It didn't occur to me that coloring was so important or that I might borrow someone else's crayons or pencils to complete the assignment; hence, the **E**. By the fourth marking period I earned an **A** in her course and had learned to follow classroom instructions better. I learned another lesson as well: you needed to have the right resources to do good work.

As it turned out, I got the highest grade on any project

ever in my life in eighth-grade history. I liked to read and I liked history and was generally well prepared. Mr. Lyons, our history teacher, had given us an assignment to do a project relating in some way to colonial America.

"For this part of American history, I'd like you to do a project that depicts colonial America," Mr. Lyons told us. "For example, you could build a house or cabin to scale, or make candles, or write a paper on the types of tools that colonists used. If you want, you could find a partner and work on a project together. The final projects must be completed and presented to me in two weeks."

I thought that this assignment was going to be a lot of work and would involve more than just coloring a few maps. I knew that outside the classroom I had very little extra time. I decided that I would need a partner. An idea about a potential project came to me as well as a person with whom I might work.

I approached Nevin Oswald whom I knew from Bible Club. "Hey, Nevin, would you be willing to work together on a project?" I asked.

"I think so," he said. "Do you have a project idea?"

I knew he could type. Most college prep students learned to type during the summer in a typing class. I had no opportunity to take classes during the summer and didn't even have access to a typewriter. I loved stories about Benjamin Franklin who was, among other things, a newspaper editor.

"Yes, I have an idea," I replied. "What do you think about creating a colonial newspaper?"

"I like it. Do you have ideas about what we would print?" he asked.

"Yes, I do."

We began to plan. He offered to get some poster-sized sheets of paper so that we could paste columns of printed stories on the sheets and form a large four-sided newspaper. I offered to write stories that he could type and paste on the sheets. The stories were easy for me to make up since I already lived in a fairly primitive setting. I knew about farm animals, shoveling snow to make a path to the barn, splitting wood, heating water on the stove for bathing, clearing fields, raising pigs for slaughter, and I even knew about the use of outhouses.

The process began. He brought to class two large poster-sized sheets of paper, which he'd attached together forming a four-sided newspaper. He'd also drawn three columns on both sides of the sheets. The plan was quite simple: I would tell him stories or write stories by hand and give them to him. He would type them out in columns on typing paper, cut out the columns of stories, and paste them onto the poster sheets. In this way we would create a newspaper, which we titled "The Colonial News."

I created stories about births, deaths, weddings, and town meetings. The stories all had authentic descriptions of the farm set in colonial times. We even had a couple of encounters with Indians to spice things up a bit. We had fun collaborating on the project. As I recall, Nevin did a lot of extra work cutting and pasting, drew a few pictures of buildings, and did some extra writing to fill up the newspaper. We met the deadline.

We submitted our project and waited for Mr. Lyons' grade. He was so pleased that he awarded us a triple **A**. We never expected it. The newspaper was put on display for the rest of the class to see with a big **AAA** written across the top. I couldn't have done the project alone. I thanked Nevin profusely, as I wanted him to know how much our success depended on his skills.

Chapter 27
The Big Stink

Richard and I were eager to earn money to supplement our small allowances. I grew vegetables on the farm and sold them. Other farmers would hire Richard to help them do heavy work because he was a good worker and very strong. There were times when we both were hired to do jobs for neighbors like Mr. Mason. He would pay us to mow his lawn and pick his strawberries. Mr. VanAlstyne hired us to mow his ten-acre field using Mr. McClelland's tractor and mower. We were paid seventy-five dollars for that job, which came with a penalty.

We had a horse-drawn mower that, by changing the hitch, could be converted so that it could be towed by our John Deere tractor. Since it was originally designed to be pulled by horses, the mower was driven by the iron wheels instead of driven by the tractor's power take-off. This meant that someone had to ride the mower when it was pulled in order to raise and lower the blade. Richard and I were sent to the VanAlstynes' field to do the mowing. Richard drove the tractor, and I bounced along behind, riding the converted horse mower.

We had just two swaths to go when the mower blade nicked one of three honeybee hives on the edge of the field.

Richard turned the tractor around and then stopped. "I think we excited those bees. Look at how they are swarming around that last hive," he said grinning.

I could see that the bees covered the white hive. "Maybe we shouldn't cut the last swath behind the hives," I suggested. "They look angry."

"VanAlstyne is paying us to do the whole field," Richard countered. "Besides, all we have to do is speed up the tractor and roar past the hives before they know what's happening."

I wasn't so sure, but I wasn't in a position to stop him. I'd already had several bad experiences with bees that hadn't ended well for me. He put the tractor in fifth gear, advanced the throttle, and pushed the clutch forward. We raced toward the hives. I clutched the seat as it jostled me around at the high speed. The mower blade chattered furiously, cutting the last strip of grass. The bees heard or saw us coming and formed a dark cloud over the hive. I knew that this was going to be a bad experience, and it was. Richard sat up front on the tractor on a high seat surrounded by tractor noise and the exhaust fumes while I was behind on a lower seat without protection. I was the target of choice.

The swarm of bees converged on me. They stung me at will. I swatted with one hand, but I had to hold on with the other. When we got to the edge of the field and far from the hives, there were no more bees. They'd given up the chase. Richard had gotten stung a couple of times, but I'd been stung many times. He was smiling, as he always did when something didn't work out quite as planned, and said, "That didn't work out so well, did it?"

"No shit," I said. I was feeling the stings all over my back, under my arms, and on my face and ears.

We went to the VanAlstynes. They'd heard the tractor roaring and had come outside to see what was going on.

"Looks like you boys lost a fight with the bees," Mr. VanAlstyne said.

"Look at this boy," said Mrs. VanAlstyne, pointing at me. "He took the worst of it. Come on inside and let's see what we can do."

Richard was all smiles, and I was in pain. Mr. VanAlstyne chuckled, "Boys!" He had grown up on a farm in Upstate New York, and we learned later that he'd had a few adventures with bees, too.

Meanwhile, Mrs. VanAlstyne had taken tweezers and pulled out over two dozen stingers from various parts of my upper torso. My old tee shirt had holes in it, and everywhere there was a hole, the bees had stung me.

I was lucky that I was not allergic to bee stings. I knew that every sting meant that a bee had given up its life to protect the hive. If we'd only been more careful not to have hit the hive and, once having hit it, had been patient enough to wait a while before finishing the job, we probably wouldn't have been stung and no bees would have lost their lives in a futile effort to drive us away. The challenge had encouraged Richard and underscored his penchant for taking risks. We did earn seventy-five dollars for the job, some of which had to be given to Mr. McClelland. The money I got eased the pain.

Another way to earn money was to trap animals for their fur. I had no concerns at that age about killing animals as long as they didn't suffer. I tried not to think about how the steel trap would hurt their legs.

Trapping was done in the cold winter months when muskrats, possums, raccoons, and skunks had the thickest fur. Once the animals were caught and killed, a man would come and collect their frozen bodies and pay me. He took them, skinned them, and sold them to a furrier.

Catching animals demanded patience and a willingness to go outside in the cold late at night and early in the morning. I'd found old traps in the shed and used them. Mom had given me a large flashlight as one of my Christmas gifts so that I could find my trap lines in the dark. The traps had to be set on animal trails in the woods, near burrows, or along the banks of streams. At about nine o'clock at night I would go out with the flashlight to check the traps. The 9 o'clock check was because an animal, especially muskrats, would chew its leg off and escape if left in the trap too long. About 5 o'clock, before the morning milking and other chores started, I would go out again to check the traps. If they were empty, I'd unset them so that they didn't catch anything during the day like a bird, a rabbit, a cat, or a dog. The traps were strung out over a distance of about two miles.

The money was good. The pelt collector paid me ten cents for possums, a dollar for muskrats, three or more dollars for raccoons, and one to three dollars for skunks, depending on how much black fur there was on it. If you ever managed to catch a fox, you got a bounty, plus five dollars. I never caught a fox, but I caught a lot of possums and muskrats. Every now and then I would catch a skunk.

I caught my first skunk when I was in seventh grade. It happened just before Christmas early one cold morning. The skunk was in the first trap I checked at the edge of the woods where I'd seen an animal trail the previous afternoon. By the beam of the flashlight, I could tell that it was at least a two-dollar skunk. I was really excited. I watched as the skunk backed further into the bushes. I only carried a club, and I would have to get really close to kill it. Getting close meant that I would certainly get sprayed. This was a problem. I decided that I better back away and get some advice. I ran to the barn.

"Richard, I've caught a skunk. How can I kill it without getting sprayed?"

"Roger, that's great! All you have to do is approach it from behind and you won't get sprayed." I hadn't yet learned that when Richard used the phrase, "All you have to do is …," that I should be on alert because it usually meant trouble for me.

"Really?" I asked.

"Yes, skunks spray over their heads," he replied.

"I didn't know that." It sounded reasonable. I rushed back

to the woods, eager to apply Richard's strategy.

When I got close to the skunk, I could see its bright black eyes reflecting the light from my flashlight. It was facing me and looked menacing. Fortunately, it had wrapped the chain tied to the trap around branches of one of the bushes. This had limited the skunk's mobility and gave me the opportunity to get behind it. I moved in slowly from behind, with the club in one hand and the flashlight in the other. Just as I was preparing to hit the skunk, it twitched its tail and I saw several big drops of musk heading straight for me. Luckily, I closed my eyes just in time. The drops hit me squarely in the face. What a smell. I jumped backwards and raced back to the barn.

I stuck my head in a bucket of ice-cold water. I wiped myself dry with a horse blanket. My face was stinging, and the smell was horrible. Then I saw Richard through my squinted eyes, grinning and maybe even laughing.

"Skunks can squirt you from behind," I said angrily.

"I'll get the .22 and shoot it," he said as he moved away from me because of the stench.

I stunk and I couldn't get rid of the smell. As farmers, we knew about skunks and how tomato juice was supposed to help kill the odor. I got some bottled tomato juice from the cellar and washed my face and shirt in it. Meanwhile, Richard took the flashlight and a gun and killed the skunk.

All of my efforts to get cleaned up seemed to help. The smell wasn't so bad by the time I'd finished my chores and gotten ready for school. However, the kids on the bus reacted with gasps and coughing and moved away from me. Apparently, I'd gotten used to the smell. I was careful to sit in the back of my homeroom class. This particular day was the day of the Christmas program, which was held in the morning for grades seven through nine.

When I went to the auditorium, I seated myself in the middle of a row about halfway up from the stage. Before long I noticed several teachers were walking slowly up and down the aisles, looking across the rows. One of the teachers zeroed in on me. He motioned to me to get up and come to him. I got up and joined him in the aisle. He didn't ask me what had happened; he marched me quietly to the back of the auditorium and out the door. He looked at me sympathetically while I explained everything to him quietly. He got a chair for me. I watched the Christmas program through the door by sitting outside the auditorium. No one wanted to be near me for the rest of the day.

An older student, Bernd Waitl, whom I knew from church, saw me. He came over and pulled back as he smelled me. He knew my real name; however, he nicknamed me "Skunkie." We became friends. The name stuck as an affectionate reference to that day.

Chapter 28
Alone on the Front

Richard was a powerful force in my life. There were times when I was angry at him and times when I liked him, but I always respected him. I observed how his hard work and good humor pleased people. I did my best to emulate his positive behaviors and to avoid copying his bad ones. He had contempt for authority figures, which he expressed in several ways. The most notable was when he gave "the bird" to one of the teachers who monitored the bus loading area in front of the school. Once when Richard dropped a piece of paper and the teacher told him to pick it up, Richard gestured to the teacher and walked away. Had it been me, I would have done as I was told. I feared consequences. Richard feared very little if anything. He had a dry sense of humor that was sharp and quick. He was funnier than I. He also liked to torment me, which was painful and sometimes very threatening.

As is common on farms, we had several guns in the house: a sawed-off pump shotgun, which Richard had sawed-off, a double-barreled twelve-gauge shotgun, and a .22 rifle with a twelve-bullet clip. Several times when Richard was particularly angry at me, he offered me a challenge.

"I'll tell you what," he'd say. "Why don't you take any one of the guns and as much ammunition as you want and go off somewhere. I'll give you a ten-minute head start, and then I'll take a gun and come after you."

Because there was a lot of anger in the air, I was tempted to do it. As unthinkable as it was, I knew that if I'd taken the challenge, I would have found a way to kill him and, thus, end any dreams I had of college and beyond. That grisly offer was made more than once and illustrated the worst in our relationship. I never doubted that he would have come after me had I accepted his offer. Because his bullying frightened me, I resolved not to do that to others who were smaller or weaker than I.

His best attribute was how skilled he was with his hands. For example, he routinely found old junked bicycles in dumps, selected working parts from various scrapped ones, and built a usable bike. He could fix the chains, handlebars, seats, forks, and brakes. Sometimes we would ride bikes that were assembled without rubber on the wheels or even a seat. I admired his skill and appreciated his work.

One of the bikes Richard put together lacked pedal tread bars. That defect didn't stop him from riding it until his foot slipped off and one of the metal brackets that would have held the missing rubber tread gouged a hole in his ankle. His ankle became infected and was painful. Richard tried not to show the pain, but it was clear it hurt and the injury impeded his work. The healing process was slow. The injury was so significant that Mom mentioned it in one of her letters to me when I was in Florida.

Richard excelled in shop. He liked using the power tools in the classroom that we lacked on the farm. During his senior year, he fabricated a set of four beautiful wooden chairs with smooth ridges and grooves along the sides and tops. They became the permanent chair set for the kitchen. He was clearly skilled at carpentry. He had a special relationship with Mr. Elfman, the shop teacher, who was encouraging Richard to become a cabinetmaker. However, Richard had a more immediate goal—to get as far away from the farm and the foster care system as soon as he legally could. Richard needed special permission from the Aid Society to join the Army since he was not going to be eighteen for a couple of months after graduation. They gave him permission without hesitation. Upon graduating high school, Richard promptly joined the Army.

When Richard left, no work was eliminated. Work was redistributed. My workload was increased the most because the McClellands were getting older and I was getting bigger and stronger. The social workers did not seem to notice or care about the impact on me since they neither discussed the issue with me nor assigned another foster child to help out on the farm. I recalled how Richard, a few years earlier, had resisted the idea of me leaving the farm and sticking him with extra work. Because he only left after he graduated, I assumed his code allowed him to leave because he'd fulfilled his obligations to the McClellands for giving him a home. I felt that the burden of my sentence had been increased by the extra work, and there was nothing I could do about it.

After basic training, Richard visited us on the farm as a young man wise in the ways of the world. Once in the Army, Richard immersed himself in fast cars and heavy vehicles. He moved into the twentieth century and was eager to show me what it offered. My experience with cars was very limited until he visited us on the farm when he was on leave.

The first time I can remember riding in a car was when I was transported from Philadelphia to the McClelland farm by the social worker. Since the McClellands had neither a car nor a truck, I rode in vehicles only when we went to church, school, or to Philadelphia with social workers. Limited access to cars or trucks meant that I didn't get to tinker with them. Thus, I didn't learn about engines, brakes, and transmissions and how they might function. I grew up not understanding them and basically became indifferent to them. I saw vehicles as only a way to transport people or goods from one place to another.

The Schaeffers across the road had an old black 1938 Chevrolet. The first time I rode in it was when they took Mrs.

McClelland and me to the Quakertown Farmers Market. On that trip I became aware of the man and machine interface. They had removed the passenger side front seat in order to create more cargo space, which forced Mom and me to ride in the back seat with Mrs. Schaeffer while Mr. Schaeffer drove. The upholstery was threadbare, and there was no carpet on the floors. Without carpeting, the road noise and the sound of shifting gears was loud. He was constantly changing gears, using the long black-handled gear shift. We lurched back and forth whenever he changed gears. Along the route to the market, we had to travel on Route 313, which had a long hill.

Mrs. Schaeffer turned to us and said, "Now be quiet. Frank has to concentrate to get us up this hill."

I thought it was strange that being silent helped a car go up a hill. Or even stranger that his concentration could get us to the top. All in all, the vehicle was slow, and it made for a long trip.

Uncle Ted and Aunt Verna, Mrs. McClelland's brother and sister-in-law, drove over from Doylestown almost every Sunday and took us to church in Chalfont. Mr. McClelland never went to church. Since Uncle Ted worked for a Chevrolet dealer, his car was new and quiet and provided a smooth ride. The routine each week ended with a big Sunday lunch at our house. We always gave them a couple dozen eggs in return for their assistance taking us to church. Since we were dependent on others to give us rides, we were always grateful and showed our appreciation for their kindness in any way we could. However, I think that Uncle Ted and Aunt Verna were kind people and would have done it without a favor in return. I learned about thoughtfulness, but at the same time I knew that accepting favors limited a person's independence.

Cars could be dangerous. Richard met boys in high school who had enough money to own cars. Although I don't recall any of them coming to the farm, I heard stories about speeding, about being ticketed by police for speeding, and about playing a game called "chicken" in their cars. There was a level stretch of road on Route 202 west of Chalfont and before Montgomeryville that was ideal for racing and playing chicken. Richard didn't have a driver's license and never participated in any of these car events, but he told stories about them. He had a friend who was small but had a lot of guts. He was known for his ability to win games of chicken. The point of the game was to have two drivers race toward each other at high speeds from opposite directions. The winner was the one who didn't steer away at the last second to avoid a collision. Richard's friend and another guy played chicken and neither veered away. Richard's friend went through the windshield and was thrown over the other car and landed on the highway on his face. He was hospitalized for a long time; when he was released, he had an ugly facial scar. The other driver was killed.

When Richard returned home on leave from the Army in his white 1952 Ford, he was eager to show me how fast he could go.

"Come on," he said, "let's go for a ride."

"Sure!" It was the first time I saw him drive a car, and I was excited to get away from the farm. I climbed in.

"Where are we going?" I asked.

"Let's go somewhere where I can show you how fast this thing will go."

"How about 202?" I suggested.

"No. Too many cops. Let's go to New Galena Road," he said. "Remember those cinnamon buns we stole from those dumb bastards and how we never got caught? We won't get caught today either."

I sensed how excited Richard was. I knew that he liked to take risks, but I felt safe in his car, which rode smoothly and was quieter than either Mr. Schaeffer's car or Uncle Ted's.

We arrived at Newville School and turned onto New Galena

Road and headed east. I watched the speedometer cross over fifty miles an hour, which was about as fast as I'd ever gone. We passed sixty and kept accelerating. I began to feel anxious when we got to seventy.

"Feel this baby hold the road. Isn't this ride great?" Richard was excited.

Our speed increased and so did my heart rate. The car began to shake and leave the ground as we flew over the ridges on the asphalt road. When the car was going eighty, I was clutching the armrest with one hand and the side of the seat with the other. I started to think about Richard's friend going through the windshield when we hit ninety. I was scared, but I was afraid to show weakness by asking Richard to slow down.

Richard was smiling and laughed out loud when we hit a hundred miles an hour. "How's that for a ride? This baby can really move."

Chapter 29
Decline, Defense, and Detection

Mom's stoic veneer was pierced after my first day of school in eighth grade. I was unloading baskets of potatoes and taking them into the basement when she came around the corner of the house holding her left arm.

Before I could ask what had happened, she gasped and said, "I need Dr. Burkhardt." As she said that, she sat down limply on the edge of the porch.

"What happened?" I asked.

"Please, just call him and tell him I had an accident and I may have broken my arm. Ask him to come right away."

I put down the basket of potatoes that I was holding, went inside, and called Dr. Burkhardt as directed. Mom was a skinny and fragile-looking woman, which hid an inner toughness and resilience that was rarely breached. Even when Paul had stabbed her in the hand, she grimaced but kept her composure and didn't indicate how much it must have hurt. This was different. She was in pain and showed it. For the first time, I sensed fear in her.

I returned to the porch, saying, "I called the doctor, and he said he wasn't far away and would be here in twenty minutes."

"Thank you."

I asked again, "What happened?"

"I was dizzy and fell. I must have landed funny on my arm."

"Here, let me help you to get up and sit on the couch," I said to her.

The wicker couch on the porch was old when I'd arrived years ago and only the dogs used it. It easily supported her light weight. She felt cool to the touch.

"Thank you. I'll wait here until Dr. Burkhardt comes."

"Can I get you some water?"

"Yes, please."

I got her water, which she drank slowly. Her hand was shaking. She said, "Finish storing those potatoes in the basement, or Daddy will begin wondering what you're up to." She waved me off.

The doctor arrived just as I finished unloading and storing the potatoes. Mr. McClelland saw the car coming down the lane and came in from the field to see what was happening.

Dr. Burkhardt had been their doctor for years and was quite old himself. He was a friend as well as the family doctor. He had an old black valise, which looked as weathered as he was. He talked softly to her while he examined her arm and listened to her heart through his stethoscope.

"What's going on here?" Mr. McClelland spoke loudly. "Son, why didn't you come and get me?"

Before I could answer, Dr. Burkhardt spoke, "John, as far as I can tell, her arm is broken. Maybe in two places. We have to take her to the hospital."

There was a pause before Mr. McClelland spoke, "Maud, what happened?"

Before she could answer, Dr. Burkhardt was standing her up and helping her off of the porch and into his car. He answered by saying, "Let's get her to the hospital. We can talk on the way."

Mr. McClelland was caught off guard. He had a puzzled expression and turned to me. "We'll finish gathering the potatoes tomorrow. I don't know how long this will take, but if you start the chores now, you can finish everything before dark. I must go with Mum."

They got into the car and drove away. I put the tractor in the garage and did as I was told. Dr. Burkhardt and Mr. McClelland returned from the hospital in the evening a few hours later without Mom. Mr. McClelland thanked the doctor and waved goodbye.

He came up to me on the porch and asked, "Did you get all the chores done?"

"Yes. Is Mom still in the hospital?"

"Yes."

"Why?"

"When the hospital doctors were checking her over and interviewing her, they were concerned. They want her to stay so that they could give her a thorough examination tomorrow and run some tests. They did set her arm in a cast. It was broken in two places. They said it may take a couple of months to heal."

He looked worried. I asked, "What else did they say?"

"Nothing. They just want to be careful because she hasn't had a medical exam in years. We have to wait and see what they tell us. I need to call Aunt Lizzie now and ask her to come up to help out."

The next day when I came home, Frank Schaeffer was there. He told me that he had taken Mr. McClelland to the hospital after the noon chores were completed, and Mr. McClelland was still at the hospital. Mr. Schaeffer told me that I was expected to do all the evening chores again. He left.

Aunt Lizzie's son, Hugh, who lived in Cross Keys near Doylestown, picked her up at the train station and drove her to the farm. After she caught up on the news, she busied herself, preparing supper for the two of us. She was a good cook and a positive person. I was glad she'd come.

Toward evening, Uncle Ted arrived with Mr. McClelland who looked tired and worried. When Aunt Lizzie and I started asking questions about Mom, he went outside. Aunt Lizzie and I ate dinner alone. When I was turning the chicken house lights on, I saw him by the barn, slumped forward, sitting on an overturned basket, smoking his pipe, clearly deep in thought.

Eggs were accumulating in the buckets near the overstuffed chair in the kitchen. Aunt Lizzie and I did the best we could to clean them, grade them, and pack them for Mr. Moyer for the next day's pickup. When I went to my room, Mr. McClelland hadn't come into the house. I heard him later in the kitchen talking to Aunt Lizzie. I slipped quietly into the McClellands' bedroom to listen through the hole in the floor.

"Tell me, John, how is Maud?"

"She has tumors."

"Oh, no. How do they know?"

"She told them that she'd been bleeding. That's maybe why she fainted and fell. They examined her and found tumors. They might be cancerous."

"Oh, my God. No."

"They won't tell me for sure if it is cancer until they operate."

"Operate—how awful. When?"

"They plan to operate on her tomorrow and take everything out. After she heals, they're talking about giving her radiation if the tumors are cancerous."

I withdrew to my room and curled up in bed. I'd seen cancers in farm animals. The animals had to be killed because they were suffering and were going to die anyway. I couldn't help but think that Mom was in a lot of pain and was going to die. I prayed for her. Previously, I'd prayed for one of the McClellands to die so that the Aid Society would move me like they did when Mr. Perry-Ferry died. Now, I didn't want Mom to die even if it meant that I had to stay on the farm.

The next few weeks were a blur. The tumors were cancerous. The operation happened. I learned through the secret listening hole in the bedroom that Mom also had a very long tapeworm that no one had mentioned to me. Mom came home after about a week in the hospital. Relatives and friends came to express concern and offer support. Some brought meals, others brought flowers, and some brought books. When churchwomen came, they left boxes and boxes of Kleenexes, which struck me as strange.

Aunt Lizzie did all the scheduling for arrivals and departures. The doctors at the hospital arranged for Mom's radiation treatments. Each radiation therapy was followed by a period of recovery. Mom, who was thin to begin with, grew thinner until her skin lay on her body like a cloth sheet. I kept going to school, did more work around the farm than was expected of me, and tried my best to stay out of everyone's way.

Aunt Lizzie was a powerhouse. She ran the household and was always kind to me. One morning on my way to school she noticed that I was wearing a pink shirt and said to me, "Pink becomes you, Roger. You should wear that shirt more often." I didn't know what that phrase meant, but I thanked her. Later my English teacher, Miss High, told me that it was a compliment. That compliment was one of the very few about my appearance I received growing up. Aunt Lizzie's praise made me feel good, and I liked her a lot. She stayed longer than she or anyone expected. In time, though, Mom got well enough to resume doing the housework on her own. Aunt Lizzie was leaving.

Before she left, she stood talking to me outside in the cold wind. "Roger, pray for Maud to grow stronger every day, and I'm sure she will. God will hear your prayers because you're a good boy." My heart sank. "Everyone is counting on you."

She added, "If you need me to come back, let me know. Otherwise, I'll come back before Christmas."

Aunt Lizzie was a perfect image of a Mrs. Santa Claus. Her stout cheeks were rosy in the cold wind. Strands of her white hair that had escaped from underneath her black hat waved in the breeze. I listened to her. I vowed to myself that she must never know what I'd previously prayed for.

"I know, Aunt Lizzie. I'll do everything I can to help. I'll pray every day for her to get better." I spoke with conviction.

The system for doing chores changed to make it better for Mom. Egg collections became a shared responsibility for Mr. McClelland and me. Other tasks, like hanging laundry and moving buckets of eggs or pots of water, were my jobs. I was doing more work, but I felt that God had spared Mom, which inspired me to be thankful and to work diligently most of the time.

Mr. McClelland kept an eye on me to be sure that I did my chores on time and without taking shortcuts. The only place where his surveillance broke down was the hayloft where I had the job of throwing down hay or straw for the animals. When I was up in the barn, I had privacy. I could watch the pigeons feeding their babies and hear them cooing to each other. Sometimes I would play with tiny kittens the cats had hidden in a straw nest. Other times I would lie down comfortably in the straw to daydream and maybe even take a short nap. There was always the threat of discovery. I would be blamed for taking too long and be cursed at for being lazy.

One late afternoon I was startled when Mr. McClelland yelled, "Roger, what's taking you so long? Get off your lazy ass and throw the hay down now!"

My mind raced. I knew I'd taken too long and was going to be in trouble. I ignored his calls and instead said loudly enough to be heard, "You should go before you're found here."

"What's that you're saying? Roger, who are you talking to?"

I added, "Did you hear that? That's my foster father. If he catches you, you'll be in really big trouble. Get out of here!"

Mr. McClelland yelled up again, "What's going on? Who's up there with you?"

The ploy was working. His response was so much better

than what I'd expected. He was distracted and not cursing me or threatening to cuff me.

I jumped to the barn floor and began to throw bales of hay outside to the ground. I went to the barn door and saw Mr. McClelland staring up at me in exactly the same place where Richard had thrown a pitchfork at him. I'd chosen a less aggressive form of rebellion. I looked down at him and pretended to look toward the back of the barn, as if to see someone leaving. At the same time, I said, "She's leaving now."

"Who's leaving now?"

"Some girl. She was hiding in our barn," I lied.

"What the hell are you talking about? Get a move on and finish your chores."

I'd dodged a bullet. I went about my work, finished in the upper barn, and went into the stables below. I fed the two cows and the bull, cleaned out the manure, and began milking the cows. However, I wasn't prepared for what happened next.

When I came out of the barn, I saw a state police car with a flashing light. Mr. McClelland was standing on the porch agitatedly talking to two policemen. Mom was leaning against the open screen door to the kitchen.

Mr. McClelland yelled, "Roger, come here!"

As I approached, I heard him say, "Yes, I'm certain that there was a runaway girl in my barn."

He pointed toward me and said, "I could hear the boy there talking to her."

The policemen turned to face me. I was scared. My maneuver to avoid punishment had backfired, and now I was facing the law. They motioned for me to come over while they said to Mr. McClelland, "We don't have any reports of missing girls."

They turned their full attention to me. One of them had a notepad. They began to question me.

"Your name, please?"

"Roger."

"Tell us about this girl. Did she give you her name? Where did she come from? How old was she? How long was she in the barn? What was she wearing?" The questions were fired at me like bullets tearing into my story. I made up answers as fast as I could, trying not to be inconsistent.

At one point in the interrogation, one of the policemen asked the question, "Was she a blonde or a brunette?" I froze. I suspected it was a trick question because I had no idea what a "brunette" was. I thought I was about to be found out, no matter how I answered the question. I went silent and the policemen looked at each other. Unexpectedly, Mr. McClelland jumped in and said, "There was someone there. I'm sure of it."

Mom looked at me hard and backed into the kitchen. The policemen looked at each other and asked me to take them to the barn and show where I'd seen her.

Once in the barn, they asked questions about who I was, how long I'd lived on the farm, if I was a foster child, and who else lived on the farm. I answered as best as I could, fearing that they were going to accuse me of lying. They did not. They left me and went back to their car and drove away slowly.

I'd told a big lie and gotten away with it. I hadn't been punished for being lazy. I've often wondered what those policemen really thought, but I never doubted that Mr. McClelland believed me. Although she never said a word, I could tell from Mom's looks that she didn't believe me. I vowed to myself to be a better worker and depend less on lies. However, even to this day, I've never been able to escape that deep internal feeling that I'm basically a lazy person who avoids work whenever possible and lies.

The next few months passed, and Mom seemed to be better although she still spent most of her time in the house. When summer came, the Aid Society arranged the second trip for me to see my mother in Miami. Richard was home on leave from the Army and helped out around the farm along with the Schaeffer boys while I was gone. When I returned from the trip, they told me that Mom's cancer had flared up again. I believed that she'd kept quiet about her worsening condition so that I could take that second trip to Florida. The one big difference between the two trips was that on the second trip there were no letters from Mom to me while I was away.

There was a growing silence in our home. An emotional aridness had taken up residence with us. The conversations were sparse and usually about the work that needed to be done. Although Aunt Lizzie would visit and other relatives of the McClellands would come and spend time, the visits were brief and only gave temporary relief. The visits did allow me to be alone and not feel the pressure to be on my best behavior in front of Mom.

It was a tangled and confusing time for me. I was living in two worlds, the world of work and the world of school. I told no one at school what was happening at home because I'd learned that no one really cared nor could understand that world. I'd begun to copy Richard's code of silence and kept to myself when it involved anything personal. At home, work was everywhere. I felt more and more trapped.

The Aid Society assigned me a male case worker, Mr. Molitor. He was a caring man. He would come to my high school and get permission for me to leave classes in order for us to meet. We would sit in his car where he would ask questions about how I was feeling. I didn't want to talk about my feelings, which were getting darker and more pessimistic. I felt sorry for him because it didn't seem fair to treat him as badly as I did, especially since he was trying so hard to communicate with me. However, I blamed the Aid Society for placing me in such a tough situation and didn't trust him enough to talk about what was really going on inside me. Besides, I had no idea when someone else would be assigned to me, so why waste my time trying to create a rapport with any social worker?

Chapter 30
Blows

One of the benefits of going to Central Bucks was that we took hot showers after gym class. Although I was embarrassed by how white my body was compared to the suntanned bodies of other boys, I liked washing and getting really clean. The Schaeffer boys felt the same way because at both our homes we bathed in water that was heated in buckets on our stoves. Richard had often joked, "We have hot running water if we run from the stove to the bathtub." In those showers we could get clean and eliminate the stink of manure and the smell of our sweat. We'd heard that other kids had talked about how we smelled, so we were glad to have the opportunity to stink less and be more like them. Showers were not the only benefit of gym class.

When I was in ninth grade, President Eisenhower launched his Presidential Youth Fitness Program designed to improve the health of America's youth. He believed it would strengthen the pool of recruits for military service. We were told about this program in gym class and how we were to be evaluated. We were expected to pass several exercise tests. These tests were offered as a contest to determine the most physically fit boy in our school. The winner of the contest would be the boy who, following the rules, could collect the most points for doing deep knee bends, squat thrusts, pull-ups, sit-ups, and push-ups.

I found that the exercises were easy to do. I finished second in the school in my ninth-grade year. The winner was a senior named Tell Schreiber whom I met for the first time during the finals of the contest. Tell was a personable athlete and a respected leader in the school. He was also known to be an excellent wrestler.

He saw how strong I was and spoke to me, "Roger, wow, you did amazingly well. Congratulations!"

"Thank you, but you did better. You won," I said.

"Thanks, but I'm in training for wrestling. You ought to go out for the team."

"Not me. I have to get home after school. There's a lot of work to be done."

"That may be, but I'll talk to Coach Williams about you anyway. You never know." He grinned and walked away.

A few days later, Coach Williams, who was also my guidance counselor, called me down to his office.

He looked at me with a broad smile and said, "Roger, I understand that you almost beat my best wrestler and the team captain in the physical fitness contest."

"Yes," I said. I knew where the conversation was headed.

"How about trying out for the team?"

"I can't. I have to work."

"Yes, Tell mentioned that you have a lot of work at home that you're expected to do that might make it impossible for you to participate."

"Yup."

"You live on a farm, right?"

"Yup."

"Do you know that there are other boys in school here who live on farms, and they go out for sports?" He went on, "I see that you are enrolled in the college preparatory curriculum. How are you doing?"

I was beginning to feel a little uneasy with all the questions, but I answered anyway, "Okay, I guess."

"If you were allowed to go out for wrestling, would you be interested?"

"Yes, I guess so, but I don't know anything about wrestling as a sport."

"Well, let me worry about that. In the meantime, give me a chance to see what I can do about your situation."

I left, wondering what he could do to get past Mr. McClelland. I knew for sure that I was not going to ask permission to go out for a sport and risk getting another no.

A few days later, when I was alone with Mom, she said, "I had an interesting call today from a Mr. Williams. He would like you to try out for the wrestling team. Would you like to do that?"

"Sure. But what about Daddy and all the work?"

"I talked to Mr. Williams about the work," she said. "He told me it was a winter sport. I thought that since the work in the winter isn't as demanding that maybe something could be arranged."

"What about Daddy?"

"He agreed to let you do this as long as all the chores get done."

I stood there amazed that I might be allowed to go out for a sport.

Mom went on, "Mr. Williams told me that if you were good enough, colleges might offer you a scholarship. That might be a way for you to go to college."

I could hardly believe what I was hearing. That was great news. Unexpected possibilities were opening up for me.

Later when I saw Mr. McClelland, he brought up the subject of staying after school to practice and how important it was that I come home on the late bus and get my chores done before dinner. I understood what he was telling me, but I had no idea about the consequences of that commitment.

I tried out for the team and made it easily since I was stronger than the other boys in my weight class. However, I quickly learned that more than strength was required to be a good wrestler. I lacked the finesse to move quickly and purposefully in order to win. There was pressure to perform as a wrestler and growing tension at home as Mom's health deteriorated.

By fall of tenth grade, Mom was going to the hospital almost every week for treatments. Aunt Lizzie was coming and staying longer, and other friends and relatives were making frequent visits. It was clear to me that Mom was dying. My work responsibilities kept increasing as did the ill will between Mr. McClelland and me. The more I had to be around him and his crude behaviors, the more I began to feel I hated him. At one point he came into the house looking for me when I was supposed to be working. He found me upstairs going through some old books. He cursed me for being lazy and not working and started to cuff me across the face and neck.

"You won't do that to me anymore!" I yelled at him. At the same time, I swung my fist and hit him squarely in the chest. It was the first time I'd ever hit him back. He fell backwards and hit the wall at the top of the stairs, too stunned to say a word. He looked at me as though I were a monster. He pushed past me and went downstairs. I followed him down and went outside and back to work. He never hit me again.

I had grown to abhor close contact with him. One of the activities that forced us to have close contact was the gothic experience of haircuts. Mr. McClelland always cut our hair, and Richard cut his until he went into the Army. After Richard left, I had to cut his hair while he continued to cut mine.

He had a barber's cloth, hand clippers, a thin comb, and a straight razor. We cut each other's hair about once a month. I could hardly tolerate the process. When he cut my hair, he would brush against me. He smelled like pigs and chickens mixed in with his body odors since he rarely bathed. His breath was heavy with the smell of old tobacco. I'm sure that his false teeth added to his awful breath. In addition, his manual dexterity had deteriorated as he aged so that he would sometimes move the hand clippers through my hair without squeezing them, which pulled my hair. The odors and hair pulling were not the worst of it.

He was an inveterate corncob pipe smoker. He would clench the pipe in his teeth while he cut my hair. I would watch warily as spittle accumulated slowly around his mouth and began to inch down the pipe stem toward its corncob bowl. The bubble of his frothy drool would grow larger and would slosh back and forth, threatening to drop on me as he moved around. I never knew when or where it would drop, but I knew that it could land on my neck, arm, or lap. Sometimes I would be lucky, and it would slip off onto the floor. I came to expect about five scalp pulls and three drops of drool per haircut.

There were times when he took the straight razor to trim my neck that I believed that he was going to do more than just nick me with the blade. In retrospect, I shouldn't have had that fear. I was, after all, an economic asset like any common laborer would be. In addition, I even brought in monthly support revenue from the Aid Society. He was a practical man. Thus, I had far less to be afraid of about him than I'd imagined at the time. In reality, I was becoming more of a threat to him and his property than he was to me. We were both caught in a tightening circle of conflict and pain as Mom wilted.

By the time winter came and my second wrestling season had arrived, Mom was confined to her chair and to the sofa in the living room, which was dark and isolated. She could no longer climb stairs. She still tried to contribute by cleaning eggs every day, but her ability to work was declining steadily. The rate of decline was reflected in fewer cleaned eggs per week. She continued to read her Bible every day.

Our minister, Reverend Linthicum, and other parishioners were coming regularly to visit with Mom. They brought gifts and cards. There were several visits from a woman representing Christian Scientists in the area, too. She prayed with Mom, who wasn't going to take the chance that the Methodists might not be as influential with God as the teachings of the Christian Scientists. We all knew she was dying a little every day and would be gone soon, but no one ever spoke about death. I knew that I was being punished by God for asking that one of the McClellands die just so that I could escape from work. I increasingly believed that I was lazy and selfish.

Wrestling was an outlet for me. Mr. Williams selected John Davis and me to go to schools in the region and put on demonstrations. John had a good build, too, and together we put on shows like those of professional wrestlers on TV. We took turns lifting each other into the air and dropping to the mat. We had fun playing in front of our young audiences.

When I was in actual matches, I wanted to succeed so badly and win that I would tense up and perform poorly and lose. Coach Williams used me strategically as a substitute in higher weight classes; since no one could pin me, it saved a couple of points for the team. My teammates would laugh when bigger wrestlers would try to pin me but were frustrated by the fact that my neck was so strong that no matter how hard they bounced me around, they could not flatten my shoulders to the mat for the pin.

Mr. McClelland didn't like the fact that wrestling made me late getting home. I despised the constant pressure to explain myself for being late after a practice or for going to an evening match. The breaking point came when I was at a league championship meet, which lasted into the evening. This particular meet was part of a series of progressive meets leading to the state championships. The wrestler from my school in my weight class was unable to wrestle because he didn't make his weight. Mr. Williams put me in as his replacement with little hope that I could win since the boy I was to wrestle was highly ranked in the state. It turned out that the boy made a mistake, and I was able to use my superior strength to pin him almost immediately. I won. I was elated and so was Mr. Williams because I was on my way to the next elimination level scheduled for the following week.

I came home late.

Mr. McClelland met me at the door and pushed me outside and out of Mom's earshot when I got home to say, "Goddammit, I thought you promised that you would get home in time to do your chores."

I started to say, "But—"

"Don't you 'but' me, you, sneaky, lazy sonofabitch."

He was raging. "Get your lazy ass out to the barn now! Milk those damn cows. I had to water all the chickens and give hay to the cows. Here I am doing all your work and you're off somewhere playing. That's the end of this wrestling joyride for you. It's over!"

He followed me all the way out to the barn, yelling the entire time. I never told him about my victory; since he was in such high dudgeon, he wouldn't have cared. What mattered was that I was late, and he had had to do some of my chores. I knew that I had to quit wrestling as punishment for being late. I was furious. He left. I threw forkfuls of manure out as far as I could, trying to get control of my anger.

I milked the first cow hurriedly. Then, I sat down on the stool to milk the second cow, whose udder was swollen with milk and probably tender to my touch when I pulled on her teats. She kicked the milk bucket and spilled the milk. Then it happened. My rage exploded. I stood up and punched her stomach and ribs over and over. I was lifting her up with the impact of my fist each time that I hit her. She cried out with a loud wail and tried to climb out of the stall, but the chain from her neck to her feed trough restrained her. Her dark eyes were wide open and showed great fear. She groaned and moaned from deep within. I'd completely lost control of myself. When it was over, breathing heavily I sat down and finished milking. I went into the house and up to my room too angry to eat supper.

The next day I quit wrestling. I told Mr. Williams that there was nothing that he could do about it. Mr. McClelland had ordered me to quit because I'd broken my word and there was too much work for him to do alone at home. There was no good explanation, but my wrestling was over and my teammates and Mr. Williams were stunned. They were not as stunned as I was later that day.

When I got home, the rendering truck was there. Mr. McClelland came up to me and told me that the cow had died in the pasture that afternoon. He'd called the vet and the vet examined the sick cow and said that she must have injured herself trying to jump over a fence. She died very soon after that. I knew that I'd killed her. At the time I didn't feel much of anything because part of me had died, too. I'd been punished after I'd been successful. I'd been denied the opportunity to be an athlete and maybe even a chance to go to college. Mr. McClelland controlled my life.

Chapter 31
Psalm 23

A gloominess, a pall hung in the air around the farm. My wrestling dreams had been squashed like an unwanted insect. My rage had killed a cow. My relationship with Mr. McClelland had become so rancorous that the only spoken words were about what work had to be done. Mom's health was steadily deteriorating. Each time Aunt Lizzie arrived to help out around the house, she pulled the shroud away and gave us new energy for a while.

Home from school one day in early April, I'd just stepped onto the porch when I overheard Aunt Lizzie scolding Mr. McClelland, "John, hurry up and clean up that blood before Roger gets here. He mustn't see that." I stopped and listened.

"He's seen plenty of blood," came the reply.

"Not Maud's blood, he hasn't."

I opened the door and saw Mr. McClelland wiping the floor with a mop. "What happened?" I asked.

"Your Mom had an accident," Aunt Lizzie said with concern.

"What kind of accident? Where is she?"

"She got sick and threw up some blood. We're waiting for Uncle Ted to arrive and take her and John to the hospital." Aunt Lizzie spoke, using her "I-am-in-charge" tone.

"John, here comes Ted now. Roger, grab Maud's suitcase upstairs. I've put some of her clean night things in it."

There was no arguing with Aunt Lizzie. Uncle Ted rushed in and carried Mom out to his car while Mr. McClelland helped. I handed the suitcase to Uncle Ted, who hurriedly tossed it into the trunk of the car.

Mr. McClelland turned to me before he closed the rear door and said, "Do all the chores, son." In that moment, I looked past him and saw Mom in her white nightgown and blood splatters on her front. Her eyes were closed, and her head was leaning back against the seat.

Aunt Lizzie and I watched silently as the car went up the lane. I wanted to know exactly what was going on.

"Aunt Lizzie, Mom's about to die, isn't she?" I asked the question even though I knew the answer. I just wanted someone to tell me.

"Yes, it seems that way. The doctors have done all they can for her. Now her fate is in God's hands. We need to pray for a miracle."

I didn't want her to die. The cow had died quickly and unexpectedly. Mom was dying slowly and predictably. I was responsible for both. Guilt surrounded me like a field of weeds.

"I'll pray for a miracle," I said without showing how hopeless I felt. The times between her relapses were getting shorter, and the strengths of her recoveries were diminishing. Recently, every day when I returned from school, I was worried about what I might find at home. Mom had lost interest in almost all that was happening around her. She slept most of the time on an improvised bed in the parlor. At times she would moan in her sleep or cry out. It was eerie, and it scared me.

Sometimes she would ask me to read from her Bible. She insisted that I start with Psalm 23 before reading verses. She would whisper it with me. The day before her last day at home, she didn't wake up. Aunt Lizzie had slept in a chair beside her bed in the parlor all night. At breakfast that morning, Aunt Lizzie had said it had been a rough sleeping night for Mom who'd moaned a lot.

I did all the chores that evening and afterwards ate the dinner that Aunt Lizzie had prepared. Little was said during dinner that night. Mr. McClelland came home after I was asleep. The next morning, I woke up before daylight and lay in bed thinking about Mom in the hospital and how bad I felt for her. She was quiet and kind. She was my safe haven. She listened to my dreams and encouraged me to do well in school. She always signed my report cards and complimented me on my grades and noticed when teachers commented on my good behaviors and habits. She was the one I could go to when I wanted to visit a friend, and then she would ask Mr. McClelland for permission. When he said no, I could see that she was sorry for me. She liked the wildflower bouquets that I would gather for her; she displayed them in a jar on the kitchen table. I wanted her to come home and be healthy again.

When daylight came, I got up and did my morning chores. After I finished, I joined Mr. McClelland and Aunt Lizzie for breakfast.

"How's Mom?" I asked.

"She's not doing well," Mr. McClelland answered. "Uncle Ted is taking me back to the hospital this afternoon. We'll see if the doctors will let her come home."

I could see that he was worried and so was Aunt Lizzie. "John, we'll pray for the best," she said to him.

When I came home that afternoon, Mr. McClelland was still at the hospital and I did the chores again. At dinner Aunt Lizzie spoke to me. "Roger, I know that today is your birthday. John was too distracted to remember this morning. I made a small chocolate cake for you. Maud and I talked about your birthday before she went to the hospital."

I could feel my eyes welling up. I couldn't let the tears start. I'd forgotten, too. Mom made chocolate cake for each of our birthdays. Sometimes Mr. McClelland's daughter and son-in-law would come with their daughters, and we would have a party.

This year they were at the hospital with Mom. I thanked Aunt Lizzie, and we each had a piece of the cake. Even though I'd eaten dinner and the cake, I still felt empty. That night for the first time in a long time, I cried in bed.

The next evening Uncle Ted took Mr. McClelland and me to the hospital to see Mom. She was by herself on a bed in the hallway of the hospital. I thought that the rooms must be too full. It didn't occur to me at the time that maybe there was no money or no hope for her and that they'd deposited her there until she died. There were tubes in her arms. She was lying on her back with her eyes closed and her mouth open. She was gasping loudly for breath. The noises were similar to the moans I heard when I was hitting the cow. The nurse told me that although she was heavily drugged and unconscious that I should speak to her. I tried to speak, but I couldn't say anything. People brushed by us in the hall and looked away.

I was afraid I was going to cry. My emotions were screaming at me to get out of the hospital and get away from the scene, which was so painful. I raced down the stairs to the outside steps and felt the damp air of the cold spring evening sweep over me. I wanted to tell her that I heard spring peepers the night before, that flowers would be blooming soon, that birds would be building nests, and that we would be planting seeds soon. I knew she wouldn't have heard me. I hoped that she would hear my thoughts and forgive me for being who I was. I wanted her to know that I would try to be a better person.

Uncle Ted drove us home, and I went to bed and fell asleep. I awoke suddenly and knew that Mom had died at that moment, which was 9:40 p.m. on my alarm clock. About ten minutes later, the telephone rang and I went downstairs. Someone from the hospital called to tell Mr. McClelland that Mom had passed. He hung up and turned to Aunt Lizzie and said, "She's gone." His face was expressionless. He wore the walled-off look of someone who had experienced many deaths.

"John, we all know it was a blessing for her to escape that horrible pain. God bless her." Aunt Lizzie had seen many deaths, too and knew how to see the good in the bad.

There were no more words, no hugs—just resignation and silence. I went back to bed with thoughts of Mom moving like shadows through my mind mixed with worries about what lay ahead. I remembered she'd said to me in one of her last coherent moments. "Roger, if you work hard, you'll do well, and if you're kind to others, you'll be happy." I wanted to have had a chance to talk about what she'd said, but I never did. She'd always worked hard. She was always kind to others. She seemed at peace.

The next morning after the chores were done, the phone rang constantly and people came and went. Reverend Linthicum came and took Mr. McClelland away. Aunt Lizzie called Richard at Fort Belvoir and told him what had happened. He promised to drive home for the funeral. Arrangements were made for a service and the burial. Everyone who had a role to play seemed to know what to do, and I faded into the background.

I was amazed by how many people showed up at the funeral service, most of whom I didn't know. Reverend Linthicum spoke about Mom's devotion to God and how she'd lived a good life and given so much to the community. It meant a lot to me that he and others knew her to be a caring and generous person who gave beyond her means.

Richard and I were pallbearers along with Uncle Ted and Brother Ed. I was grateful to have something to do. The coffin seemed to weigh only a little more than the wood it was made of. After the service many of the people came back to the farm and parked their cars around the barn, taking up all the available spaces to the point that some even parked in the field.

People gathered around the house inside and out. Some of the churchwomen had prepared food and placed it on boards, which lay across sawhorses in front of the house. Everyone was complimentary toward Mom. Eventually most of the people drove away. Some stayed and helped Aunt Lizzie to clean up. It was a gray day in my life, a day which was the gateway to living alone on the farm with Mr. McClelland.

Shortly after Mom died, Mr. Molitor visited me at school.

"Roger, tell me how you're feeling since Mrs. McClelland died?"

"I'm not feeling anything."

"Come on, Roger, you have to be feeling something."

Again, I copied Richard's approach—the less talk, the better. I felt numb and didn't want to tell anyone what I was feeling. My feelings were mixed, and they were mine. I wanted to hold on to them. I never shed a tear after Mom died, and I wasn't going to talk and maybe lose it in front of Mr. Molitor.

"This is what I know, Mr. Molitor. It's spring. There's more work to be done. I can't waste time thinking about or discussing my feelings." I pushed my body against the car door to get as far away from him as possible.

He sat silently. I stared straight ahead, feeling tense and threatened. I counted the electric poles, which I could see through the windshield.

"Roger, I've had several conversations with other staff members, some of whom knew you when they were your social worker, about your situation and what's best for you. You're sixteen and in two more years you'll age out of foster care. You've lived on the farm for the past twelve years. We don't know what's best for you. Whatever happens, we believe that it's best for you to stay in this school system. We know that you want to go to college, and changing schools and friends right now could hurt your chances. Besides, you're old enough to help make the decision."

He went on about the pros and cons of living on the farm and what the Aid Society knew from experience about moving children at my age to other families. I wasn't listening. I wanted them to make me leave the farm. I didn't want to face Mr. McClelland and tell him I wanted to leave. I felt guilty about my prayers and Mom's death, and I knew I should be punished for what I had done.

"What do you want to do, Roger?"

There it was. He'd put the dreaded question directly to me. I had to answer.

"The farm is my home. I agree that I should stay and graduate from Central Bucks High School. I'll stay." My stomach was churning and I felt awful, but I told him what I had to do. It was my penance.

Mr. Molitor seemed satisfied and relieved. Clearly, I'd made his life easier. He and the people at the Aid Society wouldn't have to search for another home for me and go through all the hassle of interviewing and evaluating potential parents.

"I'm sure that Mr. McClelland will be pleased by your decision," Mr. Molitor responded. "I think that you should tell him yourself tonight when you go home. You said that you don't talk to him very much, and maybe you could make this the start of a new chapter for the both of you."

"Yup. Thank you," I said. "I have to get back to my next class." We said our goodbyes, and I went back to school, feeling the added weight of my decision.

I didn't know what I was going to say to Mr. McClelland that night. Our relationship was almost nonexistent ever since Richard left and I'd become the only help for him on the farm. The night he berated me about being late and lazy, the night I'd killed the cow, was the night that something had snapped between us and our relationship was forever broken. Mom had been the intervener, but when she died, the decay of the relationship between Mr. McClelland and me was exposed. How was I even going to start a conversation about staying?

Aunt Lizzie was cleaning eggs, and Mr. McClelland was grading them. I was washing dishes when he spoke up, breaking the silence. "Son, you saw that man Molitor today. What happened?" I shrugged off the shudder that went through me every time he used the word "son" and said, "He thinks that it's best for everyone that I stay on the farm until I graduate." I knew that saying that I'd decided to stay could've implied that I had feelings toward him.

"That's good," he said matter-of-factly as if he knew that that was the only logical choice.

I took advantage of the relaxed moment and said, "The football coach wants me to come out for football this fall. Is that okay?"

"Football? I thought you did wrestling?"

"Wrestling is a winter sport. I thought that maybe I could do both." I didn't want to say anything to remind him of the night he ordered me to quit wrestling.

"If you play football, how much time does that take?"

"About the same as wrestling."

"Here's what I think. If we can get all the work done this spring and summer and you work hard, I'll let you go out for football in the fall."

"Promise?"

"Do you promise to work hard?"

"Yes."

There it was—an agreement witnessed by Aunt Lizzie. I knew that I could do the work. All I had to do was get through the spring and summer, and I could play football. Maybe I could get through these next two years one season at a time, and I'd be on my own.

Chapter 32
Ever Rarer Normalcy

Aunt Lizzie stayed with us for three weeks after Mom died. She prepared good meals, cleaned and organized the house, did laundry, and, most importantly, she was cheerful and pleasant to have around. She'd observed the two of us long enough to know that there would've been little or no conversation between Mr. McClelland and me without her interventions. She took it upon herself to provide the much-needed conversational lubricant between us. She asked questions and gave daily reports. She left us several pre-prepared meals in the refrigerator and departed with the promise to return in May.

After she left, it was all business. Mom's death had delayed the usual spring plowing and planting for potatoes. I'd also missed the deadline to get my third quarter report card signed. Mr. Finn, my homeroom teacher, had followed up with me to turn it in, and I knew I had to get Mr. McClelland to sign it. When I came home with that report card, he was waiting for me at his usual place at the kitchen table.

He greeted me by telling me the work lineup, "It's late in the season, but we still must plant potatoes."

I handed my report card to him and said, "Please sign this report card because my teacher, Mr. Finn, needs it." He was already getting up from his chair but sat down again and took the card. It was the first time that I ever saw him look at one.

He examined it. "Why are you taking Latin?"

"I have to have languages for college."

"No one speaks Latin anymore except Catholic priests.

You're not becoming one of them, are you?" I knew he was trying to be funny, but I wasn't going to give him anything and certainly not a smile.

He went on, "Why would any college want you to study that?" "Latin is a root language for other languages, including English," I said.

"Wouldn't it be better to take something practical like math?" "I am taking math. See, that course called plane geometry? It's a math course."

I pointed to the report card where it was abbreviated as "Pl. Geom." I momentarily felt sorry for him because the modern world had passed him. I had no idea what they'd taught him in Northern Ireland up to the time he left in eighth grade. I was sure it must have been very practical. He signed the card and pushed it toward me, saying, "I guess you know what you're doing. It's your life, but right now we have more important things to do." He got up from the table, and together we went outside to plant potatoes.

A few days later at school, the principal, Mr. Livingston, stopped me in the hall. "Roger, could you step into my office for a few minutes?"

I was startled and just a little concerned. The last time I'd been in his office he was warning me about fighting. At the time, I could tell that he was pleased that I'd beaten up the school bully, but he had the responsibility as the principal to caution me. He'd told me that fighting was not the way to settle arguments of any sort, and I'd be punished if I got in another fight.

"Roger, please sit down." He went around his big desk and seated himself.

His smile made me relax a little, and I asked, "Is everything okay?"

"Yes, everything is excellent," he said. Then, he paused and gave me a serious look. "I understand that your mother passed away a few weeks ago. I'm sorry for your loss. It must be hard."

"It'll be okay. How did you find out?"

"One of the teachers told me. She saw it in the newspaper." His expression changed, and he said, "I'm sure that she'd be very proud of you for what I'm going to tell you next."

I waited.

He went on, "Every year the faculty selects a student graduating from their sophomore year to represent our school at Boy's State. It is a one-week summer program designed to teach leadership and communication skills in a government setting. This year, Roger, we've selected you. Congratulations. It won't cost anything since we give you a scholarship to attend."

I was immediately conflicted. I knew it was an honor, and I wanted to do it. However, I knew Mr. McClelland wouldn't let me be away from the farm for a week. I managed a thank you.

He must've seen how hesitant I was. "Roger, what's the matter? You look uncertain."

"It's my father. There's too much work to do on our farm. He won't let me go."

"Really? I'm sure he can find a way to get by without you for a week."

"No, he can't. He's old, and he needs the help. There's so much extra work in the summer."

Mr. Livingston looked at me patiently and said, "Well, we'll see about that."

When I left his office, I felt bad. I knew that there was no way that I would be allowed to go. In addition, there would be a lot of trouble for me if Mr. Livingston called and tried to persuade Mr. McClelland to let me go.

I found out that I was right about trouble when I went home that day after school. Mr. McClelland was outside on the porch with his pipe clenched in his teeth. He greeted me by saying,

"Why did you have the principal call me about some damfool program? What were you thinking? You knew that you can't be going away, especially now that Mom has died."

"I didn't ask anyone to call you. I told the principal that I had too much work to do and that I had to be here."

"Don't forget, you promised me that you would work all summer. If you do, I'll let you go out for football this fall. Remember?"

"I remember. I already told them I couldn't go." The issue had been settled the only way that I knew it could be: there would be no week away. The rule was that work out-prioritized everything. I knew that breaks from work would have to be brief and had to be taken after all the work was done for the day. Bernd Waitl helped to make those breaks fun.

I knew Bernd from church and the skunk incident in seventh grade. He immigrated to the United States after World War Two. Mr. McClelland, who'd fought the Germans in World War One, was suspicious of him. Mom liked him because he went to our church in Chalfont and because he filled the role of an older brother for me after Richard left.

Bernd loved cars. He had a black Chevy convertible with a white top, which he kept in pristine condition. He would show up on the farm on summer evenings and help me with my chores, or help complete any field work that I might have been doing, and then take me to get ice cream. Sometimes on a Sunday afternoon, we would ride together with loud music playing and the top down. We would go to his favorite Italian sub shop for a hoagie. Cars became a way to escape from the farm.

Although we didn't have any vehicles, I knew that I needed a license if I were to be able to drive anyone else's car. Another friend of mine, Bill Triest, who lived nearby, was sixteen, too. He'd gotten his driver's license and was able to drive one of his parents' cars.

One evening I said, "Bill, I think I should get a driver's license."

"You don't have anything to drive," he said. "What good would it do you?"

"Maybe Harry would let me drive his car once in a while." Harry, who'd recently bought a car, was one of the foster children that lived at the Schaeffers.

"I'll talk to my mom and see what can be done, Roger," Bill said casually.

Not long after that conversation, Mrs. Triest came to our farm determined to drive me to Doylestown so that I could take the driver's test. She was always well dressed, attractive, and very polite. She got out of her jeep and said, "Hello, Mr. McClelland. I would like to take Roger to get his driver's license on Tuesday when they give the tests. What time would be best for you?"

I knew that he considered the Triests to be rich city people. I was a little worried about his reaction.

I expected him to say, "Who are you to come here and take Roger away for some tomfoolery?" Instead, he said, "Mrs. Triest, we don't have a car or a truck. There's nothing here for him to drive except the tractor, and he doesn't need a license to drive it."

"He's sixteen now. All of his friends are getting their licenses. Don't you want him to be able to drive someone's car in an emergency?" she responded respectfully.

He looked at me, "Son, is this something you want to do?"

I wasn't going to argue with Mrs. Triest. "Yes."

"Well, then, go ahead. You can tomorrow. Be quick about it. We have work to do when you get back." It was clear to me that he didn't want to look like a bad person to Mrs. Triest.

Just like that, on Tuesday, I was on my way to get a driver's license.

When I got into her vehicle and we drove away, she turned

to me with a pretty smile. "Well, I thought he might change his mind overnight. It turned out better than I thought."

"Yes" was all I could muster because I was already focused on how she was driving. The jeep was a standard with a floor shift. Mrs. Triest was very pleasant, and I wanted to please her. I couldn't tell her that I'd never driven a car. I watched how magically and smoothly she shifted the gears while still talking. I had a lot to learn before we got to Doylestown.

The driving test area was filled with cars. We had to wait in a long line. Anxiety began to overtake me. I knew that soon I'd be expected to perform driving tasks, which I'd never done. We sat there together watching policemen ahead of us. They would get into cars on the passenger side, and the young unlicensed candidate drivers would drive away with them to take the test.

My turn came. Mrs. Triest got out of the jeep, I moved over to the driver's side, and a policeman opened the passenger side door and sat down beside me. He had a clipboard. He asked me some questions and told me that I had passed the written exam and that all I had to do was follow his instructions as I was driving.

Trouble started with the turn of the key. I hadn't depressed the clutch enough. The car began lurching. I quickly depressed the clutch to the floor, the engine idled smoothly, and I exhaled a sigh of relief. I put it into gear and let the clutch out too fast, and the jeep stumbled forward.

The policeman looked at me and said, "Nervous, son?"

I started slower the next time. All went well until I gained enough speed and had to shift again. I ground the gears, hit the brakes instead of the clutch, and we jerked to a stop in the middle of the road. The policeman looked at me and asked, "Have you driven this vehicle before?"

I said, "No." He reached over and turned off the ignition and calmly got out of the jeep and walked around to my side and

motioned for me to move over to the passenger side.
He climbed in, saying, "If I drive, it'll be safer for both of us."
He started the engine and drove us back to the parking lot. When
we got there, he stepped out and handed the keys to Mrs. Triest.
"Ma'am, he did well on the written exam but failed the
driver's test. He needs to practice before coming back."

I was so embarrassed that I wanted to melt into the upholstery
and disappear. Mrs. Triest, who was an exceptionally proper lady,
said, "Roger, it would've been very helpful to know that you'd never
driven a standard shift before we drove all the way into town."

"Yes, I should've told you. I apologize for taking so much
of your time." I doubted that I would ever get another chance.
I was mistaken again because in a couple of weeks she drove up
in her Buick, which had an automatic shift. I was able to pass
the test with a different policeman. I was deeply appreciative of
her kindness and thanked her repeatedly on the way home. She
smiled in acknowledgement.

Mr. Triest also took a special interest in me that summer. He
knew that Bill and I were friends and had spoken to me a number
of times when I was at his house. I was curious about him since
he was a businessman who travelled the world to contract for
the purchase of vanilla beans. He was lanky, tall, smiled easily,
and carried himself with confidence. In every aspect, he was the
picture of what I imagined a successful international businessman
would look like.

I was flattered when he said to me, "Roger, would you like
to learn how to play tennis?"

"I don't know anything about tennis."

"Well, I love the sport, and I think that you might grow to
love it, too." He'd been an excellent tennis instructor and player
as a younger man and had shelves filled with trophies in his den
to show for it.

"I don't have much time to practice, and it looks like it takes a lot of time to be any good," I said.

"We have a place in the Poconos and have our own full-sized tennis court. How would you like to go up there with me one weekend?"

I was surprised. "I have to ask if I can go. We have a lot of work to do."

"I see. Let me worry about asking Mr. McClelland for you, Roger."

I really didn't feel comfortable about having anyone ask Mr. McClelland for me to skip work, but I thought that maybe it was better that he ask Mr. McClelland than if I did.

Mr. McClelland came to me a couple of days later and said, "What have you been up to with Mr. Triest? He came into the field this afternoon while I was cultivating and asked to take you to the Poconos for the weekend."

"He wants to teach me to play tennis."

"I thought you were going to play football?"

"They're not the same," I said.

"What, do you take me for a fool? Of course, they're not the same. This seems like one of your schemes to get out of work. That's what's the same. Another damn scheme."

I felt beaten back. What little talking we did always hurt. "What did you tell him?"

"I told him that we had too much work to do to let you go running off somewhere for a weekend. He kept pressing me and said that it might do you some good to get away from the farm for a day or two."

I was amazed that Mr. Triest pushed so hard.

"I finally told him that you could go Saturday afternoon but that you had to be back to do the evening chores on Sunday. But, we have to find someone to help out while you're gone."

I was so startled that all I could say was, "Thank you. That would be great!" I thought of Ralph, one of the foster kids who lived with the Schaeffers. I'd helped the Schaeffers when Mr. Triest had taken Ralph to a Phillies game. He was a good friend. I had no idea how good until later.

Ralph agreed to do my chores for me while I was away. Mr. Triest drove me to his summer home in the Poconos. He taught me the very basics about serving and ground strokes. He also talked nonstop about tennis and the great players at the time. He specifically emphasized an Australian tennis professional named Roy Emerson. Emerson had strong wrists because he'd milked cows; those strong wrists helped him endure long, hard volleys and helped him to beat his opponents. Although Mr. Triest never mentioned it specifically, I suspected that he thought that because I milked cows that I might have the same type of strong wrists that would help me to be a good tennis player.

The best part of the trip for me was having the full attention of a man for a few hours who was about the right age to be my father. I got to see part of the world that I knew existed for other boys, but not me.

Chapter 33
Perfectly Imperfect Pass

Mr. Molitor showed up unexpectedly in July. I was riding the combine, tying off hundred-pound bags of wheat, and tossing them down at the pre-arranged spot on the field when I first saw him. There was nothing I could do to stop the machine since the combine driver was a contractor who needed to get the job done as quickly as possible. Besides, he wouldn't have heard me over the sounds of the machine if I'd yelled out. I bagged the grain, the driver drove the combine, and Mr. Molitor stood at the edge of the field in the hot sun waiting for me to finish.

After a few more turns around the field, I saw Mr. McClelland standing there talking to Mr. Molitor. They went away and disappeared into the house. We finished harvesting the wheat, and I went from the field to the house while the contractor checked his combine and prepared it for the trip to another farmer's wheat field.

I found them sitting with glasses of water at the table. They stood when I came in, and Mr. Molitor shook my hand. Mr. McClelland brushed by me, saying, "I have to go pay Mr. Gargas for harvesting our wheat. I hope that you two won't be too long because we have to get those bags in before it storms."

I looked at Mr. Molitor to see his reaction. Seeing none, I got myself a glass of water and came back to the table and sat down. I was covered in wheat chaff and hadn't taken the time to wash it off my face and arms.

"How have you been, Roger?"

"Okay, I guess." Richard's code of silence was in full force.

"I wanted to stop by and check in on you and see how you were doing and to bring you some news. That looks like hard work throwing those bags of wheat around."

"You get used to it. It's not bad." I was aware of my sweaty dirty clothes in contrast to his white shirt and tie and gray dress pants. He was clearly a city person. I remembered that he'd told me that my sister called me a "country bumpkin," and I imagined that in his mind that I fit the description to a tee on that day. He'd been my social worker for longer than any of the others and knew more about me than they did and seemed to care more about me, as well.

There was a long pause. He appeared to be waiting for me to say something more, but I did not. Finally, he said, "Your mother has been in touch with us. She was sorry to hear from us that Mrs. McClelland died." I noted that he mentioned that she'd heard from them instead of me and sat back to hear what else he had to say.

"Her brother, Bob Laurie, who lives in Springfield just outside of Philadelphia, would like to come and see you."

"I heard about him once before. How many other relatives are there who live nearby?"

"Funny. That's exactly the same question that your dad asked, too. We don't know of any others."

"What does he want to see me for?"

"He has a son who's your cousin whom he thinks you should know. He wants to visit you."

"When does he want to come?"

"This Sunday."

"Okay. You came all the way out here just to tell me that I had a cousin in addition to an uncle nearby and to ask me if I wanted to meet with him?"

"No, actually I was out here to meet with the Thomas

brothers who live in Plumsteadville. Do you know them?"

"I've heard of them. Never met them, though."

"Roger, why don't you tell me exactly how things are?"

Mr. Molitor was a nice man. However, I wasn't going to open up and tell him much. I knew from Richard that talking about feelings was not a good idea. It would lead to more and more questions, and what would they do about it anyway? I'd resolved to stay until I graduated and then get out. One thing I was sure of was that I didn't want to live in Miami and that was the only move I figured they could make. Besides, Richard's brothers had visited us here and he stayed.

"Everything is okay. I'll be playing football this fall."

"You will? You should do well because you look strong and seem to be in excellent condition." He looked me over again and said, "Don't forget to use your clothing allowance and buy some new clothes for work and for school."

"What clothing allowance?"

"We've included an extra thirty-eight dollars per month in the checks we send here ever since we stopped giving you clothes when you visited us at the Aid Society. I assume that Mrs. McClelland handled all of that."

"I didn't know that there was a special allowance for clothes."

"Do you want me to talk to Mr. McClelland about it?"

"No, I'll handle it." The last thing I wanted was to have someone from the Aid Society ordering Mr. McClelland to hand over money to me. It would seem to him that I'd been complaining about something. He was especially sensitive about money. That would anger him for sure. It made sense, though, that Mom had been ordering my clothes from those catalogs and that she'd been getting money to do it. The last thing I could see him doing was to order clothes from a catalog for me.

I sensed that he was relieved that he didn't have to talk to

Mr. McClelland about the clothing allowance or anything else for that matter. The conversation ended, and Mr. Molitor left with the understanding that he would tell my uncle that it would be okay to visit Sunday afternoon. I wondered what that visit would be like but didn't give it much thought since there was plenty of work to do before then.

I recalled that Richard had two of his brothers visit him in his junior year. I had no idea why they suddenly appeared since Richard had had no contact with anyone from his bloodline family ever. When they arrived, Richard had sat in the kitchen about as far away from them as possible. Although they seemed friendly and wanted to talk to Richard, he sat silently staring at them as though to say, "Why are you both here anyway?" I wondered at the time why Richard was so disinterested, but I was about to gain some insight.

My uncle arrived as promised in a bright shiny new car along with his wife. Interestingly, his wife's name was Ruth, which was the same as his sister, my mother. He was a little taller than I was, had a stocky build, and had reddish blond hair with freckles on his arms. He didn't look like he was related to me. His wife didn't seem interested in being on the farm or near me.

Mr. McClelland was nowhere to be seen. We walked around the farm buildings and talked. My uncle asked a lot of questions about how I was doing in school, what courses I was taking, what sports I played, and whether I was really interested in going to college. It was more of an interview than a friendly conversation. He may have realized that he was asking too many questions. He paused to tell me some things that he remembered about me.

"Roger, I knew you as a baby before you were put in foster care. Later, I saw you when you were a little boy, a toddler. You lived in Philadelphia. The neighbor family next to your foster home at the time wanted to adopt you. They thought you were a cute baby, and they wanted a boy."

"Were they neighbors to the Perry-Ferrys?

"No, this was before you moved in with them."

"What happened?"

"Well, they went to the Aid Society and asked about you. The Aid Society discussed it with Ruth, and she wouldn't agree to it."

"Why not?"

"She believed that eventually you would live with her."

"Well, that didn't happen. Did you know my father?"

"You know that Mr. Saillant is not your real father—right?"

"I know that."

"Yes, I knew your real father," my uncle replied.

"What was he like?"

"I'm sorry to say that he wasn't a very nice person."

"Is he still alive?"

"I don't know, but it wouldn't surprise me if he weren't alive. He had a bad temper and often got into fights."

"When I was in Miami, my mother said that she thought that he might be in prison or living in South America."

"Could be. I think you're better off not knowing him."

His statements aligned perfectly with what the McClellands had always told me about my blood parents—they were no good and I was better off without them in my life. My mother was okay, but not someone I wanted to live with, certainly not in Miami.

"Why did you come today?"

"We wanted to meet you. Ruth said that you were a good boy and doing well in school and were thinking about college. I wanted to tell you that you have a cousin named Robert and he's an excellent baseball player."

"What position does he play?"

"He has a strong arm and is a good pitcher. He plays the outfield, too."

"Why didn't he come today?"

"He doesn't know we're here."

Uncle Bob's wife remained silent and stayed at a distance. I saw her looking me over several times, but she kept her thoughts to herself.

When he said that his son didn't know they were on the farm, the conversation was over for me. I believed that they wanted to check me out to see if I was good enough to be a part of their family. Based on some comments he made, I knew that he and my mother didn't get along. In addition, my biological mother never mentioned to me that she had a brother. They were pleasant to me, but when they left, I had the feeling that I would never see them again, which turned out to be true. I'd failed inspection. What a waste of my time.

As they drove up the lane, Mr. McClelland appeared on the path coming back from the pigpens. "They didn't stay long. What did they want?" he asked.

"I think that they just wanted to meet me," I replied tonelessly. I walked away, regretting that I'd talked to them and feeling abandoned again. I'd learned to put up a good front so that no one knew how sad I felt inside. Least of all, I didn't want Mr. McClelland to know. My mother had left me because she and my father were bad people. Their dark shadows loomed around me. I knew I was bad, too. That evening I did something that made me feel even worse.

The Schaeffers had multiple foster children. Their children came to them through the Lutheran Church. We referred to them as "from the Lutheran Home" as though that had a special meaning. To me, it only meant that the boys were placed there because some Lutheran families had failed to stay together and the parents couldn't raise their children. They were the same as us. Neither the Schaeffers nor the McClellands were supportive of the boys from the two families getting together as frequently as we did. There was a lot of work to be done on both farms, which helped to keep us separated. I think that both sets of parents believed that "idle hands were the devil's workshop." There certainly was some truth in that for us. But they were old and we were young, and it was difficult for them to keep track of us all of the time.

Ralph Dunstan was one of the foster children who lived with the Schaeffers. He and I were friends, but we were headed in different directions. He was a good worker, a poor student, and an excellent athlete. When we were in school, the pickup teams during recess competed to see who would have him on their team. He was never allowed to play organized sports in high school because the Schaeffers needed him to work and do chores on their farm.

I had a large old house mirror that I used to signal to him when I wanted him to come over and hang out. Late afternoon on that Sunday was one of those times. I flashed his front porch with reflected sunlight. He saw it and came over without being caught.

"Did you hear the game today?" Ralph asked, meaning the Phillies, since he was a great fan.

"No," I replied. "I had a visit from my uncle."

"I didn't know you had an uncle. Where do they live?"

"They live somewhere near Ambler."

"How did the visit go?"

"It was okay, I guess. It was a little strange, though."

"What do you mean, 'strange'?" He picked up our football and was passing it back and forth between his hands.

"He asked a lot of questions about what I was doing. He brought his wife, and they didn't stay long."

He tossed the football to me. The conversation stopped as we began to pass it back and forth in earnest. I enjoyed watching him toss perfect spiral passes to me. I couldn't help but reflect on him and his abilities and his future. If he'd been able to play organized football, I was sure that he could've developed his skills in a competitive environment and probably been a good quarterback. He needed a break or otherwise he was going to be like so many others in foster care who wouldn't make it through high school and would be employed in some unskilled job on a farm or in a factory.

While we were playing, we moved from behind the barn to an area in front of our big tractor shed in order to be out of sight from those across the street. Ralph saw a large funnel used to put gas in the tractor sitting on a sawhorse and picked it up. The rusty funnel was very large. In fact, it was so large that Ralph put it to his mouth like a megaphone and began to give a play-by-play report of a football game.

I was the quarterback, dancing back and forth on the driveway, making fake handoffs, and launching deep passes as Ralph called out the plays. We were into the moment and having fun when in an instant the idea to throw the football into the wide end of the funnel came to me. I threw a perfect pass. It hit the funnel. Ralph dropped to the ground instantly. I raced to him. His face was already covered with blood. My throw had driven the sharp edges of the funnel into his lips and broken off half of his left front tooth.

He didn't cry. As he lay there bleeding, I got some cloths soaked in water and began to wipe his face. I kept apologizing. I did what I could to staunch the bleeding. I was frantic. I'd hurt a friend. I'd taken a moment of fun and transformed it into something horrible. Slowly he got up. He was too stunned to be mad at me. We both knew that there would be big trouble for us and a lot more trouble for me if anyone found out that he'd gotten hurt playing. By now it was nighttime.

"I've got to get home." He spoke through the wet cloth that

he was pressing to his face.

"I'll go with you until we get to the road."

He nodded.

I walked across the field with him, giving him some support and apologizing all the way.

When we got to the road, he stopped me. "Roger, get out of here before they hear or see us. I'll take care of it."

I headed home, scared and worried. Mr. McClelland was watching Ed Sullivan on television when I got home. I nodded good night and went to bed.

The next day Mr. Schaeffer came through the field where we were hoeing corn. I braced myself.

Mr. Schaeffer started by saying, "Do you know what that dumb shit Ralph did last night?"

Before anyone could say anything, Mr. Schaeffer said, "He fell out of bed and cut his lip on a nail and broke his tooth. Good lawd-see, what a dumb kid." His favorite expression was "good lawd-see." I never knew what that expression meant. But for sure, that time it meant that Ralph had lied for me and spared me a lot of trouble. I owed him a lot for his loyalty. Dark shadows were growing inside me, selectively nourished by memories of the bad things I'd done.

What I didn't know at the time was that Mr. Triest was going to pay to have plastic surgery done on Ralph's disfigured lip and have the tooth repaired. He also gave Ralph the chance to try out for a minor league team.

Chapter 34
It's Who You Know

I loved to drive the tractor. We'd sold the two Belgian workhorses the day after Richard joined the Army. Selling the horses eliminated the chores around their care and increased our efficiency significantly. Furthermore, a tractor was easier to manage than a team of horses. You placed it in gear, engaged the clutch, and started to steer.

When the tractor moved, I daydreamed, isolated from the world. The loud sound of the tractor formed an impenetrable sound wall. My eyes were focused on the work in the field ahead. My hands felt the vibrations of the engine rippling through the steering wheel. I smelled the engine exhaust heading into the wind and the freshness of the newly worked field in the absence of exhaust in my face. If I'd opened my mouth, I would have tasted dust. I was working in a bubble without the fear of being called lazy while my mind wandered.

I was driving the tractor two days after I'd injured Ralph. The tractor was attached to a side delivery rake, which swept the wheat straw to form a long snake-like ribbon through the field suitable for baling. My thoughts were not on the job, which was boringly simple. "Why did my uncle come? Why was I so careless with Ralph? Would he be okay? Would he be able to keep quiet about what really happened? How am I going to address the issue of the thirty-eight dollars a month for my clothes with Mr. McClelland?"

Talking about money with him was always a problem. He was true to the Scotch-Irish stereotype. He'd given me garden space to raise vegetables and sell them when I was nine. I earned a couple of hundred dollars a year. A year after Richard left, I found that I didn't have enough time to care for a garden. I stopped raising vegetables to sell. Mr. McClelland knew that I wanted to save money for college. He offered me another opportunity to make money. When I was fourteen, he gave me a runt from one of the hog litters and a stall and told me to raise the pig and sell it. I raised it but decided not to sell it since it was a sow. I bred her and she had fifteen piglets. He gave me an acre of corn to feed the pigs, and I bought some hog feed to supplement the corn. I sold the thirteen that lived to Mr. Foley for good money. The sow was pregnant again.

I knew that he would believe that he'd been overly generous by giving me land and a pig as a way to build a bankroll for college; therefore, why should I ask him for the thirty-eight dollars when he'd already given me more money than he believed I deserved? I believed for certain that he would say, "Buy your own damn clothes. You already have plenty of money based on the opportunities I've given you."

In addition, the tension between us was growing. It created a barrier so high that almost all conversation between us was eliminated. I even feared that he might try to kill me. I knew that he'd not forgotten that I'd hit him. There were two situations which I could not forget that had really frightened me.

He'd given me the job to paint the tin roof of the house just like Richard and I had done on the barn a few years earlier. The house roof was much higher than the barn, and there were only rocks to fall onto, not a barn hill. He'd set up the job like the barn-roof painting operation with ropes and ladders anchored to the cultivator. I double-checked everything before climbing up the extension ladder to paint the roof. I worked as quickly as possible all morning and had the job about half done by noon.

After doing the noon chores and having lunch, I climbed back up to paint. When I climbed onto the ladder lying on the roof, it started to slide. In that brief moment I thought that he'd untied the rope. Instantly I was filled with fear. Fortunately, it slid only a few inches and stopped. What had probably happened was that the rope had expanded in the heat over lunch and the ladder slid to take up the slack.

Another job, which he'd given me, was to lower the extension ladder into the 20-foot well and climb down and dig out the accumulated silt. When I went down into the well, I imagined that he would pull the ladder up and leave me there. To prevent him from retrieving the ladder, I kept one foot on the bottom rung. Attached to the ladder with one foot, I was still able to dig out the silt and shovel it into a bucket, which he hoisted up and dumped into a wagon. At one point he yelled down to me, "Roger, it would be easier to dig if you'd take your foot off the ladder!"

I called back up, "Yes, I know, but the bottom seems so unstable that I might slip and fall." It took some time, but I managed to get the job done and climbed back up the ladder to safety.

My distrust of him was deeply ingrained. Looking back at the side delivery rake, I recalled a time when he'd tricked me. Richard and I were greasing the various moving parts of the rake. To grease it properly, we had to rotate the toothed bars. During one rotation, my index finger was caught between the toothed bar and the frame. The pain of the fingernail being almost ripped off was horrific. I stepped back and saw blood flowing out of my finger and the hanging fingernail. I wrapped my finger in my tee shirt and raced home to get it into water. I was yelling. When I got to the house, Mr. McClelland was already coming out to see what I was shouting about.

"What happened?" he asked.

"I got my finger caught in the rake when we were greasing it."

I wasn't crying because I knew not to be around Mr. McClelland.

"Here let me see how bad it is," he said, trying to calm me down.

I unwrapped the bloody tee shirt to show him.

He saw it. Instantly he pulled the hanging nail off my finger exactly as he had with my first loose tooth. I grimaced with pain and anger. Why had I trusted him again?

When I finished raking, my daydreaming was over for that day. I drove the tractor to the edge of the field and unhitched the rake. The next day we would bale the straw, load it on a wagon, and haul it to the barn where it would be stacked in the haymow. I looked forward to the next day because I knew that my friend, Bill Triest, would come and help.

Bill and I met one morning at the bus stop at the beginning of eighth grade. He and his older sister had been driven to the corner in their jeep and dropped off by their mother. It was the first time that I'd stood at the bus stop without Richard, and I was glad that I wasn't going to be waiting alone. He was trim and tall with short blond hair.

He started the conversation, "Hi! My name is Bill, and this is my sister Deana."

"Hi, I'm Roger."

"Where do you live?" he asked. Before I could answer, he said, "We live down on Creek Road on the property with the white fence around it."

"I live on the farm at the top of the hill on the left." It was good that I said that because Ralph Dunstan was coming down the hill to join us from his farm on the right. More introductions were made.

Bill smiled a lot. He seemed like a nice guy. "Are you in ninth grade?" I asked since he was taller than I was.

"No, I'm in eighth grade and Deana is in tenth. What grades are you guys in?"

"We're both in eighth, too," Ralph had spoken up.

At that moment Bill saw a bird overhead. "Look at that hawk!" "Hmm," I thought, "he's a city kid." Then I pointed out, "Actually, that's a buzzard."

"No, no, that's a hawk," Bill countered.

"Bill, don't start something over a bird," his sister had spoken up. He liked to argue because he was bright and liked to exercise his mind by making his points, good or bad. We became friends. Although his father was a successful businessman, Bill liked agriculture. He became a member of the Future Farmers of America at school, bought a Black Angus steer from the Weeds, a local farmer who raised cattle, and came to our farm to learn more about farming firsthand. He helped me. We had good conversations, and arguments, about multiple topics.

He had a genuine passion for anything related to agriculture. He asked as many questions as an investigative reporter, and like a good reporter he would not be deterred until he had the facts.

In his sophomore year, he became particularly interested in the economics of our farm, probably because it was a part of a project he was doing. He wanted to know how many dozens of eggs we sold a week, how many pigs we sold a year, how much feed we bought, how long we kept the chickens before we sold them, and so forth. The economics of our farm didn't make sense to him. He classified us as subsistence farmers, without including the small fee the Children's Aid Society paid the McClellands or my free labor. He was the perfect choice to discuss the problem of the clothing money and what I should do.

Bill came the next day and helped to load the bales of straw on our wagon and unload them in the barn. Mr. McClelland had two hernias, which limited the amount of lifting he could do. Bill's help made the work easier for me. Besides, while we worked, we talked.

"Bill, do you know how much money your mother spends

on your school clothes?" I asked.

"I don't know. Why do you want to know that?"

"I was wondering if thirty-eight dollars a month would be enough to get good clothes, is all."

"I think so," he said. "If you don't have to buy very expensive shoes or a suit, it should be enough. That's a pretty exact number. Is that your allowance for clothes?"

I said yes and dropped the conversation. I didn't want Bill to know that Mr. McClelland had been getting money for me and hadn't told me about it. We were friends, but there was personal stuff about me that I didn't want to share. I was afraid it might get back to his parents. Bill went home later that afternoon when the work was done. I was left with the realization that since school was starting soon, I would have to buy clothes, which meant I would have to ask Mr. McClelland for the money or take it out of my savings, which I didn't want to do. Although I did not want to ask him for anything, let alone money, I'd have to find a way to do it.

The next day Mr. McGlaughlin, who lived on Creek Road, came by to update me on what was happening for football. His son was a year behind me and played. Luckily for me, Mr. McGlaughlin came up when Mr. McClelland was there.

"Hello, John," he said. "It looks like our boys will be playing football together this fall."

Mr. McClelland nodded and turned to me and said, "Did you tell everyone?"

"He didn't tell me. Coach Maskas told me. He's excited that Roger will be going out for the team this year. I'm here to tell Roger that practice starts in two weeks."

"Are you sure? School doesn't start for another month," said Mr. McClelland.

"Oh, I'm sure alright. There are two weeks of double practices each day before school starts."

Mr. McClelland's face grew taut; he wasn't happy about the news. I didn't know about the double sessions, and my mind began racing to figure out how I could get the work done and still do two practices a day. I was glad that Mr. McGlaughlin had told him and not me.

Mr. McGlaughlin offered one more thing before he left, "I came to tell you that I can drive you the first week, Roger, but after that, you'll have to find another way. I'll be back on Monday morning two weeks from now at 8:30 sharp to pick you up."

I thanked him, and he drove away, leaving Mr. McClelland staring at me. He stood there for a few long moments before he said, "Okay. So, that's the way it's going to be. Remember, you still have to get your work done." I knew exactly what he meant. In the past, when there was a difficult request to be made of Mr. McClelland, I would talk it over with Mom and she would usually ask for me. I didn't have to ask about starting football practice because Mr. McGlaughlin had done that for me. I still needed to get clothes for school.

That weekend Aunt Lizzie arrived with her usual cheerful smile. She busied herself washing clothes, cleaning up around the house, and making meals. She noticed that Mr. McClelland and I were still not talking to each other. When I was alone with her, she asked me what was going on. I explained to her about football practice and the way Mr. McClelland found out. I also told her about the clothing allowance and the fact that I needed some new clothes for school. That evening at supper she worked her magic.

"Roger, I understand you'll be going back to school soon?"

"Yes," I answered.

"Will you be needing new clothes?"

"Yes."

"Maybe your friend Bernd can take you to the Montgomeryville Market in that new car of his?"

"That's a good idea. I could ask him."

"John, Maud had told me that the Aid Society gave you a monthly clothing allowance for Roger. Is that right?"

He shifted in his seat and said, "Yes, now that you mention it. I'll give him some money tomorrow or before he goes with Bernd to the market."

"That's wonderful. Roger, be sure to get a good pair of shoes, too."

The next day he gave me over a hundred dollars to go buy clothes. I was grateful to Aunt Lizzie and relieved that I hadn't had to ask for the money.

I kept my promise about the farm work, so when the first Monday for practice came, I was ready at the end of the lane for Mr. McGlaughlin. During that first week I had to get up early, do my chores, and wait for Mr. McGlaughlin. After the morning practice I would catch a ride back to the farm with the McGlaughlins, work until late afternoon, and ride back for the evening practices. From what I could tell, none of the other guys were doing anything more than just showing up for the practices. I was very conscientious and never late. The second week he and his son were staying at their place on the Delaware River, which meant that I had to run, walk, or hitchhike to the practices.

The early season practices ended with a scrimmage against Downingtown on a Saturday afternoon. The scrimmage was held about ten miles from my home. The longer distance made it impossible for me to do my work on the farm and get to the scrimmage on time. I was late. The coaches sat me down on the bench as punishment for being late. Mr. McGlaughlin saw me sitting at the end of the bench with tears in my eyes. He went to the coach and spoke to him quietly. I don't know what he said, but the coach then went over to some of the players and talked for a few moments. He spoke to John Davis, who stood up and pointed to me and spoke to the team. I saw that they all nodded in agreement.

Coach Maskas came over to me and said that I could play. Mr. McGlaughlin had spoken on my behalf and so had John Davis. I often lacked someone to speak up for me. I was grateful to Mr. McGlaughlin for saying something to the coach and for John Davis speaking to his teammates. I appreciated being included. I played defense that afternoon and played well.

As the football season progressed, I made more contributions. I didn't start in our first nonleague game against Bensalem. It didn't seem fair because I thought that I was the quickest and strongest defensive lineman. I was aware of parents talking to the coaches and calling attention to their sons and representing them, but it didn't really sink in just how influential the booster clubs and lobbying parents could be on coaches. I really thought it was all about pure performance. I believed that by putting the best players into a game you increased your chances of winning. My chance to play in that first game came very late. The coach walked over to me and said, "Roger, I want you to go in and block that field goal attempt." I was used to taking orders and wanted to please. I burst through the line and blocked the kick. We won the game.

On Monday, following the varsity game, there was a junior varsity (JV) game in which I was a starter. I outplayed everyone and dominated the line play. I was like King Kong, marching through lines of little people, bowling them over at will. They couldn't match my strength and speed, no more than they could match the anger in me. Football afforded me the opportunity to bash other boys legally. I hungered to unleash all my pent-up frustration from my work-and-no-play life on opposing players. The JV coach benched me after a couple of quarters, witnessing how aggressive I was. I never played JV football in high school again.

At the end of the season all kinds of awards were given out to the various players on the team. Of course, I was unaware of the award process because I'd never been part of organized sports. After the last game and before the awards banquet, Coach Maskas took me aside. He told me that in his mind I was clearly the most improved player on the team, having begun with no experience. And, yet, I'd become a starter and a real key factor, which helped the team have a winning season. However, he was going to give the most improved player award to one of the seniors because he thought it would improve his chances to get into a college. I knew who the player was, and I knew his father was president of the booster club.

Chapter 35
Simply Curiosity

"Tell me, Roger, how's school?" were the first words Mr. Molitor asked each time we met in his parked car outside of Central Bucks High School. When he asked this time, I was thinking about home and work.

"School's fine."

"Football season is over. How was that for you?"

"Practices were boring, but playing was fun. I was a starting defensive guard."

"You were. That was quite an accomplishment for your first year."

"Yeah, the coach thought I was the most improved player, but he gave the award to someone else."

"Why did he do that?"

"The kid who won is a senior and he thought he needed to be recognized to help him get into college. Besides, his father was the head of the booster club."

"How did that make you feel?"

"Like I always feel. Just not good enough."

"But the coach said you were the most improved player. That meant you were good enough, right?"

I wasn't going to show weakness to anyone, especially a social worker. "I had fun playing. That's all that matters."

"I see. What made it fun to play?"

"I got to hit others as hard as I could. It was okay as long as I played by the rules. Sometimes I hit so hard with a 'forearm shiver' that the other players had to be helped off the field."

"I can see why a coach might like that," said Mr. Molitor. "Didn't you feel a little sorry for the other players?"

"No, not at all."

He gave me a worried look. Then he asked, "How are things at home? Are you getting along okay with Mr. McClelland? There must be a lot to do around the house now that your mom is gone. Who does the cooking? Is your Aunt Lizzie still there?"

"Aunt Lizzie comes about once a month. When she's there, everything goes better. She cleans the house, washes our clothes, cooks, and when she leaves, there are extra meals in the refrigerator."

"And when she's not there, how do things go?"

"Look! A lot of work has to be done. I don't want to complain or anything, but we don't talk much. He cleans and sorts eggs like Mom used to do while I make dinner after the outside chores are done."

"Really, you cook dinner?"

"Who else is there? I don't cook anything complicated. I boil some potatoes and mash them or open a can of sauerkraut and warm it up, or maybe fry some hot dogs or chicken. Sometimes I fry scrapple for breakfast and dinner–it's good. Stuff like that."

The more questions Mr. Molitor asked, the more uncomfortable I became. My answers became shorter in an effort to avoid telling him how I really felt. I wasn't going to tell him that playing football made things worse at home. On top of that, when I came home one day, Mr. McClelland had thrown the newspaper across the table at me and said, "I thought you were playing football? They describe all of these other players on the sports page but never mention you." I told him that they were backs and that I was a lineman, and that linemen never get mentioned. He shrugged as if to say, "What a waste of time." Mr. Molitor seemed to be a nice person. He was the first male social worker I had, which made me wonder why he took the job. Maybe he couldn't do anything else? I believed that he had no idea what I really felt.

I knew my muscles made me stronger than the other kids. But there were negatives, too. One day Ron Shane, who was riding alongside of me on the school bus, said out of the blue, "My father told me that you'll die young. Since you have all those muscles, you also have an enlarged heart." I knew that Ron's father was a butcher in the meatpacking business and probably saw a lot of hearts. Outwardly, I ignored what he said, but inwardly I wondered what I'd done to provoke that comment and whether there was some truth to it. What hurt even more was that Ron was on the wrestling team with me and was one of the better wrestlers. I felt ashamed of the whiteness of my body compared to the tanned bodies of the other kids in gym, but my muscles helped to offset that deficiency in appearance. I felt good about my strength when Bill Triest admired my physique, but Ron's pessimistic assessment fit into a growing pattern of self-pity and self-hate.

I was an abandoned child. When Richard left, I was abandoned again. The only reason families kept me was because the Aid Society paid them money to keep me. I was a thief who stole from stores and from other kids like Eddie Boyle. I broke into people's homes. I'd set fire to the Wolfe's garage. I was lazy and worthless. I'd killed one of our two milk cows with my bare hands. I'd prayed that one of the McClellands would die. When Mom died, I felt overwhelmed with guilt. I deserved to stay on the farm and work as punishment for my terrible thoughts and prayers. Deep down, I knew I was a bad person. Miss Hanisch was right—I wasn't that smart. I'd researched so-called 'gifted children' in the school library and found that I wasn't gifted. I'd met others who were. I'd scarred Ralph for life. I was a phony.

I smiled and pretended to be a good kid when I wasn't. These gloomy thoughts tumbled around inside of me and became part of my life whenever I was alone.

There was no way that I was going to talk to Mr. Molitor about these thoughts. If I told him how bad I felt, I'd have to explain all the awful things I'd done. Then what would he do?

I couldn't tell him that I would sit in class filling sheets of paper with the sentences: *Roger is ugly. Roger is bad. I hate Roger.*

I began to think about suicide. It felt better and better to think about killing myself. It felt so good to think about it. It began to excite me. I felt worthless and lazy, and the more I thought about it, the more seductive the idea of suicide became. Suicidal ideation was nourishing something deep and ugly inside me. I was becoming addicted to dark thoughts. The dark mood was drawing me in, swallowing me.

I remembered that when I was about seven years old, Dr. Binswanger, our veterinarian at the time, killed himself with a shotgun. They said he'd set the gun on the floor, put the barrel in his mouth, and used his toe to push the trigger. No one understood why he'd done it, or at least no one talked about it to me so that I would've understood why he killed himself.

I became fixated on my .22 and how I could kill myself with it. I was afraid of trying to kill myself by jumping off the barn roof. I'd fallen from that roof and had not been hurt. I worried that if I jumped and was just paralyzed, I'd be a cripple for the rest of my life and be even more despised than I already was. No, jumping was too risky; the gun was the right and certain way to do it.

The suicidal ideation grew stronger and stronger. The justification for self-punishment grew, and triggered addictive chemistries in me. I was wallowing in the stream of those chemicals triggered by self-loathing. The more I hated myself, the better it felt. The thoughts of ending my life created a slippery slope, and I was on it.

The week before Christmas, I took the .22 and went to the grain storage room in the barn. I stuck the .22 in my mouth. My teeth gripped the hard barrel. The cold barrel on my lips sent shivers through me. I could taste the rusty steel on my tongue.

I sat there with the barrel in my mouth, willing my finger to pull the trigger. I tried to summon the courage to end my life. I kept going over and over what it would mean to be dead. I was curious about my future. I knew that I only had to live on the farm for seventeen more months. The first time I tried to kill myself and did not, I blamed myself for being a coward. The next day I tried and failed again. I didn't stop from pulling the trigger because I suddenly felt loved, or cared for, or that I was really not that lazy or had any worthwhile abilities. I just couldn't make myself pull the trigger because I was curious about what I might eventually miss.

Even if no one else cared about me, I felt selfishly that things could change if I stayed alive, but nothing would change if I killed myself. My life would just end without my experiencing the possibility of really good things happening to me.

Dancing with the darkness was electrifying and seductive. Being helpless and feeling hopeless added to the seduction. I believed that no one, not anyone anywhere, cared whether or not I lived or died.

What happened to me? What made me stop? Simply—curiosity. I was curious about what my life might offer. I was curious about getting answers to all sorts of questions, from scientific ones to ideas that I might discover in books. I knew for certain that if I died, there would be no answers.

Chapter 36
Rumination and Regret

I was in my eleventh-grade history class when an announcement came over the PA system. "There's been an accident in the cafeteria. The sirens you may hear are for an ambulance and a firetruck. Everyone should remain calm and stay in their current class. We will tell you when it is all clear to proceed to your next class."

Although we'd heard the sirens, we had no idea that it pertained to our school. My classmates whispered but abruptly stopped when our teacher spoke, "Settle down. We're all curious about what's happened, but now is not the time to add to the confusion."

When the all-clear message came, we went to our next class. The hallways were filled with students making guesses about what had happened. I found out immediately since my next class was chemistry. Mr. Schaeffer told us.

"Boys and girls, as I've told you, chemicals can be dangerous. What just happened was a careless accident. One of our seniors was standing in line, holding a test tube filled with chemicals. Apparently, the heat of his hand was sufficient to initiate a detonation. The explosion badly damaged some of his fingers and ignited the blouse of the girl standing in front of him. They've both been taken to the hospital for treatment."

One of the students asked the obvious questions, "Who's the guy? Who's the girl?"

"I'm not free to say right now," said Mr. Schaeffer. He added, "Fortunately, they were the only two people involved in the accident."

Another student asked, "What were the chemicals?"

"I'm not going to share that information with you. Chemicals can be very dangerous, especially in the hands of untrained people. We don't need another accident. I've frequently told you that you shouldn't handle chemicals outside of the laboratory. We can all take that to heart based on today's accident."

A week or so later just before Christmas, I spoke to Garry Spear, the boy who was holding the test tube when it exploded.

"Garry, glad to see you back in school. How are you? What exactly happened anyway?"

He held up his heavily bandaged right hand and said, "Blew two fingers off at the first knuckle and my little finger. That's what happened."

"That's awful," I said sympathetically. "What were the chemicals?"

He studied me thoughtfully for a moment before he responded cryptically, "Let's say that not everything mixes well with sugar. I'm not supposed to say anything about the chemicals." When he said that, he moved away and went down the hall where other students had started to gather to talk to him. Garry was a quiet person who kept to himself most of the time.

I left school that day, trying to guess what chemicals he could've possibly mixed with sugar to make it explode. The next day was a Friday, which was the day before Christmas. The first Christmas without Mom. It wasn't going to be fun because the weather was very cold and the ground was starting to freeze. If the ground were frozen hard enough, it meant that we would haul manure. Richard used to say, "It's Christmas Day, you can't play, you can't sit, gotta get going to haul the shit." I missed his humor. Over the holidays, I was faced with a few days of working alone with Mr. McClelland.

Hauling manure in the winter was a lot better than some other outside jobs. We threw forks filled with manure out of the pigpens, chicken coops, and henhouses and made piles. These piles gradually decomposed, giving off heat. When we dug into the piles with our forks to load the manure spreader, the heat warmed us. There was less smell in the winter, too, compared to the summer. We loaded together silently. When we had a full load, I would drive the tractor to the field where I would spread the manure. The two of us working together got a lot done that day. My mind was very active and fully aligned with the devil.

I was angry. I was alone with a man whom I despised. He was making me work on Christmas and most any other time that I was available. I was allowed to play sports if it didn't interfere with my chores and other farming responsibilities. He was always dirty. He had repulsive personal habits. I was disgusted by his behaviors. I resented the situation I was in and wanted to find a way out.

I'd turned from thinking of killing myself to killing him. I justified my thoughts by ruminating on the many times he'd sabotaged my fun.

I thought about the time Mr. VanAlstyne asked him if we could go fishing on a Sunday. Mr. McClelland agreed to let me go as long as I got back in time to do the evening chores. Mr. VanAlstyne and I drove to Barnegat Lighthouse State Park and talked all the way down and back. He needed a son, and I needed a real father.

"Roger, I love to fish. When we were boys like you growing up, we used to go fishing all the time."

"What kind of fish did you catch?" I asked. "One time I caught a sucker."

"Well, boy, we fished for bass and trout. Suckers are too bony."

"Uncle Jack, what kind of fish are we going to catch today?" He liked it when I called him Uncle Jack.

"That's the spirit. You're positive. You didn't say, 'What kind of fish are we going to fish for today?' Too many people think 'trying' is all you have to do. You have to believe that you'll be successful, and nine times out of ten you will be."

"You grew up in New York—right?"

"Elmira, in fact. Not far from Ithaca and Cornell University. We used to play pranks on the so-called 'Cornell Men.'"

"Like what?"

"We'd go up the hill to where they parked with their girls and put potatoes in their exhaust pipes. Sometimes we would let the air out of their tires."

"Then what?"

"We would pull up beside them and blow the horn of our car. They'd try to start their cars and couldn't, and we'd laugh."

On that trip he relived his childhood while he taught me how to surf-fish. We each caught a bluefish. I knew Mr. McClelland would be excited to get fresh fish for dinner. When we got home, it was dusk. We opened the trunk to show him the fish. Mr. McClelland cursed Mr. VanAlstyne for making me late.

Mr. VanAlstyne was quiet. He tried to give him my fish. "Here's the fish the boy caught for you," he said.

Mr. McClelland cursed, "I don't want your damn fish. Keep it. I told you to get him home in time for his chores. You're over an hour late, and the work still has to be done."

The memory of how Mr. McClelland treated Mr. VanAlstyne that evening and how slowly he drove away clung to me like the smell of manure.

There were times when Bernd would drive up in his '49 Chevy, anxious to go somewhere and have fun. Bernd had to help me finish my work if I were going to go with him. If we did slip away to get some ice cream or go get a Philly cheesesteak sandwich, we always had to come straight back to the farm. We'd eat the treats behind the barn as if we'd stolen them and had to hide. Everyone who came, whether it was one of the Schaeffer boys or Bill Triest, was expected to work in order to free me to do something with them.

That Christmas Day was filled with a lot of bad memories. Inside, I was filled with malice toward Mr. McClelland, and like a loaded capacitor, I was going to discharge that anger in some way. At the end of that day, I resolved to build a bomb. A bomb might kill him, injure him, or scare him. It didn't matter what happened because it would guarantee that I'd be able to leave the farm. My anger and frustration blinded me. I had no concern about what the consequences for me might be for committing a horrific act—a crime.

I needed to get Garry Spear to tell me what he had in that test tube. When I went back to school after the holiday, I tracked Garry down in study hall. His hand was still bandaged.

"Garry, what chemicals were in that test tube besides sugar?"

"I'm not allowed to say," he answered. I could tell that he wanted to tell me something but was afraid to.

He spoke to me, "This is the second time you've expressed an interest in knowing about the contents of that test tube. Why are you so interested?"

I was ready for the question. "I like chemistry and I like to experiment. Besides, I live on a farm and we have groundhogs, and I'd like to figure out how to get rid of them. I was thinking that I could blast them out of their holes."

"I thought maybe you lived on a farm. Here's what I can suggest. Go to the library and study the composition of fertilizers." After he told me that, he walked away.

When I had a chance, I did go to the library and learned a lot about fertilizers. Garry was right; the farm had all that I needed to make a mixture that would explode—a bomb. I handcrafted a crude prototype and tested it in the field behind the barn. It detonated but didn't go off at the desired time. However, when it did explode, there was a loud *pop* and it burned the area where it was placed. By the time I made another device, there'd been a snowstorm with snow so deep that we had to shovel the snow from the lane and make paths to the various outbuildings. I thought that the snow would make a perfect cover.

On the Saturday afternoon after the snowstorm, I waited until Mr. McClelland left the house to collect eggs. I knew his routine well, and I knew how long he would be out and which path he would follow on his return. I placed the makeshift bomb in the snowbank where I could witness the explosion from the house. I waited for him to return. While I was watching, I began to realize for the first time that what I was doing could really kill him or injure him so badly that I would be sent to jail. I'd been so absorbed by the idea of making the bomb and doing harm, and so filled with hate that I'd lost my ability to think. My rage had hijacked my rational thought processes. I was about to kill a man this time and not a cow.

I saw him coming up the path with two buckets filled with eggs, one in each hand. He was walking, bent into the north wind with flurries of snow blowing by him. He looked small wrapped in multiple old gray sweaters. He didn't have a jacket. He added and subtracted sweaters based on the temperature. He was wearing an old-fashioned Irish herringbone flat hat pulled down low on his forehead. He looked frail and cold with his pipe sticking out of the side of his mouth.

In that instant, I regretted what I'd been thinking and what I'd set up to happen. I prayed that the bomb wouldn't go off. He seemed to go too slowly past where I'd placed it. I breathed a deep sigh of relief and thanked God when he was safely on the walk to the house. As he came in, I slipped out the other porch

door in order to retrieve the bomb before it went off.
I used a long-handled pitchfork to lift it out of the snow and
move it to the pasture. I think it didn't detonate because of the
coldness of the snow.

Chapter 37
The Mountains of Tennessee

I liked English. I was in English class just after New Year's when a note was delivered to my classroom telling me to report to the office. I was certain that I'd done nothing wrong but still wondered what was up. Mr. Molitor greeted me when I arrived. Instead of taking me outside to his car, he took me to a wide-open area adjacent to the auditorium where a few desks and chairs were located. We sat down close to where I'd sat when I was reeking with skunk odor.

Mr. Molitor began by saying, "I apologize for the unexpected visit."

"This is a surprise," I said. I was on full alert.

"Yes, I'm sure it is, but I was in the area and thought I'd check up on you since I haven't seen you for almost a month."

Then, he began with his usual social worker talk. "Tell me, Roger, how are things in school?"

"Pretty good, I guess."

"I know I pulled you out of English class. What are you studying now?"

"Right now, we're reading some of the works of Edgar Allan Poe."

"He wrote scary short stories, right?"

"Yes, he wrote poetry, too. I like his poem 'The Bells,'" I said.

"Really, what's that about?"

"It's a great example of writing using onomatopoeia. He's trying to create the sound of bells by the words he uses in the poem. He has one line that I really like where he used *tintinnabulation*, a word that he made up."

"I seem to recall that word from my school days. Remind me of the line."

"I don't remember that line, just the word. The lines I do remember are: 'While the stars that oversprinkle / All the heavens, seem to twinkle.'"

"Why do you like those lines compared to all the rest?" he asked.

"Because when we're shoveling snow late at night and I stop and look up, I see the heavens filled with bright stars twinkling at me. I'm so filled with awe that I don't feel cold or tired. His words remind me of those night skies."

Mr. Molitor paused for a few moments and then said, "I see. Why are you working late at night shoveling snow?"

"We have to clear the lane so that trucks can come and deliver feed and pick up our eggs the next day."

"Don't you have a snowplow?"

"It's okay. Shoveling snow is a lot better than shoveling manure."

At that moment the bell rang to end the period. The hallways immediately filled with students, some of whom looked at us sitting at the desk as they passed by.

Mr. Molitor stayed a while longer and asked questions about how things were at home and whether Mr. McClelland and I were talking much. I avoided answering the questions. When he asked me what I'd gotten for Christmas, I knew I had to say something specific. I didn't want to tell him that Mom always handled Christmas for us and that Mr. McClelland never gave us anything.

"This Christmas was different without Mom," I said.

"How so?"

"She used to make or buy treats for us like a cake or cookies, and she always gave us shirts and socks. We didn't make treats this year. Mr. McClelland doesn't shop."

"What did Mr. McClelland give you?" He asked that question

with a firmness that was out of character for him.

I squirmed and said, "He gave me ammunition for my .22, some money, and a good pair of work gloves." I had to say something. I didn't want to say he only gave me some money. I knew he rarely left the farm and certainly would never go out just to shop. I was uncertain that my answers satisfied Mr. Molitor. He told me that the next time he would like to talk to my guidance counselor and maybe one or two of my teachers. I said that it was fine with me. Privately, I thought that it was better that he speak to them rather than to me anyway. That session had made me feel uncomfortable. I felt like he was probing me harder than usual and that there was something else on his mind.

When he got up to go, he said, "I'll be back to see you in a couple of weeks. I'll let you know the next time before I arrive."

We parted and I went to my next class. When I arrived in class, several of the students looked at me as if to inquire about why I could be late without permission. I sat next to Scott Pierson. He was a friend whom I'd met in seventh grade. He was a very good student and a good athlete. We got along well. Once I settled into my desk, he leaned over to me and whispered, "Who was that guy you were with?"

"Let's talk later."

He persisted with one more question. "Is that your social worker?"

I nodded yes.

Later outside of class, Scott asked, "How's it going at home? Are you still working all the time?"

"You know, Scott. This won't last."

"What do you mean by saying, 'It won't last'?"

"I have a plan."

"What kind of plan?"

"Scott, let's just say that you won't see me around here when spring comes and the weather is warm." I knew I had to wait until warmer weather because there had been an amazing snowstorm two years ago in March of 1958. The snow was so deep that the roads were blocked for days. The drifts were very high, and I had made several tunnels through them so that I could get to the chicken houses. I didn't want to run away and get caught in a big snowstorm.

"Are they going to move you?"

"No, I'm going to move me."

"Are you thinking about running away?"

"No one will find me in the mountains of Tennessee." I was beginning to tell him my dream plan. I'd first become aware of Tennessee because of the Davy Crockett song and stories. I liked the pictures of the lush green mountains and the idea of hunting and fishing and living off the land. I would be free.

"I don't think that would be a good idea. What about college?"

"The only thing I care about now is getting away from the farm."

"I have to go home, but we should talk more about this tomorrow. You have a lot of friends here, Roger, who would miss you."

His statement about friends saddened me. Even though I knew I had friends intellectually, emotionally I was alone. I believed that I was like the character in Hawthorne's story "Rappaccini's Daughter"—toxic to everyone around me.

When I went home that evening, I was greeted by an agitated Mr. McClelland.

"That guy, Molitor from Children's Aid, stopped by to see me this afternoon. Do you know anything about that?"

"I don't know anything about him stopping by to see you," I said. "What did he want?"

"He asked a lot of questions about our business here. He

was even nosing around the buildings and asking if we had a snowplow. What do you suppose he was up to? Did you see him today at school?"

"Yes."

"What did you tell him?"

"We just talked about school and English class."

"You must've said something more than that to have him come here like he did."

"Nothing that I know of. He's a city person. You never know what they're thinking about."

"You should be careful about what you say to him from now on. I don't want him snooping around again like he was today."

That conversation was more than we'd had in weeks, if not months. I knew why Mr. Molitor was there, and I knew that he hadn't believed me about shoveling the lane. He thought I was a liar. I resolved to keep to myself around him for sure. Richard was right again. Talking frankly to social workers had bad repercussions. They couldn't be trusted because they had no idea what happened around the farm, and they didn't really want to know. For some reason this time, he'd come by to check things out. I wondered why he was suddenly showing interest in my situation. Not knowing, I shrugged and did my chores.

Things were quiet for the next several weeks until one evening Mr. McClelland stopped cleaning eggs and spoke to me.

"Mr. Molitor called today. He told me to tell you that he'd be at school tomorrow and wants to see you."

"Did he say why?"

"No, he just said that he'd see you at the same time as the last visit."

"Okay."

"This time you need to be more careful what you say to him."

"Sure," I said. I didn't care what Mr. McClelland told me to say when I was talking to Mr. Molitor. I didn't want Mr. Molitor prying into my feelings, but as far as the farm situation was concerned, I would say what I wanted.

The next day I was pulled from English class again to meet Mr. Molitor. This time he took me to our class guidance counselor's office, the office of Mr. Williams who left when we entered. I could tell that they knew each other and that something was up. Mr. Molitor sat down alongside me instead of behind Mr. Williams's desk. Sitting as close as we were, I noticed the dark mole on the cheek of his pale white face. I tried not to stare at it. There was tension. I knew I was in some kind of trouble.

"Tell me, Roger, how are things in school?"

"They're okay. I assume that Mr. Williams knows better than I do." I made the assumption since I believed that they'd been talking.

"He has a good opinion of you and your work here."

"Phew! For a minute there, I thought I might be in trouble."

"No, you're not in trouble. In fact, I understand that you're running for student council president."

"Yes. I'm considered a long shot."

"Well, you never know how those things can turn out."

The small talk was making me even more uncomfortable. It continued for a few more minutes, and then he got to the point.

"Roger, we're taking you out of Mr. McClelland's care tomorrow."

My heart skipped. I felt lightheaded. "Holy mackerel," I thought, "I'm being moved." I sat there stunned.

Mr. Molitor looked at me as if bracing himself for an explosive reaction. "Do you understand what I just said? We're moving you tomorrow."

"I have work to do. Mr. McClelland depends on me."

"We know that. He depends on you too much. We've let this

situation persist far too long after Mrs. McClelland died."

"Does he know?"

"Yes, I told him before I came to school. Didn't he tell you last night that I was stopping to see him, too?"

"He only told me that you were coming to see me, not anything about you visiting him. How did he take it?"

"Well, frankly, he told me to go to hell and left me standing on the porch."

I wasn't surprised by that reaction. I felt guilty about leaving him with all that work. At the same time, I was deeply relieved to be getting out of there. I felt excitement growing inside me.

"Where are you moving me to?"

"I understand that you and Scott Pierson are good friends."

"Yes."

"His parents have agreed to be your new foster parents."

I didn't know his parents or anyone in his family other than Scott, for that matter. I did recall that he'd introduced me to his mother at the National Honor Society ceremony a few months ago. I was swept up by many thoughts until his words dragged me back to the conversation.

"What are Scott's parents like? What's his family like?"

"They're good people. There are three other children in the family besides Scott. I've met them all except for the oldest son, Bob, who's in college. He's studying to be a chemist, by the way. Mr. Pierson is a landscape architect. Mrs. Pierson teaches school at Buckingham Friends. Scott has a younger brother named Dennis, and a much younger sister named Susan. I'm sure you'll like them."

"Are any of them foster children?"

"No, they're all biological children of Mr. and Mrs. Pierson."

"They live in Buckingham—right?"

"Yes, they do. You'll meet them tomorrow

at their house."

"How will I get there?"

"You've been excused from school tomorrow. I'll pick you up at the farm at 11 a.m. Be packed and ready to go."

"What should I say to Mr. McClelland?" I had some fear that there could be a macabre incident like in the Poe stories and I could end up in a crypt somewhere.

"I recommend that you say as little as possible. Pack and be ready. If there's any talking to be done, I'll do it."

I went home that day knowing that it would be the last time I would do chores on that farm, make dinner in that kitchen, or sleep in that house. I'd been trapped in a maze. No matter what I'd thought or what path I took, I hadn't been able to find a way out or find the cheese. And now suddenly, the walls of the maze had disappeared and there was going to be cheese everywhere. There was no explanation; it was a blessing. A miracle that I didn't deserve. I was abandoning the farm before I was "aged out" of the foster care system. It didn't feel right to move into another home. Richard would be really upset. In his mind he'd stayed loyal to the family that had raised him. I had not.

I did not see Mr. McClelland when I got home. I knew what my chores were and I did them. For dinner I boiled some potatoes and mashed them and fried some liver with onions; they were warming on the coal stove ready to be served when he showed up at dinner time. He did not speak a word and just sat down at his place at the table. I served the dinner, and, although I had very little appetite, I ate. The room was thick with silence. Even the dogs were unusually quiet. Then he spoke.

"You realize what's happening here, don't you? After all that Mum and I did to give you a home when no one else cared about you, you're just leaving me to run this place by myself. We gave you land to have a garden and raise vegetables to sell, we gave you pigs to raise, we gave you corn to feed the pigs, and we gave you opportunities to earn extra money doing work for others. I was going to support you if you wanted to go to the National Farm School in Doylestown. You're throwing all that away to go live somewhere else. Now those people in that family will get all the fame and glory, and I'll get nothing."

I sat silently while he raged at me for being ungrateful. Eventually, I got up, cleared the table, fed the dogs the scraps, and washed the dishes. I took two cardboard boxes from the shed, carried them up to my room, and packed.

Chapter 38
Fresh Start

The next day was partly cloudy and unusually warm for early March. I had cloudy and warm feelings, too. I felt some gloominess about leaving, mixed with tempered optimism about what might lay ahead.

I took my time doing my chores and tried to avoid Mr. McClelland. We passed each other a couple of times, and when we did, he looked at the ground and said nothing. I was toughened to his behavior of abusing me with his silence, while his actions galvanized my feelings about escaping. When I finished my chores and went to the house, he'd already gone out to harrow one of the fields. I made some scrapple and eggs for breakfast, ate, washed the dishes, and sat down. I waited in one of Richard's chairs by the kitchen window so that I could see Mr. Molitor's car when it came down the lane.

When I saw him coming, I carried my packed boxes out and set them down at the edge of the driveway. Mr. Molitor parked the car, got out, and opened the trunk.

"Good morning, Roger. Are you ready to go?"

"Yes," I said and loaded the two boxes and the little brown travel case that I'd used for my trip to Florida in the trunk.

He gave me a puzzled look and said, "Is this all you have?"

"Yes, I have everything I need. I have some stuff from my past, I have what I need for the present, and in this box are some things for my future," I said as I pointed to each container.

"I see," he said with a smile. "You seem pretty well organized."

He looked around and asked, "Where's Mr. McClelland?

Don't you want to say goodbye?"

"He's harrowing that field over there," I said, pointing toward the Schaeffer farm. We could hear the *putt-putt* of the tractor in the distance and see Mr. McClelland with his flat tweed hat pulled down on his forehead with the usual corncob pipe jutting from the side of his mouth. As we drove out the lane that day, I felt I'd betrayed him by leaving the farm and all of the work that he'd have to do alone. Bernd Waitl told me a few weeks later that Mr. McClelland sold all the pigs, chickens, and cows, as well as the corn in the cribs the day after I left. I felt better knowing that he wasn't struggling to manage the farm by himself.

We rode along for a mile or so until Mr. Molitor spoke. "Roger, I'm curious about what you said about dividing your belongings into three categories. What did you mean by past, present, and future?"

"I meant that I have things from my past like report cards, a couple of letters from Mom, a Bible, the first novel I read, and a few pictures. You know—memories. In another box I have everything I need right now like underclothes, socks, some school shirts, a pair of clean pants, and my good shoes."

Materially, I was prepared; emotionally, I didn't know what to expect. My mind wandered to the time when I moved from the Perry-Ferrys to the McClellands. I recalled the bottles of ginger ale and how I'd clutched them. I wondered if I were clutching the small suitcase on this move. There was also the parallel that a parent's death eventually led to a move again.

"How old are the Piersons?" I asked.

"I would say that they are in their late-forties."

Before I could ask something else, Mr. Molitor questioned me, "What do you have in the future box?"

I answered even though I was a little embarrassed to share my dream. "I've been preparing for college. When I was in eighth grade, I bought a dictionary, which I think I'll need. When I was in ninth grade, I purchased a book of famous quotations. And, last year I bought a Tower typewriter."

"Really! You've been thinking ahead. The Piersons will be a perfect home for you."

"Why is that?" I asked.

"Both Mr. and Mrs. Pierson are college educated. Their oldest son, Robert, is in college, and you know Scott is definitely going to go to college. They value education. Your goals will align perfectly with their expectations for their children."

"Tell me more about them." This was the first time that Mr. Molitor had discussed Scott's family with me.

"The Piersons are sophisticated. They use proper language. They don't swear. They have good manners. They are particular about cleanliness."

I made the commitment to myself that I wouldn't swear. "Do they have hot running water and a shower?"

"I'm sure they do," he said with a smile.

"What do you mean when you say that they're sophisticated?" I knew the McClellands were not sophisticated. That probably meant that I wasn't either.

"Well, for example, they love music. They play instruments and sing."

This made sense to me since I heard Scott play the piano in school and he could draw. I didn't know that the whole family was musical. I knew I was neither artistic nor musical. A tinge of apprehension was creeping into my mind. I might not fit in as well as I'd hoped.

"What does Mr. Pierson do?"

"He's a landscape architect. I believe he works for the Bucks County Land Conservancy."

"Mrs. Pierson teaches school, right?" I asked.

"Yes, she does. She teaches at the Buckingham Friends School. The Piersons are Quakers."

"Oh, boy," I thought. I was glad that I left my gun at Mr. McClelland's farm. "Are they pacifists?"

"Let's put it this way, they care a lot about the common good."

"What does the 'common good' mean?"

"That's in reference to people who work in jobs or volunteer to serve the whole community. Jobs in schools, law enforcement, or public parks are considered to be for the common good."

"Do you think that they're taking me because it serves the common good?"

"They are very good people. I think they see what they're doing for you as a way to help you out of a difficult situation."

"If I disappoint them, will they ask to have me taken away?"

"Roger, you'll do just fine by being yourself. In a little over a year, you'll probably be going to college. You'll be on your own soon enough. I'm sure that nothing will happen to make them change their mind in that time about you."

I knew that just being myself wouldn't work. I had to be better than before. I was pleased that the trip was almost over since Mr. Molitor's helpful comments were beginning to make me wonder about this move. All I wanted to do was fit in and please them. That seemed like it might be harder to do than I'd expected.

The Piersons lived in Buckingham, which was a small village at the intersection of three highways. We turned up a hill at the intersection, drove a short distance, and then pulled up a tight driveway alongside their house that was perched on the side of the hill. This was going to be my new family, and I intended to do my best even though they were sophisticated city people.

We were greeted warmly by Scott and his parents when we got out of the car. They were really young-looking even though Mr. Pierson was bald. Mrs. Pierson was pretty with reddish hair and refined features. Mr. Pierson was sturdily built and looked me straight in the eye when he gave me a strong handshake and said, "Welcome to our house and your new home, Roger."

"Very nice to see you again," said Mrs. Pierson. "I was so sorry to learn about Mrs. McClelland. I'm glad that you're here and going to live with us now."

I smiled and said, "Thank you." I liked them instantly and was filled with hope about this home.

Scott was home, too. He apparently didn't have to go to school either because of my move. He greeted me with a big smile and politely shook Mr. Molitor's hand. I felt self-conscious when everyone gathered around and watched Scott and me unload the boxes from the trunk of the car.

The introductory awkwardness eased when the Piersons invited Mr. Molitor inside to talk while Scott helped me move into my new room upstairs. The house was small and very clean. I noticed a lot of bookshelves filled with books and a piano in the living room. My room was tucked into the third floor and had two windows, a bed, and a bureau alongside a small desk. We set my stuff on the bed and went downstairs.

I saw that Mr. and Mrs. Pierson were engaged in a conversation with Mr. Molitor in the kitchen. None of them seemed to notice Scott and me. Scott grabbed my arm and said, "Come on, let's go outside and go for a bike ride. I want to show you the neighborhood."

The bikes were English bikes with handbrakes and gear shifts. The bikes were light and easy to pedal compared to the old heavy American bikes we had. Clearly, the Piersons were rich.

Scott loved to ride his bicycle, and he had bulging calf muscles to show for it. I had trouble keeping up with him as he told me who lived in what homes and what they did. The first road we went down was Anderson Road where the Histand family lived.

Mr. Histand was a businessman who owned the Histand Brothers Roofing Company in Doylestown. He had two children, Mike and Beth. I knew them both since Mike was a good wrestler and an excellent student. Beth was a good athlete and a cheerleader. Their stone house with white trim set back from the road on the terraced lawn looked like an old estate. It was clear that they were well-to-do, too. As we rode along on the hilly roads, many well-groomed properties caught my eye, which made me feel lucky to be suddenly a part of this community.

When we got back to the Piersons, they were standing there waiting for us.

Mr. Molitor spoke first, "Did you boys take a tour of the area?"

"We did!" we chorused and laughed.

"Well, I'm going to leave you now," said Mr. Molitor. He extended his hand. I reached out and shook it.

"I'll be in touch in a couple of weeks to see how things are going, Roger. It looks like you're off to a good start."

He and the Piersons said their goodbyes, and he got into his car and backed down the driveway and was gone.

Just like that, I was alone with an old friend who had just become my foster brother in a new home with his family.

Chapter 39
Adjusting to New Reality

My worldview underwent a seismic shift when I moved into the Pierson's household. I jumped from the eighteenth century to the twentieth century. I had moved from a blue-collar world to a white-collar one. I'd only imagined what the transition would be like; in no way was I prepared for the reality of the Pierson's home and family dynamics, nor were they prepared for me.

Our first dinner was a little uncomfortable since everyone was trying their best to be polite, especially me. I tried to size everyone up without staring while still exhibiting good manners. I loved their milk.

"Roger, you had cows on the farm, right?" asked Mrs. Pierson suddenly.

"Yes, we did," I said. Then I realized that she'd been watching me drink several glasses full. "This milk is so great; I really like it—it's pasteurized, right?"

She smiled and said, "Glad that you like it so much." Then she changed the subject. "When you brought your things in, I didn't notice that you had any dress clothes. Do you have a suit?"

"No, I don't. I used to have one, but it doesn't fit anymore."

"Bob, tomorrow is Saturday. I want to take Roger into town to Musselmans and buy some dress clothes. Scott should come, too. Unless, of course, you have something else planned for him."

Mr. Pierson looked at us both and grinned and said, "Maybe we can get two dressed up for the price of one?"

I hoped that Mr. Molitor had given them money to buy clothes for me.

Denny and Susan, Scott's younger brother and sister, listened and ate quietly. I believed, based on what Mr. Molitor said, that they both went to the Friends School where Mrs. Pierson taught. So, it didn't surprise me that they were so quiet.

"Roger, what church did Mr. and Mrs. McClelland go to?" asked Mrs. Pierson.

"He didn't go to church. Mom and I went to the Methodist Church in Chalfont. I was baptized there."

"Methodists are good people," Mr. Pierson said approvingly.

"Phew," I thought. I was glad that he wasn't against them like Mr. McClelland hated Catholics.

"Mr. Pierson, Mr. Molitor told me that you are Quakers."

"We are. Buckingham Friends is the place where Quakers meet," he answered. "Buckingham Friends is one of the oldest Quaker meeting houses in the country." He paused and added, "Roger, we'd like you to call us Mom and Dad instead of Mr. and Mrs. Pierson. Is that okay?"

I felt uncomfortable about calling them that since I'd just met them and had already used those terms in other homes. "Sure," I said. "I'll try my best to do that."

Sensing that there was a little awkwardness, Mrs. Pierson spoke up, "Roger, there are six at the table now, and when Bob is home, there will be seven of us. That means there will be chores to be done like setting the table, clearing the dishes after we eat, washing the dishes, and taking out the garbage, especially at dinner."

I knew where this conversation was headed and could see that doing these chores was going to be a lot easier than farm chores. "I'll be happy to do those jobs," I said eagerly. They looked at me with surprised expressions, and Dennis and Susan smiled at each other.

"No, no, you misunderstood," said Mrs. Pierson. "I was

talking about chores, which are assigned to each of you to do separately. On the calendar by the door to the basement I write once a week who does what for each day of that week."

There was an uncomfortable pause, and then Dennis spoke up, "We go to the Buckingham Friends Meeting every Sunday."

"Not every Sunday," Scott clarified.

"Well, we're going for sure this Sunday!" Mrs. Pierson said with finality. "We need to introduce Roger to all of our activities."

We went to Musselmans the next day, and Mrs. Pierson bought a white shirt, a pair of dress pants that were too tight around the thighs, and some socks for me. Later at home, she tailored my pants. During the process, I learned that she was part of a group of ladies in Buckingham called "Sew What." The ladies met about once a month to sew and catch up on what was happening in Buckingham and Doylestown. Mrs. Pierson sewed both by hand and with a sewing machine. Mrs. McClelland had done all her sewing by hand; because her eyesight had been poor, she'd often asked me to thread needles for her so that she could repair torn clothes.

After she adjusted my pants, I tried them on and they fit perfectly. She was a good seamstress. While she'd been sewing, Scott was playing the piano in the background. When she went into the kitchen, I experienced the full blast of Scott's musical talent. He played with such enthusiastic force that he could be heard throughout the house and even outside.

When he paused, I asked, "Scott, it's fantastic—what are you playing?" I'd never heard anything like it.

"I'm practicing for my piano teacher. That piece is called 'Malaguena' by Lecuona. I practice every day."

Mrs. Pierson had overheard me admiring Scott's playing and had come into the room. "Do you play any instruments, Roger?" she asked.

"No. Scott can really play."

"If you'd like, we could arrange to have you take lessons. What instrument would you like to learn to play?"

"I'm not musical."

"Oh, we all have some musical talent even if we don't play an instrument," Mrs. Pierson said with kindness in her voice.

"My real sister, Karen, sings, and she can play the piano, too."

"Really. See, there's musical talent in your family. You must have some, too."

I knew I had no musical talent. I stood silently until she repeated herself, "Roger, we could arrange for you to take lessons on the piano or any other instrument that you might prefer."

"Thank you. Let me think about it," I said. I was hoping that she wouldn't pursue the idea.

I was so grateful to the Piersons for giving me a home that I was afraid that I didn't have enough talent to be worthy of their family. The thought came to me that I might be able to impress them with my knowledge of the Bible in the Quaker meeting on Sunday.

Quaker meetings offered a completely different experience than the Methodist Church. There was no singing, no stained-glass windows, no visible minister, and worst of all for me, there were no Bible readings. Overall, the setting was austere with hard wooden benches facing each other. The walls were exposed wood, and the ceilings were made of rough-hewn beams. The services lasted about an hour. We sat mostly in silence unless the Spirit moved someone to speak. The Spirit only appeared to move elder men. When moved, they spoke eloquently about world peace and the need for love and compassion in the world. I believed that the Spirit was truly speaking through them because they spoke so well. Through the Quaker meetings, I learned about the power of silence and the power of meditation, how sacred each person's beliefs are, and that each person had to be respected for their beliefs. The flow I'd felt at times working in the fields was similar to the experience of being in a Quaker meeting.

I appreciated Quaker meetings. I liked the silence, and, although I never felt moved to speak, I often took time to reflect on my spiritual growth.

My birth mother was Catholic, which probably meant that I was first baptized in a Catholic church in Philadelphia. Going to church must've been a part of my life before the McClellands because I was never uncomfortable going to church when I lived with Mrs. McClelland. Mom made sure that I went through catechism and was baptized in the Methodist Church as soon as I was old enough.

Mr. McClelland never attended church, but I believe he was a Protestant. I never heard him say a negative word about Mrs. McClelland's beliefs, no more than I ever heard her swear, which was his specialty. She also believed in Christian Science and healing through faith.

I began reading the Bible at an early age and was puzzled by all of the "begats." As long as the list of begats was, the calendar time didn't seem long enough to go from Adam and Eve to the time of Abraham and ultimately, the birth of Jesus. When I asked our minister about the possible temporal discrepancies, I was told to have more faith in the teachings of the Bible. The idea of having faith and believing struck me as very important. Faith as small as a mustard seed could move mountains.

The Bible was clear that people had wandered in the desert for forty years and that their faith in God had been rewarded when He delivered them into the Promised Land. Their faith had been tested, and those who hadn't wavered were rewarded by God. When I was younger, I believed that I had a lot of faith and I'd wanted to prove it to God. If I believed in Him, God would show me that He cared and protect me. I'd trusted that my faith was strong enough to support me enough so that I could walk on air. In order to test this belief, I placed a plank between two sawhorses, climbed up, and stepped off with the idea that I wouldn't fall to the ground. Every time I did this, I fell to the ground. Clearly, I didn't have enough faith. Then it occurred to me that I'd failed on the plank test because by using a safe height it wasn't really a test in God's mind, so it wouldn't be worthy of his effort to save me from falling.

I'd wanted to prove to Him, and myself, how much faith I had. To do this, I began to practice believing with all my strength. I would clear my mind and focus so hard that it made my head tense; it even hurt sometimes. After I'd done this for about a week, I knew I was ready. I went into the barn, believing that my faith was very strong due to my faith-building exercises, and that now I could really walk on thin air. I climbed up onto the highest rafter. The idea behind this test approach was to introduce an element of real danger and maybe even death if my faith were not strong enough when I stepped off the beam. I stood on the top beam without fear. Below me on one side, a long way down, was the barn floor made of hard planks. On the other side, not as far down, was the hayloft.

No matter how much I'd wanted to step off into the air over the hard wooden floor, I couldn't do it. I tried it over the hayloft several times and fell into the hay. I knew that I just didn't have enough faith. I was disappointed in myself because my fear was greater than my faith. However, I hadn't been injured at all when I fell off the barn roof, which suggested that God did care for me and would protect me.

The Bible had great stories and messages. I could relate to the David and Goliath story because it seemed to be a lot like Richard and me. Although he was much bigger than I was, I had ways to outsmart him like David did. Although there was never a formal battle to the death between us, it seemed like there could have been one at any moment. Sometimes I felt like I'd been sold into slavery like Joseph. Other times I felt that God was testing me like Job because there were always disappointments and challenges in front of me. I admired how God protected Daniel in the lion's den and hoped that I would be worthy of being protected like he was. I really liked Samson's great strength, but had some fear about trusting women like Delilah, especially after what my mother had done to me. I was drawn to the wisdom of Solomon and hoped that I would grow up to be really smart.

I wasn't as interested in the New Testament because I could never understand why Jesus was crucified and why he knowingly let Judas betray him. However, I readily agreed with his Golden Rule and tried to live by it as best as I could. When I would fail to live up to it, I felt shame and guilt. I became the president of the Bible Club in eighth grade, probably because of going to church and reading the Bible, which I readily quoted from when appropriate.

As hard as the work was in the fields, especially hoeing, I found that it was soothing and quieted some of my internal demons. The rhythm of hoeing and feeling the "flow" of it was like an accidental meditation practice. Praying felt structured and ritualistic to me. I had to be thankful, which was hard as a foster child. I would often ask God for something instead of filling myself with gratitude. Always asking didn't seem right. When I began to pray that either Mr. or Mrs. McClelland would die, that especially didn't seem right. When I was rescued from the farm and moved to the Piersons, I went from an Old Testament life to a New Testament one. I'd been saved.

At the time I was attending the Quaker meetings, I was reading the works of Ralph Waldo Emerson and David Thoreau.

Based on what I'd learned in the fields and woods of the farm, the idea that man and all of nature were connected divinely made a lot of sense to me. I liked the metaphor from Transcendentalism, which taught that each of our souls is deposited on the beach like puddles after a wave, only to be swept up by the next ocean wave and absorbed into the Perfect Whole. Those teachings seemed so much bigger than the ideas within the organized religion I'd known and seemed to align better with Quakerism.

I felt a lot of pressure to be a better person, and this fresh start in a new family and the ways of the Quakers became part of my development.

Chapter 40
Abundant Free Time

I'd lived at the Piersons for about a week when one evening Mrs. Pierson asked, "Roger, what did you do when you came home after school on the McClelland farm?"

"It depended a lot on the time of the year. In the spring we prepared the ground and planted. In the fall we harvested crops. We always had chores to do every day regardless of the season."

"I see," she said furrowing her brow. "But, when did you study?"

"I usually tried to get my schoolwork done in class or in study hall. Once in a while I would do homework after my chores were done but not very often."

"You've probably noticed that Scott practices the piano every day after school. When he finishes playing the piano, he does his schoolwork. Denny and Susan have the same routine."

"Yes. They have very good study habits," I said. I was listening intently. She'd spoken precisely without taking her eyes off of me.

"I know there's a lot for you to get used to in our family. You may not have noticed that if you come home and ask Scott to go for a bike ride and he goes out with you, his routine is disrupted. He doesn't want to say no to you. Maybe after he's completed his piano practice and schoolwork would be a better time to ask him to do something."

I tensed. I wanted to please the Piersons. I could see that I'd not been careful enough. They were good to me, and I'd been clumsy.

"I understand," I said, trying not to show how bad I felt for being disrespectful of the Piersons' routine.

Mrs. Pierson smiled and said, "Besides, if you studied like Scott, you might have a better chance of being accepted by a college."

I knew she was right.

"I'll bring books home and do schoolwork here," I said firmly. I felt like I was being forced to study in the Pierson home like I'd been forced to do chores at the McClellands.

I brought books home and tried to look like I was doing homework. However, I was too restless to study every day. I needed to be physically active. I knew that I couldn't interrupt Scott or the others again. I tried to be very quiet around the house. When the weather was good, I went for long bike rides and stayed out of everyone's way. My behavior led to another conversation.

Mrs. Pierson called Scott and me together to discuss another idea. "I know that you both like to read. As seniors next year, you'll be expected to write long papers on various topics. I've been reading about the Great Books of the Western World and was wondering what you would think if I ordered a set for our use. Would you use them?"

Scott and I both smiled enthusiastically. Scott spoke first. "How many books are there? Who are the authors?"

"There are over fifty volumes. The authors include ancient Greeks like Aristotle and Plato and continue right up until today. Scott, there's even a book by Goethe, which could help you in your German class. It would be like having your own library right here."

"Are there works by Edgar Allen Poe, Hawthorne, and Longfellow?" I asked.

"I have the list right here. Let me see," she said as she looked at the folder that she was holding. "I don't see them, but I do see that Mark Twain, Charles Dickens, and Tolstoy are included. I think that they only selected the really major writers."

She gave me the folder, and I saw names that I'd never heard of. I noticed that the whole set cost over four hundred dollars. "The set is expensive."

"Yes, it is. Bob and I have discussed the cost and the opportunity it offers all of you, and we think that it would be a wise investment for your futures. I'm going to order them now so that you can have them available to read during the summer."

I was thinking about the two books I'd bought in the past in preparation for college and knew this was a much greater commitment. I was eager to get started on them, knowing that Mrs. Pierson was steering me away from distracting the others by giving me something to read.

Not long after that conversation, Mrs. Pierson had another idea to address my restlessness. "Roger, I spoke to the manager at Musselmans today, and he said that he could hire you after school as a box boy. It would mean that you could earn some money for college."

"What does a box boy do?" I asked.

"He opens delivery boxes, places items on shelves, and is a general help around the store," she replied. "I'm told that it's very clean work."

"Thank you. How much do they pay? When would I start?"

"You can start next Monday after school. They will pay you one dollar and fifty cents an hour."

"How long would I work each day?"

"We thought you could work from three thirty to six o'clock each day and come home with Bob after he finishes at the office."

The following Monday after school I was working at Musselmans. I wanted to do well. Mr. Fischer, the manager, showed me where shipments were delivered, how to open the boxes so that nothing happened to the clothes, and how to clean up around the store. The work was much easier than farm work. I wasn't employed very long before an incident happened, which frustrated Mr. Fischer.

"Roger, do you have a driver's license?" Mr. Fischer asked.

"Sure do," I said.

"Here are three boxes that have to be delivered to Cross Keys Chevrolet. They contain their new uniforms." He handed me the boxes and the keys to his car.

"The car is a two-tone 1955 Buick parked behind the store. It should only take you twenty-five minutes or so."

I was glad to get out of the store and do something different. I was pleased that he trusted me with his car and was excited to take on the additional role of delivery boy. The Buick was bright and shiny, and I saw with relief that it was an automatic. I turned the key on and nothing happened. I turned it off and on again and still nothing happened. I looked at the floor to see if there was a starter button. There was no starter. I thought that maybe the battery was dead, so I tried the radio, which worked when the key was on. I even turned on the lights and got outside to see if they were on, and they were. I became concerned because time was passing, and I'd not even been able to start the car. I felt about the same as the time I'd failed my driver's test. I sat there stuck. I didn't want to go back inside and ask Mr. Fischer how to start his car after saying that I could drive.

My hands were sweating, and I could feel the trickle of sweat roll down under my arms. I was frustrated. I began to feel tense and panicky. I just wanted to do the job. I kept searching the instrument panel to be sure that there wasn't another button that I'd missed. I sat in the car trying to will it to start. In my frustration I stamped down on the floor and accidentally hit the accelerator and the engine started.

I was surprised and relieved. I drove to Cross Keys and dropped off the packages but kept the car running while I was inside. When I returned, Mr. Fischer was waiting for me at the back door to the store.

"What took you so long?" he asked.

"I couldn't get the car started," I said.

"I thought you said that you could drive." Before I could answer he took the keys and said, "Never mind now, we have to clean up the store before closing." Two days later he told me that he no longer needed my help at Musselmans because the full-time employee who did my job and other jobs had returned. I knew I'd been fired.

On the way home that evening Mr. Pierson said, "Roger, you don't have to worry about a job. There are plenty of jobs around for boys who are willing to work. In fact, I would like you and Scott to help me plant trees at Brittany Farms in Chalfont this weekend."

"That sounds like fun," I said. I knew that working with Scott would be different than working with Richard. Besides, I was eager to do something to earn my way.

"Where are you getting the trees, and what kind of trees are they?" I asked.

"You know the trees that are growing in our backyard?"

"Yes."

"Well, I have a contract to plant the trees in the new development in Chalfont." I hadn't realized that he was raising the trees to be sold and planted. I thought he was only a tree hobbyist since he was a skilled landscape architect employed by the county. He was raising the trees just like I raised vegetables to sell. I was impressed.

He continued. "We'll plant pin oaks, white oaks, red oaks, and some red maples. We'll only select the trees that are over six feet tall."

That Saturday, Scott, Mr. Pierson, and I dug up trees, hauled them in his trailer, and planted them in the front lawns and backyards of the newly built homes in the development. We followed the layout Mr. Pierson had created, which called for three trees per lot. We spent three Saturdays sweating and planting trees.

Scott was strong, a good athlete, and a great bike rider; however, he didn't seem as comfortable using the pick and the shovel as I was. My farming experience had prepared me well for jobs like planting trees. Mr. Pierson appreciated our work, and I felt good to do something for him. Later in the summer he put us both to work to dig a hole for a new septic system for the house. I actually loved digging the hole and kept at it longer than Scott. We were able to finish the work more quickly than Mr. Pierson had expected, which pleased him again.

Mr. Pierson and Scott never swore when they were frustrated at whatever task they were engaged in. Working without swearing was a new experience for me. Mr. Molitor had told me that the Piersons were well mannered—and they were. I had to keep my guard up and not curse.

The campaign to keep me busy and to earn money continued. Next, I was introduced to Mr. and Mrs. Milton C. DelManzo. She was a skilled artist and weaver of fabrics, and he was a retired provost of Columbia University. They needed yard work to be done. Scott and I were available on weekends and I also worked after school. An extra benefit for me was that I met and got to know their granddaughter, Beth Histand. She was an attractive cheerleader and was one year behind me in school.

Eventually, Mr. Pierson introduced me to John Diemand who owned a hundred-acre farm. I was paid one dollar an hour to help Mr. Van Luvanee who was the farm manager. The work was exactly like what I'd been doing on the McClelland farm except that there were a lot more cows to milk and the Diemand farm had many acres of fruit trees. I surprised Mr. Van Luvanee and Mr. Diemand by how hard I worked and by how much work I got done. There were two drawbacks. I smelled like the cow barn when I went home, and I was always very hungry by dinner time.

The first time I came home from the Diemand farm, Mrs.

Pierson said that I had to take off my shoes and pants outside and take a bath before dinner. Soon, I learned that I ate so much that it made Mrs. Pierson cry in frustration because all the dinner was gone so quickly. I was able to alleviate some of my appetite by stopping at a Dairy Queen on my way home and eating a banana split before dinner. I was beginning to feel like an intruder and that they had regrets for taking me in. Several times in those early months of living at the Piersons they had a family meeting that intentionally didn't include me. I thought that they were trying to figure out a good strategy for dealing with me.

I began to wonder if I might be causing Mrs. Pierson the migraine headaches that she was getting. Sometimes she would stay in her bedroom several days in a row. In addition, Susan was losing some of her hair, which might have been caused by me as well. I liked her and didn't want her to suffer because of me. I was trying to be a good family member or even just a good guest in their house. I was thankful to be there, but it was clear that I disrupted their lives. I feared that whatever badness I had was beginning to infect their household. Rappaccini again.

After the big move, Mr. Molitor visited every couple of weeks at school to see how things were going. I knew that he wanted everything to be going well, so I told him it was great living with the Piersons and how much they were encouraging me to study and how they were helping me to earn money for college. That worked for a couple of visits. Eventually, he started to ask more pointed questions.

"Roger, you're telling me a lot about earning money, the Great Books, and trying to be respectful of Scott's study habits and those of his brother and sister. How do you believe that you're fitting in?"

"They're really good people—all of them. I know that I'm not as smart as they are. I know that I'm not as cultured as they are. I know that they're very musical. I know that they have to make a lot of adjustments because of me."

"How does that make you feel?"

"It makes me feel like I want to be out of their way as much as possible. I don't feel that I'm good enough to live with them."

"Have you tried to tell them how you're feeling?"

I knew that I'd already violated Richard's rule of telling a social worker too much. I didn't want to talk about it anymore.

"I guess the answer to my question is that you haven't spoken to them directly about how you're feeling." He looked past me and tried another tack. "What are you doing for fun?"

"First of all, it's good not to have to work so much. I go for bike rides. Scott and I collect butterflies. Things like that."

"Do either of you have girlfriends?"

"Well, maybe, I guess you could call Beth Histand a girlfriend." I didn't want to talk about Beth at all. Why was he asking about girlfriends at all unless he'd been talking to Mrs. Pierson?

"Are you spending much time together?"

Mrs. Pierson had suggested to me that I might be spending too much of my free time with Beth. I reasoned that Mrs. Pierson must have said something to Mr. Molitor.

"I don't think we're spending that much time together. We intend to go to the junior prom together, though."

"Well, that seems fine to me," he said in an effort to be aligned with my thinking that I wasn't spending too much time with her.

He finally got to his point. "Do you remember that time between first and second grade when you were given a series of tests?"

"Yes."

"We would like to have you enter into a conversation with a specialist who evaluates boys and girls your age."

"Why?"

"Well, it could help you with some of those difficult conversations you might like to have with the Piersons."

"I don't have to have those conversations with the Piersons if I just behave better."

"Let's just say that there are many times in our lives when we're confronted with situations that make us uncomfortable. When that happens, it's useful to have the benefit of some tools to help us to get through those times."

"What type of specialist?"

"The man we have in mind is Dr. Bonan. He's a psychotherapist."

"You mean, he's like one of those guys who treats patients in the Norristown mental hospital?" I could sense that they were going to go to work on me with a professional and my defenses were going up.

Mr. Molitor squirmed and forced a smile and said, "No, this is about a developmental evaluation and help. This could be good for your personal growth. It would only be for six sessions or so. The weekly sessions would start as soon as the school year ended."

I knew that I didn't want to do it; I had no choice. I was glad that Mrs. Pierson had bought the books, which included the writings of Freud.

I wondered what Richard would think about this.

Chapter 41
My Second Evaluation

As promised, Mr. Molitor called Mrs. Pierson at the end of the school year. He told her to tell me to be ready for him to pick me up on the following Tuesday at noon. Mrs. Pierson seemed relieved when she told me to be ready. Mr. Van Luvanee was not happy to learn that I had to leave work every Tuesday before noon for six weeks. I didn't like the idea of having to see a therapist and being treated like I was a crazy person. Nevertheless, I washed and was ready to go when Mr. Molitor arrived.

Once we were in the car, Mr. Molitor began the conversation, "Roger, have you ever been to Conshohocken before?"

"No."

"I've typed out the directions for you. Since you'll be driving the rest of the time, here they are." He slid the typed piece of paper across the seat to me while he drove.

I took a cursory glance at the directions. They were clear enough, but I wasn't going to be distracted from my concern about the purpose of these appointments.

I sat silently staring at the black mole on the side of Mr. Molitor's face. I couldn't help but think of it as a door to a safe, which held lots of secrets about me and other foster kids. His untanned face was pale and made the mole-safe even more obvious. He'd been my caseworker for nearly four years, but I knew nothing about him except that he was soft-spoken and always dressed in white shirts and wore a thin, dark tie. He always deflected my questions about him. His deflections didn't stop me from wondering about him. *Why is he working as a social worker anyway when all the social workers were women? He looked like he could be employed as a clerk in a bank rather than driving back and forth to see foster kids. Does he have children of his own? Is he even married?*

He broke my train of thought by asking, "I understand that the Piersons' older son, Bob, is home from college. How are you getting along with him?"

"He's very smart and plans to get a PhD in chemistry when he graduates from Juniata College next year. He plays the violin and is designing a model car for a contest."

"You're telling me about him. I asked, 'How are you getting along with him?'"

"I think we're getting along fine. Certainly, better than I got along with Richard. We're just learning about each other. He asks me a lot of questions when we're alone. He has a good sense of humor and makes us laugh at dinner. Things go better when he's around."

"What do you mean, 'Things go better when he's around'?"

I realized that I'd said too much and opened the door to a discussion that I didn't want to have. "I meant that he speaks up if there are quiet moments and makes things happen. He's always curious. That's all."

"I see."

Eager to change the subject, I asked, "Why are you making me see this therapist?"

There was an uncomfortable silence. Finally, he looked away from the road and at me, "Roger, do you know that Scott tells his mom what you tell him?"

"What do you mean?"

"I mean that the stories you tell him about what you did or what happened on the farm get repeated to Mrs. Pierson. They may even get exaggerated in the process."

"So?" I was on full alert again. My

mind raced to recall exactly what I'd told Scott.

"The stories worry her; maybe they even scare her." His words hung in the air like a dark cloud, and I tingled as if I'd already been struck by lightning. The idea that the Piersons had only wanted to help me and all I was doing was scaring them disturbed me. The tingling sensation was replaced by a wave of sadness. I'd only wanted to amuse Scott, not scare the family. "Are you saying that I'm being sent to see a psychiatrist because I scared the Piersons?"

"No. We all believe that you've been through some major difficulties, and it would be a good idea for you to meet with a professional who might be able to help you think through all that you've experienced."

"Who are the 'we'?"

"The Piersons, others in the Aid Society, and me." At that moment we entered the fancy neighborhood of Conshohocken. There were sprawling lawns, shade trees, and flowers everywhere. We turned up a driveway that had a large parking area.

"Why are we stopping here?"

"Dr. Bonan's office is in his house. The door to his office is over there," Mr. Molitor said as he pointed to the left. "Don't use the main front entrance. That's the entrance to his home."

We entered the nondescript door to the left. The waiting area was cool and sterile. Two chairs, a brown sofa, and a small table with a lamp filled the room. There was another door with a green glowing light above it and a button beside it. Mr. Molitor pressed the button, and the door opened. "You wait here, Roger. I need a few moments alone with Dr. Bonan."

I was left alone in a place that I didn't want to be, speculating about why I was really there. I'd said too much to Scott, I'd behaved badly or done something else that upset the Piersons. Maybe all three. Richard had never had this happen to him. He was too careful to have let it happen. I reminded myself that I needed to be careful, too.

The door opened, and Mr. Molitor emerged, saying, "Roger, you can go in now. I'll wait outside."

I went through the door into a cooler room.

"Hello, Roger. I'm Dr. Bonan." He followed his greeting with an extended hand. I shook his hand, mumbled a response, and sat down on the chair that he'd motioned to. My heart was racing. I felt like I was floating in a dream. He sat down across from me. He was a stocky man with a disproportionately large, clean-shaven head.

"Roger, we're going to have several sessions for me to get to know you better. Let me start by letting you know that I've read your file." He said this as he pointed to a thick brown folder, lying open on his desk. "However, a file isn't a person. I'm hopeful that you'll trust me enough to share some of your thoughts and feelings about your past and what's happening in your life now."

"Why am I here?"

"The Aid Society has asked me to make an assessment of your developmental progress since your situation has had some unusual challenges."

"What will they do with the assessment?"

"They just want to understand where you are in your life and how you are coping."

"You mean they want to see if I'm crazy?" I didn't know exactly how far the Norristown lunatic hospital was from Conshohocken, but I knew it wasn't far.

"No. Not at all. For now, let's talk about you and not discuss what the motives of others might be. I know that you were placed in foster care when you weren't even nine months old and have been in several foster homes over the years. Could you tell me how that makes you feel?"

I didn't want to tell this man, a total stranger, how I felt about anything. Besides, I was doing okay. Why couldn't people see that and just leave me alone? If I told them too much and they didn't like what I said, I was afraid that they could decide to send me somewhere else for treatment or even somewhere else to live.

"How would you feel?" I asked.

"I can't be helpful to you if you challenge me and resist telling me more about you."

"Why do you and everyone else seem to believe that I need help? I didn't ask to be here. I was told to be here."

"You appear very angry, which is justifiable under your circumstances."

"You know what makes me angry? All my life people have told me where to live. What to do. When to do it. How to do it. Now you're telling me what I need to do to make this session successful. Successful for who? I've been taking care of myself for most of my life, and I don't need some total stranger peeking into my life and telling me what to do."

The first session with Dr. Bonan was a declaration of war on my part rather than a caring therapeutic exchange between a professional and a patient. The remaining five meetings with him were similar. I went home that afternoon and began to read the works of Freud. The subsequent meetings were punctuated with questions and answers. My answers were governed by what I was reading in Freud, which didn't improve our relationship after the first encounter.

He would ask questions like: How did I feel about my mother? Was I dating and what did I do with my date? Did I dream and what did I dream about? What career was I interested in? What did I do when I was angry?

I would answer: Which mother? Yes, I was dating, and I even kissed a girl once. My dreams were about flying and being above the land and free like a bird. I liked English and chemistry, but I hadn't fixed on a career. I wanted to go to college and would decide then. When I was angry, I liked to hit things, which was why I enjoyed football.

"People are not things," he said. "You mean, you like to hit people when you are angry?"

"I like to protect people who are being picked on. My team is being attacked. So, I want to help them by protecting them. That's all." I was squirming and didn't want to bring up what had happened to the cow or that I'd hit Mr. McClelland.

"I see." There was a long pause until he said, "You've been in foster care longer than most boys I've met. How does it make you feel?"

"Let me tell you something about being in foster care. When I meet people, mostly adults, and I say my full name, they almost always ask, 'Is that French?' or 'Are you French?' I immediately have to decide if I'm going to lie or tell the truth. That's what it's like for me as a foster child."

"What do you mean?"

"The name Saillant is French, and if I imply that I'm French, that's a lie. However, my birth father is not Mr. Saillant. Then I have the pleasure of explaining that I'm a bastard and was placed in foster care as a baby. That leads to more personal questions. I don't like it."

"I see."

By the time the first session ended our dance had begun. The tone was set. He asked questions, and I did my best to deflect them.

On the second trip, my friend Ed Satterthwaite drove me. Ed was one of the best students in my class. I needed the ride and had asked him to drive since I knew that he would not talk about the trip. He was not a talker. Scott never went with me, nor did he and I discuss the sessions. I was afraid that he might share what I thought with Mrs. Pierson, whom I suspected was probably getting reports from Mr. Molitor, anyway.

On the way home, Ed asked, "Why are they making you do this?"

"Good question. It's one that I've asked as well and haven't gotten a satisfactory answer for. The only thing I can come up with is that the Aid Society people suspect that I might be too angry to be successful in life and might harm other people. They want to know if I'm a real threat to others." The part I kept to myself was that they thought I might be suicidal, too.

"From what I know, I think that you'll be fine." He was a good friend. It felt good to know that a judge's son was optimistic about my future.

The last session with Dr. Bonan didn't go as well as the first.

Toward the end of the session he said, "Roger, do you have any final comments to make?"

I couldn't help myself and blurted out, "You know, Dr. Bonan, your clean-shaven head makes me think of a penis." I think reading Freud made me do it.

He was clearly jolted by my ill-advised remark but gathered himself and said, "Roger, these sessions have been difficult for both of us. You've deflected each of my efforts to have a meaningful conversation with you. They've felt more like sparring matches than therapy sessions. That being said, I do have some final thoughts for you. You're smart enough to get straight As at Harvard. However, you won't. I recommend that if you do go to college, you study something that will assure you of a good income because you'll need it to support the many years of therapy that you'll need to become a healthy and happy person."

Chapter 42
Dating Steps and Missteps

Although the sessions with Dr. Bonan were awkward and not useful to me, they did provoke questions about some of my behaviors that stayed with me afterwards. I reflected on my dating practices and my overall relationship with girls.

Richard and I never discussed anything about girls or sex growing up. In fact, he never went out with a girl while he lived on the farm. He was tall, good-looking, and strong, characteristics that should've afforded him ample opportunities to date in high school. The fact that there were no vehicles on the farm and that he always avoided asking anyone for anything may have contributed to his lack of dating.

Once he joined the Army, he changed. He brought home a woman who stayed with him in his room at night. A behavior that was only tolerated by the McClellands. A while after his enlistment, I received a birthday gift subscription to *Playboy* magazine. I was surprised and pleased. My enthusiasm for getting the mail increased.

I hid the magazines in the haymow, and, when I could, I shared them with the Schaeffer boys and Bill Triest. Our imaginations were kindled and fantasies sprang up among us like weeds. I did my best to suppress them, but they were persistent. One particularly hardy weed grew between Bill Triest and me about Cookie Teresa who was a year or two ahead of us at Central Bucks. She was pretty and seemed to have a Playboy-like figure under her riding clothes. When she rode through the fields on her horse, our imaginations often spiked. Luckily for us and her, our fantasies bore no fruit.

In the fall of my junior year, unlike Richard, I had my first date while living on the farm. Ed Satterthwaite drove his girlfriend, Ruth Carwithen, my date, Ann Nuse, and me to a dance. Escaping from the farm on that date was a one-time experience and very proper. After I moved to the Piersons, I met Beth Histand; she and I saw each other frequently since her family lived close by.

Beth was a sophomore, artistic, a good student, and a cheerleader. Her mother was the daughter of the DelManzos and a good friend of Mrs. Pierson. Her father owned and operated the family roofing business and knew about me and thought of me as a good football player and a good worker. I took her to the junior prom. Upon reflection, after the Bonan visits I could see that Mrs. Pierson might have been concerned about just how close Beth and I had become and she'd shared her anxiety with Mr. Molitor and that led to some uncomfortable probing by Dr. Bonan. They'd underestimated just how restrained Beth and I were. We both believed that unmarried intimacy was wrong.

I dated Beth well into the fall of my senior year when an unfortunate accident happened. I never went to parties after football games, which most players and cheerleaders did. We beat Springfield High School by an unexpected big margin, and everyone urged me to come to the party. I agreed and borrowed Mr. Pierson's favorite car, an old, black, hardtop Austin. Beth and I were riding together talking when the car in front of us stopped suddenly to make a left-hand turn. Although I slammed on the brakes, they seemed not to grab well, and I rolled into the rear end of the car in front of us. My head collided with an exposed metal edge in the roof whose headliner had been torn away years before. Beth tried to stop herself from being thrown into the dashboard with her arm. She broke her arm and bruised her face. I had a deep cut in my scalp, which required stitches.

We both were taken by ambulance to the hospital.

I got a reckless driving ticket and a suspension for fifteen days.

Mr. Pierson was very upset and tried his best to control his anger at my carelessness that had not only injured us but had seriously damaged his car. I felt awful. Beth's parents were appropriately upset. I couldn't play in the football game the following week, which was our only loss of the season; the coaches blamed me. My relationship with Beth cratered, and we never dated seriously again. My carelessness only added to my dark feelings about myself. I believed that I was not only unprepared to date but also unworthy of dating anyone.

The only relationship that I saw that seemed steady and even-keeled among my peers was the one that existed between Ruth Carwithen and Ed Satterthwaite. They started dating in eighth grade, and although they went through their own ups and downs, they held it together better than any other high school couple I knew. They were individually very bright, and together offered an inspiring model of maturity for us all. I wanted to replicate it. A seemingly fresh opportunity came after the holidays of my senior year.

Jean Mathers arrived as a new student in my French class in January. She was quiet, pretty, dressed conservatively, and smart. As I got to know her, I learned just how fast her mind worked and was glad that she was willing to be friendly. However, her description of our first meeting was awkward and not flattering for me. She described my introduction like this:

"Hello, my name is Roger Saillant, and I'm the vice president of the student council. I just missed being president by sixteen votes."

That's about as uncool an introduction as I could've possibly made to someone that I wanted to impress.

Over the next few days, I learned that she didn't particularly care about French class. She'd moved to Central Bucks midterm from a school near Harrisburg, Pennsylvania. Her father had been making career moves, and those moves had caused her to be uprooted eight times. Although she never changed families like I had, I thought that it was probably just as bad for her to grow up having to change communities many times and having to find new friends each time she moved.

I asked her to go out with Scott and me. Our first outing was bobsledding one evening on a hill in Doylestown. We teamed up and rode down a busy hill in the park several times. Each downhill trip had a mishap. On one trip, we struck a tree. On another trip, we hit a rock and fell off the toboggan. We even bumped into another bobsled on the crowded hill. By the time we took Jean home, she had bruises on her arms and legs and a couple of scratches on her face. Her mother thought that sledding with me was a bad idea.

We were still in touch when Valentine's Day arrived. I liked her. Scott was a good artist and clever. Since I saw him creating a card for Bonnie Swartley, I thought I'd do the same for Jean. Since her father worked for the Bell Telephone Company of Pennsylvania, I thought it would be original to design a Valentine's card using a phone theme. We hadn't started taking any steps toward a real relationship like kissing, sharing hugs, or even holding hands. Thus, the problem for me was how to design a card that conveyed interest without overstepping some behavioral model. I decided that I'd draw several telephones in the shape of hearts on the outside of the card. I labelled them as follows: acquaintance, friend, best friend, lover, and passionate lover. Inside the card I wrote, "Which line should I dial you on?" In retrospect, I'm sure that her parents didn't appreciate seeing "lover" and especially "passionate lover" written on the card. Jean's reaction was so polite and tactful that it was unmemorable.

She seemed to like science, especially biology and chemistry. Scott and I had been doing experiments in the basement of our house. I thought it would impress her to see our lab and maybe do a lab demonstration or two. I invited her over and took her into the basement where Scott and I had set up some flasks, vials, tubing, and other laboratory paraphernalia with assorted chemicals. I showed her how to make several compounds from what we had available. Two of the compounds were chlorine gas and hydrogen chloride. Since they were heavier than air, they flowed down onto the floor. I noticed in the demonstration process that our cat moved from around our feet to a position higher up on the stairs. What I didn't notice was that Jean's nylons were dissolving. The nylon loss was pointed out to me later by her mother.

I think these early interactions with Jean could best be summarized by noting that she went to the senior prom with Mike Smith. I went to the prom with Bonnie Swartley, another bright and talented girl in our class.

Chapter 43
The Green Gene

I looked forward to my senior year for two reasons. First, it was my last year in high school, and second, I was going to be in the newly added honors English class. Although I'd been selected for honors history in my junior year, I hadn't qualified for honors English like Scott and my other friends had. My friends were the types of students that Miss Hanisch had forewarned me about: smart with good study habits. They had all scored well on their Preliminary Scholastic Aptitude Tests (PSAT), and I hadn't. I was sure they were going to college. I believed that a good grade in honors English would improve my college chances.

Most of my friends had solid career goals. My goal was blurry. I recalled how Mrs. VanAlstyne (Aunt Margaret) had spoken to me.

"Roger, you remind me of Rogers Hornsby," she said. "You love baseball. Maybe you'll be a great ballplayer like he was."

I knew that her thinking was governed by my name, not my skills. I went along with her words and said, "It takes a lot of practice. I don't play on any organized teams because of work."

"Oh, never mind being a baseball player, then. You still have a great smile and tell stories just like Will Rogers used to do."

"Thank you, Aunt Margaret, but he was a cowboy."

Uncle Jack looked up with a wry smile and said, "Boy, you have cows, don't you? That's a start."

Exchanges like these happened when I made my weekly egg delivery trips to their house. I felt encouraged by their remarks to think about what I wanted to be when I grew up. I secretly wanted to be a writer like Jack London. I'd read his biography and knew that he was so poor that he worked in a cannery for ten cents an hour. I loved his stories about the outdoors. I knew that I would get a chance to practice writing in Mrs. Porter's honors English class.

Some members of the recently graduated class at Central Bucks had a party on their senior trip. They drank and misbehaved so loudly that the police were called to the hotel. The chaperones and school administrators were embarrassed to the point that Dr. B. Anton Hess, our superintendent, declared that my class, the class of 1961, would not have a senior trip the following spring. Many of my classmates were upset and felt cheated. Since I liked the poet Ogden Nash, I thought that I could mimic his poetic style and address this injustice like he might have. So, just after the trip cancellation had been declared and while my classmates' frustration was highest, I went into action.

In my honors English class before Mrs. Porter arrived, I went to the blackboard and wrote the following poem:

We're the class of sixty-one,
We're the class that has no fun.
We can't go here,
We can't go there.
In fact, we can't go anywhere!

The other students read what was written and liked it so much that they were chanting it just as Mrs. Porter came into the room. She looked at what was written, slapped her books down on her desk, and turned to us with narrowed eyes and asked, "Who did this?"

The classroom became as silent as a funeral parlor. The chanters-turned mourners- looked toward me.

"Roger, did you write this?" Mrs. Porter asked disbelievingly.

I was just having some fun and couldn't understand what had upset her so much. I answered meekly, "Yes." I actually thought it was pretty clever but kept that to myself. I'd believed that she would appreciate just how much it resembled the works of Ogden Nash. I realized quickly that I'd crossed a line.

"I hope that each of you knows how difficult this decision was for the faculty and the administration. We recognized what an important tradition the senior trip to Washington has been; however, we had to send a message to everyone that behaviors that we witnessed last year will not be tolerated. To mock our decision in this way shows a lack of respect for authority and is especially unbecoming to the status given to honors students such as yourselves." She continued, but I'd tuned her out as I began to wonder what she would do to me. I waited, and then she addressed me, "Roger, I want to see you immediately after school today."

Fall classes had started several weeks earlier, and I was already in trouble. When Mrs. Porter's back was turned, one of the girls in the class poked me and handed me a note. On it she'd written, "Way to go, Ogden."

I had a sense of foreboding about meeting with Mrs. Porter. First, if it lasted too long, I'd be late for football practice. Second, was my offensive action sufficient to get me kicked out of honors English? If that happened, would it ruin my college chances? And, third, would the Piersons find out and would I slip down another notch in their minds?

At the designated time, I was in Mrs. Porter's office.

"Thank you for being prompt, Roger. This shouldn't take too long." We were standing, which suggested a brief meeting.

"Before I begin, Roger, I want you to know that I see you as a natural leader as do many other students in your class. Since you are a role model, what you do and say influences their behaviors. Do you understand?"

"Yes."

"Well, do you understand that if the other students see you

as a role model, I expect more of you as their leader?"

"I think so."

We both relaxed a little. She continued, "That little poem you wrote today was cute, but disrespectful. You can't challenge the decisions that the administration makes. They're in charge here, not the students."

I knew that teachers were in charge. From where I stood, someone else always seemed to be in charge. "I understand that, Mrs. Porter. I was just having some fun."

'Well, here's an opportunity for you to have some more fun. I want you to hand in an original thousand-word short story by Friday's class."

"Is that my punishment?"

"No, it's a challenge. You can model a behavior that reminds others that my class is an honors English class and not a place for clowning around."

I wanted to clarify and asked, "Can it be about anything I want?"

"Yes, but it has to be at least one thousand words," she repeated. "And it has to be handed in by Friday."

I was being punished and tested. What could I write about? I knew about farming, but how could I create a short story that was interesting about farming? These and other thoughts raced through my mind as I practiced football, showered, went home, ate, and went to my room. Then, an idea came to me.

I handed in my short story at the beginning of class on Friday as requested. Mrs. Porter didn't seem surprised. She thanked me and told me that she would read it over the weekend and tell me what she thought on Monday.

That Friday night we trounced Upper Perkiomen, and I didn't give another thought to Mrs. Porter and the incident in her class until Monday. She said nothing to me during the class. At the end of class, she said, "Roger, could you come to my office

312 THE POWER OF BEING SEEN

this afternoon after school?"

"Sure," I said, a bit puzzled by a second visit to her office. I knew that it had to be about what I'd written. I wondered if I'd miscounted the number of words. Other than that, I had no idea what the problem could be. When I entered her office, she got up from her desk, closed the door behind me, and motioned for me to sit down in the chair next to her.

"Roger, this is an excellent piece of fiction, or is it?"

"It's science fiction," I replied.

"Really?" she replied. "I think it is a fantasy desire of yours and is more like an allegory."

"What do you mean?" I said as I tried to read what she'd written on the margin of the story.

"You've given the story the title 'The Green Gene,' which suggests that it is about something scientific. However, on reading the story I learned that it's about freedom and independence given to children who've been abandoned because they have a green appearance. However, if the children survive, they find that they don't need food in the way other people do. The reason they don't need food is that they have a gene, which allows their bodies to convert sunlight directly to nourishment."

"Well, you've summarized the story correctly, but you haven't mentioned why people are scared of them and why they try to imprison them."

"Roger, I know more about you than you think. The reason I closed the door is to make this a private and an honest conversation. You see, I know that you're a foster child. I know that you have lived in multiple homes. I discussed your situation with Mr. Williams before you were selected for the honors English class."

I could tell that she was excited to explain her thoughts to me. She had my full attention.

"Because you're a foster child, you've experienced rejection multiple times for various reasons. In your allegorical story, food is the nourishment that comes from relationships that others need in order to nourish and sustain themselves. As a foster child you've had to learn to be less dependent on relationships. Others feel threatened by you, not only because you're physically strong, but also because you're not socially dependent on others. You believe that you really don't need other people in your life to survive. I'm meeting with you to tell you that you do need others in your life to survive."

I really believed that what she was saying about foster children, me, in this case, was true. We can be independent and free as long as we don't make too many bad choices. Her statements resonated with me better than anything Dr. Bonan or Mr. Molitor had said. I listened without making any comments.

She continued, "Roger, you're wrong to think that you don't need others in your life to be happy and successful. Human beings are social animals, and we all need others. I think your story would be better if those children with the advantage of the green genes would learn how to cooperate with those without. Foster children like you have experiences about the world that have heightened your social awareness. It isn't all about independence. It is about sharing, too. Learn from each other and become interdependent by combining your strengths with theirs."

Her enthusiastic analysis of my story and how it might have related to my life excited me.

"I'm glad that you liked my story," I said with as much monotone as I could manage.

"When I was reading your story and reflecting on how you've been shifted from one place to another, I think I understand why you wrote that poem. Your life has been governed by decisions made by others. They've told you where you'll live, with whom you'll live, and even restricted how you live. Your poem was an act of rebellion against authority. You experienced our decision to eliminate the class trip as another example of others controlling you."

I knew she was right. I hated being controlled by others.

"Roger, all of us at Central Bucks have seen who you are. We want you to reach your full potential which seems ample. We want to help you learn and grow. You have a lot to offer. We're here to support your growth. You need to adopt behaviors that are useful to you, not harmful. You must learn to accept what we are offering. In your remaining few months in school, we can help you make better choices. Take advantage of us. Don't dismiss us."

"Thank you," I said. Some of her words stung, but only because they were on target. I realized that after more than five years at Central Bucks my story was better known than I thought. I had been seen. I had felt the full power of its impact for the first time during that conversation with Mrs. Porter.

When I left her office, I felt relieved, vindicated, and even understood. I vowed to be more open to others and show more willingness to be trustful and dependent. The world of Richard and other foster children that had influenced me to be strong and silent didn't have to be my world.

Chapter 44
Aging Out

Mrs. Porter's thoughts had an impact. She opened my mind to the idea that isolation from the rest of society may appear to be safe, but it was unnatural and unhealthy. Her point was that we are interconnected and interdependent, whether we know it or not. I began to appreciate her thinking as I reflected on my situation.

Scott Pierson had listened to my stories about the farm and my plans to run away. Although I didn't realize it at the time, those stories were cries for help. When Scott repeated them to his parents, the Piersons reacted empathetically and reached out to the Aid Society to see what they could do to help. Their response in service to the common good had facilitated my escape from the farm.

Although I'd experienced the farm as harsh, other people had cared for me and invested in me so that I could become a successful adult. The McClellands had given me a stable environment albeit not typical for a child of that time. I learned that hard work had payoffs, thanks to Mr. Moyer and others. Mrs. McClelland's value system and that of the church had shown a way for me to act in the world. Teachers had given me feedback and encouraged me to perform. The VanAlstynes and the Triests had exposed me to more normal young adult activities. People had invested in me.

I knew that in a few months, I would age out of the Aid Society. Richard enlisted in the Army more than three months before he was eighteen, the formal age to leave foster care. I was going to be eighteen in early April, about two months before graduation. I felt confident that I could live with the Piersons for a while since it seemed like I was part of their family. What would happen if I didn't get into a college? I might end up in a green gene situation after all. I needed to talk to Mr. Molitor.

When Mr. Molitor met me on his next visit at school, I was ready.

"How are things going?" he said.

"I have a question."

"You do?"

I'd startled him. He was used to asking me questions, not the other way around.

"When I'm eighteen in April, will the Aid Society stop paying the Piersons?"

"A timely question. Your situation has been a discussion topic with the staff for a while. We know that you'll age out in April, which is about two months before graduation."

He continued, "When I had my first few conversations with the Piersons, it was clear to me that they wanted you to be part of their family. Their expectation was that you would live with them until you graduated. Based on their commitment, we will extend payments to them until after you graduate."

"I didn't know that. Thank you. Has the Aid Society ever done that before?"

"Yes, under certain circumstances. Our policies don't always line up with birth dates."

"What happens to me after graduation?"

The Piersons were good people and had altered their family setting to accommodate me. I also knew that cuckoo birds were known to lay an egg in another bird's nest and dupe that bird (the foster parent bird) into hatching the egg and raising the cuckoo chick. I learned later that the cuckoo species and others who exhibit that behavior are called "brood parasites," a term which fit my mother exactly. I didn't want to take advantage of the Piersons' goodwill in that way.

"I think that you and the Piersons should talk about your future. My expectation is that you'll be able to live with them if you go to college."

I believed that I would go to college, but the stakes had increased a bit more since I heard the conditionality in his comment.

That evening the Piersons asked to speak to me alone in the living room. Even though I'd lived with them for a year, it was still hard to call them "Mom and Dad," but I did the best I could.

"Roger, we spoke to Mr. Molitor today about what happens after you become eighteen," Mom said. "We want you to know that you'll always have a place with us here in our home. You're part of our family now."

I felt a surge of gratitude. I managed a quiet, "Thank you," while I fought back tears. They were doing their best to integrate me into their family, and this was a bigger step than taking me in for just fifteen months. My natural mother had taken advantage of the goodwill of people like the McClellands and the Piersons and made them responsible for raising me. I wanted to do more than say thank you, but I knew I would cry if I did. Crying would have exposed me too much. I wanted to please them for caring for me. I knew that they would feel that they'd fulfilled their intentions if I got into a college. Getting into a college would demonstrate my gratitude.

My close friends, including Scott, had done well on national tests. In addition, they had excellent grades that would help them to earn scholarships. Even without scholarships, some of their parents could afford to help them go to college. Scott was an excellent student, played the piano well, and was a skilled soccer player. We all knew he would get into a good college and maybe even receive financial aid. Besides, his parents were college graduates, and his brother, Bob, was such a good college student that he was going on to graduate school to get his PhD in biochemistry. All these factors made Scott a good candidate for college. Scott wanted to go to Oberlin College. I believed that he would be accepted easily.

Because I thought that my chances of getting into a good school were limited, I decided to be systematic in my college selection approach and apply to a few appropriate colleges. I spent two dollars and bought *The College Handbook* and started going through the schools alphabetically. When I got to the letter B and read about Bowdoin College and learned that Hawthorne and Longfellow had gone there, I decided that it was the right college for me. I discussed my choice with Mr. Williams, my guidance counselor, who pointed out that Bowdoin had high academic standards, was expensive, didn't offer athletic scholarships, and Maine was a long way from Doylestown. He urged me to apply to more than just Bowdoin.

Syracuse University held my attention for about an hour. A front office secretary interrupted Mr. Seidle's physics class with a note for me that instructed me to report to the gym at 11 o'clock to meet with a coach from Syracuse University. Because Coach Maskas had told us that colleges might contact some of us and since I had been selected by coaches and writers for the All Bux-Mont football team, I thought this might be my big chance for a college scholarship.

I was in the gym promptly at 11 o'clock with Joe Arcade, who was over six feet tall, and Nathaniel Duckett, who was one of the best high school running backs in the country. We waited inside the gym doors until Coach Maskas saw us and motioned to us to go over to him. "Here, boys, is one of the assistant coaches for the Syracuse Orangemen. Coach Schwartzwalder couldn't be here today because of other commitments."

I was sorry that the legendary coach of the famous running back, Ernie Davis, couldn't be there, but I was happy to meet his assistant. He walked up to me, ignoring Joe and Nate for the moment, and sized me up. His only words were, "Son, you can go back to class."

Coach Maskas spoke to me later, "Roger, the coach told me that you were too small and too light to be a lineman in their program. I'm sure that other coaches from less high-profile colleges and universities will be interested in you."

What struck me was the curt rejection and how he knew nothing about me other than my size. Our coaches had repeatedly drilled into us, "It's not the size of the dog in the fight, but rather the size of the fight in the dog that matters." This guy had no idea about the size of the fight in me when he rejected me. In reality, the Piersons had influenced me to think that football was a rough sport and had dampened my enthusiasm about playing football anyway. Besides, I didn't want to go to college knowing that I would have to play football as a condition of enrollment. However, it was disappointing to be rejected again. That wasn't my last disappointment.

I'd been dating a girl that was interesting and attractive. I'd taken her home from a friend's house on a Saturday afternoon. As I left her house, her father came outside and said, "Roger, may I speak to you for a minute?"

"Sure."

"I understand that you're living with the Piersons. Is that true?"

"Yes."

"Are you an orphan?"

"Oh, no. I'm a foster child."

"Really. Where are your parents?"

"My mother lives in Florida. I don't know where my father is."

"You don't know where Mr. Saillant lives?"

"Mr. Saillant isn't my father. I don't know where he lives either."

His eyes narrowed and then looked away. "Thank you for

being so honest."

"No problem," I said uneasily.

"Roger, I'm sorry to have to say this to you, but I'm thinking of my daughter and her reputation. I'm sure you'll understand me when I tell you that I don't want you dating her."

His tone was measured, and it pushed me backward like a sudden cold wind. Before I could say anything, even if I'd known what to say, he'd turned and gone back into his house. It was as though I'd been found out for doing something evil. I only spoke to Mr. Molitor about what had happened.

"Mr. Molitor, do foster kids often get rejected by the parents of their friends?"

"What do you mean?"

I described what had happened.

"Well, regrettably parents do say things like that."

"Why? What are they afraid of?"

"Often foster children have problems that spill over onto their friends. Parents just want to protect their children, especially daughters. Telling you not to go out with his daughter was his way of not taking a chance."

On the surface, I thought that I had a good record, so I said, "I haven't done anything to make him afraid of me, nor would I harm her."

"I know, Roger, but there are some who believe that an illegitimate boy in foster care is more likely to get their daughter pregnant."

"I wouldn't do that."

"He doesn't know that. He knows that you're a senior and assumes that soon you won't be living with the Piersons. I guess he may be worried about what might happen when you're on your own."

"I plan to go to college." I knew that a plan was only a plan.

I was also learning that adults didn't necessarily judge you simply on your merits. They also judged you on the status of your parents. There were exceptions.

Many of us were selected to take the state high school physics exam. I saw the state exam as another opportunity to distinguish myself. After all, I'd been given a certificate of merit by the Philadelphia Science Council. I hadn't understood at the time that the certificate was more like being recognized for participation and interest rather than for achievement. After taking the state physics exam, I knew that I hadn't done well. And certainly not as well as two of the brightest students in our class, Ed Satterthwaite and Phelps Freeborn, who had exceptional abilities in the sciences.

When the results came, Mr. Seidle was breathless to tell the class that we all had done great on the exam. He walked over to my desk and proudly announced in a loud voice, "Roger finished third in the state on the physics exam!"

My heart practically jumped out of my chest. Excitement swept over me, followed by skepticism. "This can't be true," I said. "May I see the letter?"

He handed it to me with a big smile. I scanned the summary of the results for our school. Without thinking I said loudly, "This says I am in the third quintile, not third place." The room went silent and the excitement dropped from Mr. Seidle's face.

He took the letter back, read it, and looked deflated. I realized that I'd embarrassed him and felt bad that I'd not been more discreet. The stunned Mr. Seidle turned red and walked back to his desk without speaking while the students in the classroom whispered among themselves. Suddenly, I felt awful. There was an awkwardness in class that day. I knew that I couldn't ask him for a letter of recommendation for college after that. Needless to say, I should have because of what he said to me months later just before graduation.

Letters had started to arrive from colleges for my friends. The belief was that thick letters were good news and thin letters were not. Scott got a thick letter from Oberlin the same day I got a thin letter from Princeton. We all celebrated his acceptance into the fall term. The next day I got two thick letters, one from Muhlenberg and one from Saint Lawrence. Neither letter of acceptance offered scholarship monies. The following day I got a thin letter from Bowdoin. I was sure that I'd been rejected. When I opened it and read that I had been accepted with a full tuition scholarship, my eyes filled with so many tears that they ran down my cheeks. My dream from long ago had become real. I was college timber. In addition, I was to be assigned to live in nine Maine Hall, the exact room where Hawthorne and Longfellow had been roommates. My roommate was to be the son of the Director of Admissions, Hugh Shaw. Joy shot through me. I was living with the angels. I shared the news. Everyone congratulated me. It was the best moment of my life at the time.

Weeks later, Mr. Seidle called me to his office. He looked up at me and smiled and said, "Roger, please sit down." I sat down, wondering what was about to happen.

He began, "I saw you when you first arrived here from that one-room school. I was a parking lot monitor and admired how you'd beaten that bully. I only know about some of the obstacles that you've overcome. Whatever you encountered in your life so far didn't deter you from trying to do your best. You smiled, you listened, and you did well."

He continued, "No wonder the Rotarians chose you for their Boy of the Year Award. I have twin sons. I would be so proud of them if they were to grow up to be just like you."

I was stunned. I was simultaneously relieved and touched by his kind words. "Mr. Seidle, thank you so much for telling me. I enjoyed learning about physics." I should've said that I had learned about character, too. "Thank you!" I shook his hand. He was a good man whose character rose above what could have been pettiness based on how I'd embarrassed him in class that day. Another teacher had touched my life and modelled good behavior.

I was about to enter the next phase of my life in a world knowing that how you treat others, how you behave, and how you engage the world matters. I only wasted time if I adopted a bad attitude based on blaming my social workers, my foster parents, or my real parents. Many people helped me to develop a values-based internal gyroscope that tugged at me when I strayed off course, which I often did.

Upon reflection, it was clear that all I needed was to be sensitive to others, so as to benefit from their counsel, and be willing to help others as appropriate, like others helped me.

Postscript

Mr. McClelland died of starvation alone in his apartment in Philadelphia at the age of eighty-seven. I was the executor of his estate. Ruth Saillant died as a pauper at age ninety-seven in a group home in Miami.

Richard trained in the Army to become a skilled heavy equipment operator and later became a long-haul truck driver. His independent spirit and irreverence toward authority led to a number of traffic violations. The best way, in my mind, to describe Richard is to think of him as having a code, living by it, and not letting anything stand in his way - a Clint Eastwood character. Eventually, he became a partner with his wife in a small business where he's respected for his hard work and gritty humor.

I remained in contact with the Pierson family until after college, but gradually we drifted apart because of my moves away from Doylestown. I never thanked them for their role in redirecting my life. I learned months after it happened that Scott Pierson died of a heart attack when he was riding his bike home from work at age 57. Robert lives in Philadelphia and was founder of Farm to City, serving the common good, and is a known leader in the Philadelphia local food movement. Susan still lives on the Pierson farm in Doylestown township and also serves the community as an environmental services professional.

Karen Saillant became a successful opera singer with an MFA from Temple and toured Europe for several years. She founded the International Opera Theater as well as a venue called The Fire for aspiring musical talent in Philadelphia.

Rory Saillant became a talented interior designer and resides in Florida.

I have individually re-connected with Bernd Waitl, Bill Triest, John Davis, and Ron Shane after many years. They are good men, each filled with enthusiasm and good values.

I graduated from Bowdoin College in 1965, earned a PhD in chemistry from Indiana in 1969, and a post doctorate at UCLA in 1970. I was employed by the Ford Motor Company and Visteon Corporation, a spinoff of Ford, for a total of thirty years where I served in many national and international senior management roles. After Ford and Visteon, I became the CEO of Plug Power, a fuel cell company, and later was appointed the executive director of The Fowler Center for Business as an Agent of World Benefit at Case Western Reserve University. I attribute my successes to the ability to collaborate with others and being able to adapt to people needing to be seen in various settings throughout the world. I was never afraid to experience change nor was I slowed down by the risk of being fired for doing what was necessary and right.

After Jean Mathers' father had me investigated by a detective, we were married. We had three daughters, Martha, Meredith, and Megan. They enjoy successful careers while raising families of their own. Jean and I divorced after twenty-nine years of marriage. Fifteen years later, I married Mary Lou Pinckney with whom I've lived happily for the past thirteen years.

Dr. Bonan was right. I did need the help of therapists, and, luckily, I was able to afford them.

Commentary

By Raymond Schimmer, Retired CEO, Northern Rivers Family Services

No form of behavior is accompanied by stronger feeling than is attachment behavior. The figures toward whom it is directed are loved and their advent is greeted with joy. So long as a child is in the unchallenged presence of a principal attachment figure, or within easy reach, he feels secure. A threat of loss creates anxiety, and actual loss sorrow; both, moreover, are likely to arouse anger.

Roger Saillant's *The Power of Being Seen* describes the progress of a child in a particular place—rural Pennsylvania—at a particular time—the 1950s—and in a special set of circumstances that would affect him then and for the rest of his life. Roger's special circumstances included separation from his mother at nine months of age and his subsequent journey through family foster care under the auspices of a private Philadelphia social services agency. His awareness of his peril as a child without a family and his reactions to this most literal of existential threats are at the core of the book.

Sigmund Freud's daughter Anna and her partner Dorothy Burlingham wrote a book during World War II with the heartbreaking title *Infants Without Families*. The book was based on their observations in the nursery the two administered in wartime England. The book raised an interesting question—why, despite the fact that the babies and toddlers were cared for with ample provision and continuous kindness, were so many utterly miserable? Researchers and institutions—including John Bowlby,

Mary Ainsworth, John Robertson, the World Health Organization, and many others—pursued these and other fundamental questions after the war. How do babies and mothers—or more accurately, if more awkwardly, primary parental figures—become attached? Why do they attach, and why so desperately? What happens when an existing attachment is shattered? What if it never develops?

Bowlby in particular laid down a foundation for the following set of answers—babies become attached to mothers and mothers to babies because they must. A neonate Homo sapiens cannot live more than a few hours without a protective, nurturing adult, and a parent cannot project their genetic endowment if the tiny offspring is eaten by dogs, starves miserably, or becomes fatally hypothermic.

Many successfully attached children survive and their caring adults' behaviors are perpetuated over two hundred generations. Many of those individuals who do not or cannot attach vanish from the gene pool. The drive to connect is uncompromising, and the consequences of its frustration are profoundly disturbing, both behaviorally and psychologically.

Confronted with large numbers of children left unattached and unprotected because of parental death or disability, communities have tried to build "systems" that can provide the functions of missing or damaged families. As a man-made patch for an evolutionarily-driven natural family, foster care is necessarily and obviously imperfect by definition. It is also historically mutable, driven by wildly fluctuating demand, social and political considerations, and increasingly, by scientific research. Today's complex, multi-variant, governmentally directed institution bears limited resemblance to the version that tried so unevenly to keep young Roger Saillant whole after his mother gave her nine-month-old infant to a company of strangers in Philadelphia seventy-five years ago.

The archived records of my former employer's historic predecessor, the Albany Orphan Asylum, document vividly a foster care world based on dramatically different assumptions and practices that strike the modern eye as barbaric. The mid-nineteenth century system was at least in part one of unpaid labor in exchange for room and board. No one expected families that were themselves living at a subsistence level—as were the McClellands in mid-twentieth century Pennsylvania—to care for children solely out of the goodness of their hearts. Contracts were explicit, and people were not shy about bringing back to the asylum children who did not work out.

Roger Saillant arrived in foster care at the twilight of an earlier phase, perhaps at that time when the system hypocritically relied on the free-labor concept while pretending it did not exist. The McClellands fed Roger, accepted his unpaid work as their due, and congratulated themselves for providing him with a vocational education that would give him the opportunity to be a successful subsistence farmer. Until Mr. Molitor arrived, the agency's social workers offered implicit consent for this arrangement. Although some of the practices Roger experienced are now largely historical artifacts, he was also harshly affected by several of the system's fundamental problems—problems as relevant to the confusion today as they were in 1850 and 1950. Let me outline some of those problems and the resulting confusion.

Foster care is plagued by transience that is antithetical to a developing child's need for reliable provision of care and affection. In Roger's case, transience included the loss of three mothers—Mrs. Saillant at nine months, Mrs. Perry-Ferry, and Mrs. McClelland; two fathers—Mr. Saillant and Mr. Perry-Ferry; and innumerable social workers—i.e, case managers— along the way. Roger had multiple home placements, but even then, he was far luckier than Paul, who appears to have enjoyed nothing like the relative continuity with respect to home and school that Roger had during his extended placement with the McClellands. Foster care is an institutional system, and like all such systems, deals with imperatives, e.g., staff turnover and bureaucratic regulations—e.g., Mrs. Perry-Ferry excluded from foster caring as a single parent—that will be served irrespective of the nominal clients. And then we have death and other natural stressors.

Foster care, as are all institutional systems, is plagued by confusion and incomplete communication. Consider that no single strata in the many layers of foster care knows enough about any of the others. The agency administrators don't know what the social workers know, who don't know what the families know, who don't know what the children know. And the confusion passes back up the hierarchy with the same effect. The various participants depend upon eavesdropping, e.g., Roger listening to the McClellands through the heating vent; speculation, e.g., Mr. and Mrs. McClelland trying to predict what the agency was up to based on such news as they have, in addition to their own dark suspicions; and professional interrogation, e.g., line social workers like Miss Burns and Mr. Molitor probing the foster parents and interviewing the children. No one knows everything, and no one can—the institutional barriers wall off each participant from all the others. Paranoia ensues.

Without conscious management, foster care can be a source of cultural conflict. The institution shakes participants up like a bartender shakes a martini. Roger had little cultural conflict at the outset (terror, stress, and disorientation notwithstanding) because of his youth and ethnicity (he was of the same ethnicity as his foster parents, community, and social workers), but he eventually became an out-of-place farm kid in a rapidly transitioning locality dominated by the post-World War II middle class. As a foster child his reality was completely invisible to the likes of his grade-school friends and neighbors Doris and Carl Weik. He watches his biological mother and Mrs. McClelland greet one another. He travels, in one afternoon on an airplane, from Andrew Jackson's two-seater America to Miami Beach, where his biological relatives make fun of him when he uses their modern bathroom. We have the near-comic scene in which he and the Piersons unwittingly exchange different definitions of the word chore. And perhaps most tragically, we have Roger trying to explain honor society and college prep to Mr. McClelland, an uneducated immigrant subsistence farmer, who, as Roger's foster father, has final say regarding Roger's activities in the outside world.

The cultural confusion for the late-arriving temporary foster children Paul and Leon at the McClelland farm was so great as to be unbridgeable. Leon simply checked out and withdrew, but Paul's rage exploded in a fireball of violence. These sorts of tectonic cultural collisions remain a continuing threat in foster care today, albeit reduced to some degree by an enhanced contemporary awareness among administrators and foster parents.

In foster care, peers may parent peers. This is a phenomenon I do not recall seeing commented upon much in the contemporary literature about foster children, but the beautiful and sensitive portrait of Roger's relationship with Richard brings me back to "An Experiment in Group Upbringing," a paper written by Anna Freud and Sophie Dann based on their experiences with orphans immediately following World War II. The Allies discovered concentration camps that contained only children, the Nazis having pioneered new forms of separation and attachment disorder. Freud and Dann perceived within the child population grotesque parodies of normative family structure. It was clear that the children, driven by irrepressible instinct, tried to make what they needed out of what they had, and in place of adults, they had other children.

Out of Richard, Roger created an approximation of an older, caring, teaching adult. And sometimes that's exactly what Richard was. At other times he was just Richard, another foster kid with his own anger and his own unmet needs. At those bad times Roger felt the shock of betrayal—Richard, like all his other parental figures, let him down and hurt him right to the core. In any case, the bond between the two foster brothers—for good and for bad—was all the stronger because of the tentative nature of the bonds between each of them and the McClellands.

One last note about "An Experiment in Group Upbringing": in the concentration camp, the only material possessions the children owned as individuals were the metal spoons with which they ate. The children called these the "little thing" and despite the material excesses with which the soldiers showered on them after liberation, their possessiveness about the little spoons endured. Young Roger's fierce connections to his farewell ginger ale and to his small suitcase are similar—symbols of his deep need for the assurance of provision and of his indisputable, if achingly limited, personal agency.

Until recently, foster care ended at age eighteen, irrespective of all other considerations. For decades—including Roger's time in care—the responsibility of funders and care providers terminated abruptly on the eighteenth birthday of the child. If devoted individuals like the Piersons wanted to extend support beyond that arbitrary date, they did so on their own and with their own resources. Absent Roger's intelligence and college scholarship, he would certainly have found himself at large in the community with his knowledge of nineteenth-century farming as the sum of his vocational skills after over seventeen years in care.

The absence or ineffectiveness of independent living instruction in foster care almost certainly contributes in some degree to the dismal contemporary outcomes for Americans who are discharged from foster care. The Annie E. Casey Foundation, Child Welfare Information Gateway, and Adopt US Kids reported that around 40-50 percent of aged-out foster children become homeless within eighteen months of emancipation. About 25 percent are in prison within two years of aging out of their foster homes. Almost 50 percent of prison inmates have spent time in foster care. The incarceration rate for male foster children is about 51 percent compared to the general population of their peers of about 17 percent. Although the data show that the average stay in foster care is about two years, foster children suffer six times the rate of PTSD found in the general population.

Those data are a point-in-time assessment of post-foster-care outcomes. In addition to raising concern about independent living training as offered within the system, it also reflects changes in the nature and applications of foster care's contemporary varieties of service. There has been over the last thirty years a proliferation of community-based family support services, expressly designed to enable stressed families to retain their roles as protectors and providers for their own children. Foster care is largely a tertiary, rather than primary, resort in contemporary social services; consequently, those youth who enter it may do so with already difficult experimental profiles.

Seventy years ago, John Bowlby wrote: "If a community values its children, it must cherish their parents."

The Power of Being Seen is never, though, only a book about growing up in foster care. It is as well, and perhaps chiefly, about the universal pain, challenge, and triumph of growth and development. A child's individual circumstances are terribly important, but Roger's memoir argues that they are not determinant. There are universal experiences that transcend circumstance, and Roger treats these beautifully. Every child is going to learn to manage their bowels, and many are going to be humiliated and frightened at various points in the process. Children wonder if they are inherently good or bad, and many struggle with the question. Every adolescent is going to be drawn to the outside world, and many will return with questions about their own homes and the people in them. It goes without saying that Roger's foster care situation affected the form and intensity of his developmental progression, but this memoir does a great job detailing the psychological staging between four and eighteen years of age, foster care or not.

In a book about a young man's developmental progress, lost innocence stories are essential, and there are a flock of them here, some laugh-out-loud funny and some deeply troubling: the theft of Eddie Boyle's cap gun, the filching of the farm soil test kit, the killing of Mrs. McClelland's nightshade plant, the stealing of baked goods, the Wolfe garage arson, the murder of the cow, and the many instances of shoplifting. Roger's career as youthful criminal is perhaps on the right-hand side of the bell curve but leaves him short of an ax murder. My point is that in these criminal matters Roger certainly fell on the far end of normal, but he may not have ever been in danger of becoming a singularity or an unprecedented monster. Why not?

One fundamental caregiver theory—one that underscored much of my own training and program activity—was that brain chemistry aside, the difference between the developmental outcomes of sociopathy on the one hand and functional citizenship on the other has to do with how much approval, protection, and provision we can offer a troubled child to offset the contempt, negligence, and deprivation that they have already endured. Ours was the obverse of W.H. Auden's proposition:

I and the public know
What all schoolchildren learn;
Those to whom evil is done

Do evil in return.

And maybe, those to whom good is done and kindness is given, do good in return. It was always a race against time, and we were fighting against both the child's personal history and those systemic flaws in foster care discussed earlier. In Roger's case, the combination of personal constitutional endowment and make-up nurturance he received from various nonfamily sources was enough to tip the balance and then some. Who were these "doers of good"? And why did they behave as they did with a struggling child?

The paid workers who went out of their way to help Roger included teachers like Miss Hanisch, Miss Freking, Miss Gebhardt, Mrs. Porter, and Mr. Seidel. There are the nurses who attended the hernia surgery, and even the stewardess who flew with Roger to Miami that first time. Then we have the extraordinary social worker, Mr. Molitor, who would not take Roger's many no's for an answer and who simply drilled his way through Mr. McClelland's prevarications, probably without much thanks from his superiors, whose lives Mr. Molitor undoubtedly complicated when he closed the McClelland farm as a placement option.

Finally, there is Mom—Mrs. McClelland—a paid foster mother. She was quiet and kind. She was Roger's safe haven. She listened to his dreams and encouraged him to do well in school. She always signed his report cards, complimented him on his grades, and noticed when teachers commented on his good behaviors and habits. Anna Freud famously observed: "When the attachment to parents is destroyed, there is no sense anymore in being good, clean, or unselfish." Although she wasn't his birth mother, Mrs. McClelland gave Roger a reason to be good. She told him it made sense. A lot of people were paid to help Roger, and he got more than his money's worth from some of them.

There were angels, too, in Roger's life—those people who

stepped off the apparently straight paths of their own lives and went over to help when they noticed Roger thrashing around in the weeds. They didn't have to, but they did. Uncle Hugh and Aunt Lizzie, the VanAlstynes, Mr. Moyer, the willfully-blind and deaf Mr. Mason, the not-blind Mr. McGlaughlin, and the almost absurdly naive Triest and Pierson families. Not only did they ameliorate Roger's condition and treat his wounds, but they showed him a potential for life that, given the mean and narrow circumstances of his foster-care situation, he hadn't even imagined. They offered him a sense of possibility. He took the gun out of his mouth because he was curious about where his life would go. That such curiosity existed at all was because, at least in part, these angels had shown him where his life could go.

To what do we ascribe such behavior? Were the paid heroes just a handful of exceptionally good craftsmen who saw in Roger promising raw material and the potential for an extraordinary product? Were the angels simply aggrandizing their own self-images as noble Christians or Quakers? Advertising their "goodness" to the community or themselves? Did they want to get some credit for the development of his obviously extraordinary natural gifts? Or were they just charmed by his boyish smile?

Over forty years ago, biologist and naturalist E.O. Wilson wrote in his book *On Human Nature:*

Human altruism appears to be substantially hard core when directed at closest relatives, although still to a much lesser degree than in the case of the social insects and the colonial invertebrates. The remainder of our altruism is essentially soft. The predicted result is a meange of ambivalence, deceit, and guilt that continuously troubles the individual mind.

This cold-blooded appraisal of human charitable motives seems to go hard on Roger's angels, but in recent years Wilson has executed what some critics call a U-turn. He has very controversially discussed concepts like "eusocial" and "prosocial" behaviors as relevant to some degree within our own species. The alleged existence of these hard altruistic tendencies supposes that our species has evolutionarily-determined behaviors that benefit individuals and their kin genetically and other behaviors that benefit the species as a group.

One of the phrases associated with eusocial theory is that of the open nest, i.e., that at least some members of the species are inclined to take in young who have been disconnected from their own parents. This behavior may not benefit the practitioner directly in any genetic sense, but, as in Roger's case, it may reduce the chances for development of an unsocialized, destructive individual who would be harmful to the group while at the same time retaining for the species such special gifts as the disconnected individual may possess. This is a hotly contested proposition because it doesn't easily comport with mainstream Darwinian theory. Perhaps not, but can we any more easily explain the behavior of the Piersons, Mr. Seidel, or the Triests?

In The Power of Being Seen, Roger refers to his mother as a "brood parasite," a remark that stands as a measure of the depth and longevity of the anger that Bowlby observed in the betrayed, abandoned, and unattached child. But young Roger also knew the Triests, Piersons, and VanAlstynes. They stepped forward, not as duped victims, but as voluntary, open-nest hosts. For them, young Roger Saillant was not a detested, parasitic cowbird but a valued fellow traveler in a hard world, one whom they were happy to give a hand up. Among its many other achievements, *The Power of Being Seen* memorializes them with gratitude and affection.

Raymond Schimmer worked in special education and child and family behavioral health in Massachusetts before becoming the CEO of Northern Rivers Family Services in Albany, New York. At Northern Rivers he administered a wide range of group- and family-based foster care and adoption services.

Acknowledgements

I am grateful to my daughters Martha, Meredith, and Megan for starting me on this memoir writing journey several years ago. Their initial encouragement and enthusiasm were critical for me to begin to write short stories at first in an effort to document the adventures of growing up. The writing led to my realization that I felt deep gratitude to the many who **saw** me and helped me to develop a course toward productive citizenship.

My wife, Mary Lou, and our friends, Doctors Howard and Amy Malamood, saw the potential to weave my stories into a book. Their chuckles and conversations energized me to do the work necessary to complete this project. I never felt so encouraged as when I would hear my wife laugh out loud when she read a new chapter for the first time or when she would pop her head into my office and say, "This is really good." Importantly, she would also say from time to time that I could do better. Mary Lou deserves my deepest gratitude for her unbridled enthusiasm and love during the completion of this project.

Thank you to Bonnie Martin for reading, rereading, and proofreading all of my drafts. Since she was a schoolmate from ninth grade on, she also helped to verify certain facts.

Doug and Ruth Grant were enthusiastic readers who made suggestions that motivated me and were persistent in telling me that I must publish this book.

Thank you to Mickey Moulder and Katherine Gullett who read late drafts of the book, applauded my efforts, and made many helpful suggestions. They pointed out certain traits and values I exhibited as an adult, which prompted me to see where they originated in my childhood.

My half-sister, Vicki McGroarty, shared her perspectives about our mother and gave me confidence to describe our mother as I did. I am grateful for her insights. Vicki was abandoned, too. She liked the draft of the book she read and encouraged me, as well. Thank you.

I am filled with gratitude for the remarks by Raymond Schimmer found in the commentary. His professional experience with the foster care system and his perspective will help us all to appreciate the pitfalls that challenge the developmental journeys of foster children. He highlighted critical traits in my childhood that most foster children experience to help us all to be alert to them.

Finally, I want to thank my editor, Nancy Pile, who jumped into the book and became an enthusiastic supporter of what and how it was written and was critical and thorough in making many suggestions. She was an excellent partner in the final stages of polishing this memoir prior to publication.